Communicating
Fashion

Communicating Fashion

Clothing, Culture, and Media

Myles Ethan Lascity

BLOOMSBURY VISUAL ARTS
LONDON • NEW YORK • OXFORD • NEW DELHI • SYDNEY

BLOOMSBURY VISUAL ARTS
Bloomsbury Publishing Plc
50 Bedford Square, London, WC1B 3DP, UK
1385 Broadway, New York, NY 10018, USA
29 Earlsfort Terrace, Dublin 2, Ireland

BLOOMSBURY, BLOOMSBURY VISUAL ARTS and the Diana logo are trademarks of
Bloomsbury Publishing Plc

First published in Great Britain 2021

Cover design by Holly Bell
Cover image © Brunel Johnson

A catalogue record for this book is available from the British Library.

Library of Congress Cataloging-in-Publication Data
Names: Lascity, Myles Ethan, author.
Title: Communicating fashion : clothing, culture, and media / Myles Ethan Lascity.
Description: New York : Bloomsbury Publishing (UK), 2021. |
Includes bibliographical references and index.
Identifiers: LCCN 2020033578 (print) | LCCN 2020033579 (ebook) |
ISBN 9781350112230 (paperback) | ISBN 9781350112247 (hardback) |
ISBN 9781350112254 (epub) | ISBN 9781350112261 (pdf)
Subjects: LCSH: Fashion—Philosophy. | Clothing and dress—Social aspects. |
Social media—Influence.
Classification: LCC GT521 .L32 2021 (print) | LCC GT521 (ebook) | DDC 391—dc23
LC record available at https://lccn.loc.gov/2020033578
LC ebook record available at https://lccn.loc.gov/2020033579

ISBN: HB: 978-1-3501-1224-7
        PB: 978-1-3501-1223-0
        ePDF: 978-1-3501-1226-1
        eBook: 978-1-3501-1225-4

Typeset by RefineCatch Limited, Bungay, Suffolk
Printed and bound in India

To find out more about our authors and books visit www.bloomsbury.com
and sign up for our newsletters.

Contents

List of Figures

Acknowledgments

Like any large project the inspiration and ideas we draw off of come from more places than we can fully count. To start, this project was only possible thanks to the support from my colleagues in the division of journalism at Southern Methodist University, and my former colleagues in the department of English and communication at Chestnut Hill College. Without the time, space and intellectual curiosity they provided this undertaking wouldn't have been possible.

Specifically, many thanks to Camille Kraeplin, Melinda Sebastian and especially Candice D. Roberts for reading parts of this book in both proposal and more complete forms. I'm also indebted to Georgia Kennedy for her guidance throughout the entire process, Faith Marsland, Belinda Campbell and the entire team at Bloomsbury; as well as Paula Divine and Merv Honeywood for helping get this publication-ready. And, I'd like to thank all of the anonymous reviewers — I hope you know who you are! — who offered helpful insights and suggestions throughout the process.

On a personal note, a special thanks goes out to my friends, family and partner for allowing me to talk incessantly about this project for the better part of three years.

Finally, I'd be remiss if I didn't thank the hundreds of students who have passed through my classes over the years. Students have an amazing ability to make you re-examine your knowledge and think through concepts, theories and arguments in new and exciting ways. Hopefully, this book can be a catalyst for others to do the same.

Preface

Clothing communicates.

On the surface this is a relatively simple concept, one that many of us take for granted. The clothing we decide to put on our body and how and where we decide to wear it informs our actions and—rightly or wrongly—will be interpreted by other people. The "messages" people take from our clothing and our personal appearance may not be the same as we intend to send, but the garments and how people visually see us informs how they interact with us.

Researchers and fashion theorists have often argued over this point and whether clothing can be considered a form of communication if we can't communicate clear messages through it. This argument will be better addressed within Chapter 1, but communication is always complicated, and even when we think communication is clear-cut, such as through simple language, it is still dependent upon significant cultural and interpersonal contexts for messages to be properly understood. Nowhere is this more obvious than through social media where messages are frequently stripped of their context and circulate with new or modified contexts attached. Without getting too into the weeds of various arguments here, many others have focused on *how* clothing communicates (Is it a structured language? Is it a "quasi code"?) or *if* it communicates at all (since the input and output are generally different).

However, these are not the starting places of this book.

Instead, this book starts from the statement above: *clothing communicates*.

Whether we would admit to this publicly or not, we use clothing as a way to make sense of each other. It is steeped in all sorts of unsavory ideas— racism, sexism and classism, among them—but this does not change the fact that we all do it. In fact, one could argue that interpreting clothing is part of human nature.

As such, while this book is indebted to the work of Malcolm Barnard's *Fashion* as *Communication*, which makes a compelling case to see clothing and fashion as a form of communication, the perspective presented in this book is more akin to Elizabeth Wilson's understanding in "Magic Fashion," where she writes, "... garments, like other objects, can take on imagined and/or subjectively experienced properties that go far beyond the flaunting of wealth or refined taste. It is *because* we live in a society dominated by capital and consumption that we commandeer material goods for the symbolic expression of values remote from materialism."[1]

While Wilson is making the case that clothing is magic because we assign subjective meanings to it—through superstition and the like—"magic" can be understood in a more practical way. The meaning attributed to clothing and personal appearance can never be fully or clearly articulated; simply put, there are too many mitigating factors for a structured understanding of how and what clothing communicates. And, since clothing and its meaning is subjective, each of us encounter idiosyncratic understandings due to a variety of factors and life experiences we likely can't fully understand ourselves. In that sense, the way clothing communicates to us will always be "magic" in that it will never be fully understood.

That said, we do make sense of the world through a mixture of personal experiences and various forms of media that we consume—the "mediated construction of reality" in the words of Nick Couldry and Andreas Hepp.[2] Taking this fact to its logical conclusion then, we can assume we understand clothing in much the same way: through our experiences with it and the media that tells us about it. As such, this book starts from a simple paradox: Clothing communicates and we communicate about clothing. It is at this intersection where we develop and sustain meanings for specific material items as well as larger trends and appearances.

While research on clothing and fashion studies has grown substantially over the past three decades,[3] these topics have been less represented within American communication and media studies. Instead, fields like anthropology, sociology, home economics (and later design), business, merchandising and even American studies have filled this void within the US academy. I suspect this is largely because American communication studies starts from one of two angles—interpersonal interactions (communication studies) *or* the mass media (media studies)—and clothing and fashion doesn't neatly fit into either. Clothing frames our interpersonal interactions, but does so with the support of the fashion system vis-à-vis the mass media.

As such, this book seeks to overcome these divisions as an introductory text for the study of *fashion communication*. The structure of this book may look somewhat familiar to those who have taught (or taken) introductory courses in communication and media studies. The first three chapters follow the general structure of a communication studies text. Chapter 1 explores the models of the communication (and defines some fashion terminology), before looking at clothing in individual and interpersonal communication, and group communication in Chapters 2 and 3, respectively. Chapter 4 introduces conceptualizations of the fashion system and how material objects are provided with a cultural meaning. This chapter acts as a bridge to the rest of the book which connects media forms and theory to fashion and clothing. The remaining chapters each tackle a medium (print, film and television, the internet) and the cultural institutions which help create the fashion system (advertising and the art world). Along the way, this book explains how theories like agenda-setting, framing and other media theories affect the fashion system.

Communication and media scholars have not considered fashion-related communication with the same seriousness given to political, business or environmental communication. This seems especially pronounced within the US, where even books on nonverbal communication only give a passing glance to clothing. Internationally, this omission seems to be in the process of being rectified thanks to the efforts of Nadzeya Kalbaska, Teresa Sádaba and Lorenzo Cantoni, who have recently organized a special issue of the journal *Studies in Communication Sciences* on "Fashion Communication"[4] and, along with Francesca Cominelli, began a dedicated conference series on "Digital Fashion Communication"; both of which I feel lucky to have contributed to. Still, as other subdisciplines of communication have had decades of attention, it will undoubtedly take years of work for fashion communication to be given the attention it rightly deserves. This book hopes to be one brick on the road to that end.

Figure 1.1 *The Devil Knows Cerulean. Anne Hathaway plays hapless assistant and fashion victim Andy Sachs in* The Devil Wears Prada *(2006), dir. David Frankel, 20th Century Fox.*

1

Communicating Fashion

"Oh. Okay. I see," *Runway* magazine editor Miranda Priestly begins pointedly in reprimanding her assistant, Andy Sachs, after Andy scoffed at the magazine's editors debating between two similar belts.

> You think this has nothing to do with you. You go to your closet and you select ... I don't know ... that lumpy blue sweater for instance because you're trying to tell the world that you take yourself too seriously to care about what you put on your back. But what you don't know is that, that sweater is not just blue, it's not turquoise. It's not lapis. It's actually cerulean. And you're also blithely unaware of that fact that in 2002 Oscar de la Renta did a collection of cerulean gowns. And then I think it was Yves Saint Laurent ... wasn't it who showed cerulean military jackets? ... And then cerulean quickly showed up in the collection of eight different designers. And then it, uh, filtered down through the department stores and then trickled down into some tragic casual corner where you, no doubt, fished it out of some clearance bin. However, that blue represents millions of dollars and countless jobs and its sort of comical how you think that you've made a choice that exempts you from the fashion industry when, in fact, you're wearing a sweater that was selected for you by people in this room ... from a pile of stuff.

The scene is one of the most memorable from *The Devil Wears Prada* (2006). Based on the book of the same name, the film follows Andy, played by Anne Hathaway, as she navigates the ins and out of the fictional *Runway* magazine and its demanding editor, Miranda Priestly, played by Meryl Streep. (The film and book are largely understood to be references to *Vogue* and its long-time editor, Anna Wintour.) While fictional, the scene manages to capture a few obvious truths regarding our clothing.

1 We communicate through our clothing, even when we try not to.

2 We communicate *about* clothing, whether in conversation with each other or on the pages of a magazine.

3 These processes of communication take place in an elaborate and complex system with many different participants located around the globe.

While these statements may seem commonplace or border on being trite, the truth is that popular cultural assumptions still dismiss what we put on our bodies, and those who talk about it, as superficial, frivolous or unserious. Even those who do take it seriously often emphasize the processes and practices rather than how or what it communicates and instead focus on the structures and activities that go into it. This book squarely focuses on the intersection of clothing and personal adornment—and relatedly fashion, style and beauty—and communication, in all of its forms.

In order to do that, we first need to set some foundational terms. The next several pages will define and explain ideas behind both the study of communication and clothing. You'll notice that I did not use the term *fashion* here, because, as will be explained, I'll be using "fashion" to describe the wider cultural system, which includes clothing, but also includes things like hairstyles, furniture and even food. First, we'll explore how we understand and model communication and the various levels at which we communicate. Then, we'll take a brief inventory of terminology used when discussing personal adornment and delineate key terms including clothing, fashion and style.

From there, the rest of the book will largely be structured around how clothing and personal adornment works within various communicative processes; the first chapters of the book will explore how we use clothing on an individual level. Chapter 2 will explore how clothing works *intra*personally to help us develop our sense of self and *inter*personally to communicate with each other through our appearance and how we make sense of others. Chapter 3 will extend these discussions toward how clothing, appearance and personal adornment works on a group level, helping people fit in with particular social groups and/or identifying various traits from gender to religious affiliation.

The book then turns its attention to the fashion system and how clothing is given meaning on a cultural level. Chapter 4 explores several of the conceptualizations of fashion and discusses how researchers have attempted to make sense of the meaning of clothing. The chapters that follow will each explore a particular medium which together constitutes the fashion system and provides meaning for clothing and trends. Chapter 5 focuses on print media and journalism, paying particular attention to fashion magazines and the idea of taste. Film and television are discussed in Chapter 6 and the importance of representation within visual mediums will be addressed. In Chapter 7, we turn our attention toward advertising to explore how branding efforts help give meaning to particular goods. How all of these systems—print media, film and television production, and branding—have been upended with the rise of the internet, especially social media, will be addressed in Chapter 8. We'll explore digital communication broadly to see how influencers, customization and social media promotions have all reshaped the way we talk about fashion and even produce clothing. Finally, Chapter 9 will look at a critical debate about clothing and asks: Is it art? Addressing this topic, we'll better understand how we can see clothing and fashion interact with art, music and cultural insitutitons and the processes that help us decide and bestow importance on particular objects and designers.

Ultimately, this is a lot of ground to cover, so each chapter will come with a reading list that will further explain some of the key research concepts within both communication and fashion studies. Moreover, we'll make several stops along the way to practically apply these ideas. By the time we're done, we'll have a solid understanding of how we both express ourselves via clothing and how clothing receives its meaning, and will be ready to continue to explore these intersections moving forward.

What is Communication?

Like many terms and concepts, the idea of "communication" has been much debated and defined in various different ways.[1] At its most basic level, communication can be understood as "the process of acting on information"[2] and this is often done with the purpose of creating joint meaning, helping to construct our social reality.[3] However, at times, communication can take place without human involvement—think about two computers transferring information. Because communication is so vital and is involved in so many different aspects of life, we often discuss communication within various contexts or levels[4]—the largest and most persistent division is between interpersonal communication and the mass media.[5]

Communication and the Self

The most basic level of communication is that which we do with ourselves, usually referred to as intrapersonal communication. Have you ever watched a movie or television show where a character shares their thoughts in a voice over? This would be an example of intrapersonal communication; the character is making sense of what is going on around them. Moreover, if you ever thought to yourself, "I really like that guy's shoes! I wonder where he got them?" then you've engaged intrapersonal communication. It is important because it helps us to make sense of the world around us. In fact, it is largely understood that our ability to think reflexively about ourselves is a key difference between us and other living things.

Interpersonal Communication

Now, let's for a minute go back to the guy's shoes. Let's imagine you walked up to him—we'll call him Kyle—and struck up a conversation about his shoes. Perhaps, the conversation goes something like this:

You   Hi, I couldn't help but notice your shoes—I love them! Can I ask where you got them?

Kyle   Hey . . . thanks! I don't remember the name, but I got them from this independent shop downtown . . . not far from the Broadway metro stop.

You   Is that the one along Broadway and like, Seventh Street?

Kyle   Yeah—that one! They always have such great finds.

You   I know exactly what you mean; I love that store!

In such an exchange, both participants in the exchange are communicating verbally (e.g. through talking) and doing so in real time. Together, you're helping to create joint meaning. While Kyle wasn't sure of the store, together you put the pieces together to figure out which store he meant. Interpersonal communication often has varying influences. For example, this exchange was started by you admiring Kyle's shoes, but things like context (Are you standing in line at a coffee shop? Or walking down the street?) and what you and Kyle are both wearing (if Kyle's shoes were old and dilapidated, he might take offense at your compliment) all play into the exchange. These are things that might not factor into the exchange if the two of you were not interacting in person.

Group Communication

Often times, teams and small groups are understood as a distinct form of communication because of their size. Largely, we assume that teams and small groups—formations of people that have specific purposes—range between three and fifteen people since it's difficult for everyone to participate in the exchange with more participants than that. However, groups also help us form social bonds and connect with one another. This also happens through shared experience and communication—and can present itself through wearing similar clothing or participating in similar activites. For instance, take two football teams. All players will wear similar clothing and protective gear to help them run and score, and we can distinguish the individuals are football players due to their uniforms. However, each competing team will wear different color uniforms, helping the players (and the fans) distinguish each side.

Mediated Communication

When communication takes place between individuals, but is not done in person, we refer to it as "mediated communication." While it is true that all communication is mediated in *some* way (even language isn't able to convey all of the feelings), we usually see mediated communication separately because (a) it cuts down on a lot of the context involved and (b) the communication is often asynchronous, meaning it doesn't take place in real time. Mediated communication involves everything from scribbling a note to sending a text to—as will be discussed much more in-depth—wearing particular clothing.

The Mass Media

Until relatively recently, the ability to communicate with a mass audience was difficult and expensive and, as such, was reserved for organizations who could coordinate and fund large-scale operations. Colloquially, we often refer to the amalgamation of publishers, radio and television networks, movie studios and the like as "the media," but ultimately each represents a particular medium (print publications, broadcasting/cable shows, films) that each had used to communicate. The communication here is largely different because the sources are often complex, profit-driven institutions, their audience is largely anonymous and specialized technology and equipment is needed for communication.[6] A fashion magazine like *Vogue* has an editorial staff, who write the articles; a photography and design staff, who take the photos and lay out the pages; a printing staff, who program the machines which physically print the magazine; and a distribution staff, who get the magazine into the mail or onto the newsstands. Ignoring subscriptions for a minute (which requires its own staff), there is no guarantee anyone will actually read the issue. The producers of the mass media might aim their content at specific individuals, but there is no guarantee that the target audience will be interested. Like all mediated communication, it takes some effort on the part of the audience to actually consume the messages presented.

New/Digital and Social Media

For decades, the institutions of the mass media had an oligarchy who could communicate with a large audience. However, with the advent of the internet, digital technologies and (especially) social media, individuals increasingly have the ability to communicate on the same scale. The internet has had two profound effects on the mass media. First, it has sparked an era of media convergence through multimedia capabilities.[7] Not only does *Vogue* publish a monthly magazine, but it also produces a podcast and online videos, including a series asking celebrities seventy-three questions and providing coverage of the important fashion weeks. Second, as the internet made social media platforms more prominent, there was a large democratization of the mass media. Initially heralded through the easy access of blogs in the early 2000s, people believed that the mass media could no longer remain "gatekeepers" and that everyone could participate in the publishing industry.[8] This radically transformed news and magazines, and opened the doors to streetstyle bloggers and other forms of influencers.[9] While this has come with considerable ethical questions, social media sites like YouTube and Instagram have helped give people platforms who might not have had access otherwise.

Modeling Communication

Despite the changing means of communication, one persistant feature is the communication model. Initially, Harold D. Lasswell set out some questions to help form the study of communication. Lasswell wrote, "A convenient way to describe an act of communication is to answer the following questions:

Who?
Says what?
In which channel?
To whom?
With what effect?"[10]

While others have added questions about context and intentions around Lasswell's initial construction,[11] this largely remains a nimble shorthand to use when thinking about communication. Still, as a formal research process, much communication research comes back not to Lasswell's construction, but to another model set out by Claude Shannon and Warren Weaver.[12]

This model (see Figure 1.2) goes by several different names including the "mathematical transition model of communication,"[13] also known as the "SMCR model,"[14] or the "communication as action" model.[15] Coming from

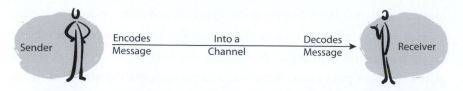

Figure 1.2 *Communication as Action Model. The "Communication as Action" Model sees communication as a unidirectional undertaking where a sender encodes a message in a specific channel to be sent to the receiver who decodes it.*

an engineering standpoint, Shannon was interested in how communication could be mediated and set forth a mathematical system to explain the process. According to this model, a sender encodes a message within a specific channel that is sent to the receiver, who decodes it. Throughout this process, noise can interfere with the communication, making it difficult or impossible for the receiver to get or interpret the message.

To put this in practical terms, imagine Sandy, a fashion-obsessed college student, gets to go to an Alexander Wang show. As the models strut down the runway, Sandy takes a quick Snapchat video of their favorite look and sends it to their best friend forever, Claudia, who wasn't able to score a ticket. In this scenario, Sandy is the sender and they encoded their message (e.g. their favorite look) into a channel (e.g. a Snapchat video). Claudia, the receiver, would get the message and have to decode it—especially if Sandy didn't include a caption or filter! Anything that interfered with the message, say Sandy's shot was out of focus or Claudia's connection was too slow to load the snap, would be considered "noise" because it interfered with the successful transfer of Sandy's message to Claudia.

To be certain, the above example is simplified and, since digitalization, several layers of communication have been added. Sandy's Snapchat message would have to be converted to a digital communication and communicated between the Snapchat application to Sandy's phone which would tie into their cell network (or WiFi) and through any number of computers until it reached Claudia's phone. (Think of how much simpler it would have been if Sandy had just written a letter!) However, the mechanical—now digital—processes are what the transmission model was intended to describe. These communications don't involve interpretation or context; the channel simply acts as a medium.

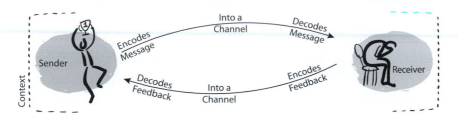

Figure 1.3 *Communication as Interaction Model. Both feedback and context are included in the "Communication as Interaction" Model which expands on the "Communication as Action" model.*

However, others found that the model was inadequate for addressing communication—especially human communication. Marvin DeFleur added feedback to the communication process and also noted that communication only occurs when there is "correspondence" in the message.[16] (We'll come back to this point.) A similar adaptation of the process which adds in feedback and also the context in which communication occurs, has been dubbed "communication as interaction"[17] (Figure 1.3). In this telling, a sender encodes a message into a specific channel to be sent to the receiver, but the receiver then encodes a return message and sends it back to the sender.

Now, imagine that after Claudia receives Sandy's Snapchat and, in reply, Claudia writes back, "So jealous! Way better than this lecture!" Claudia now became the sender as she encoded her own message and sent it back to Sandy (e.g. the feedback); she both acknowledged Sandy's message and responded in turn. Today, our phones take care of some of that for us—some apps like Snapchat let users know when their message has been viewed and everyone is aware of the dreaded "read receipts;" however, in years past, responding to the process was much more pronounced and took much longer. Moreover, Claudia and Sandy understand their messages in context; they understand how Snapchat works and have a pre-existing relationship, which helps make sense of each other's message. If Sandy sent the snap to their significant other, dad, or just broadcast it widely, the receiver might not have the same reaction—or might not even understand what is happening.

Still, this process of encoding, sending and decoding messages takes time and, while it might appropriately explain communication via letter or snap, it

Figure 1.4 *Circular Communication Model. The "Circular Communication Model" reduces the time lag between messages being sent and feedback being given.*

doesn't take into account real time of interpersonal communication (i.e. in-person communication between two people). That's where the "circular"[18] or the "communication as transaction" model[19] comes into play (Figure 1.4). In this model, both participants in communication act as the sender and receiver, constantly encoding, interpreting and decoding messages. Imagine that Sandy doesn't snap Claudia with their favorite look from the show, but instead takes a photo and waits until the next day to tell Claudia. Over coffee, Sandy explains the entire day including their favorite outfit. As they tell Claudia about their experience, Claudia nods along and interjects where appropriate. Here, Sandy and Claudia are both being senders and receivers; Claudia is listening to the story and Sandy is reading her nonverbal communication as a sign to keep going. If Claudia was on her phone or rolling her eyes during Sandy's story, Sandy would instantly know Claudia wasn't interested. Likewise, imagine what would happen if Claudia simply sat in still silence—listening, but not responding—to Sandy's entire story and only responded once Sandy stopped talking.

The communication as transaction acknowledges that during real-time communication we are constantly both sender *and* receiver; likewise, we are constantly encoding *and* decoding messages from whomever we're communicating with. Often, this type of communication takes place in person, but with things like Skype and Google Hangouts we have more ability to interact simultaneously through different channels. This model essentially collapses the time it takes to encode, decode and send feedback, while acknowledging that it all happens within specific contexts. For example, if

Sandy and Claudia were talking about the fashion show in the middle of a lecture hall, their discussion would be understood differently than if they had it at their local coffee shop. Likewise, if Sandy had an extra ticket and didn't invite Claudia, the dynamics of the conversation would change.

Other Factors in Communication

All these models attempt to take various aspects of communication into account, notably accounting for the increased speed and immediacy of communication. However, there are some other elements of communication that are equally important; namely (a) that communication is irreversible and builds on itself, (b) that communication helps us make sense of or "construct" the world, and (c) communication is complicated.[20]

To refer back to Sandy and Claudia, the two are good friends and have a history to draw on. Likely, Sandy told Claudia about going to fashion week before sending her a snap from the event. If Sandy sent Claudia the snap out of the blue—or if they had sent it to a friend they weren't as close to—Claudia might not know how to make sense of the message. Perhaps she would be surprised to see Sandy was at a fashion show (rather than in class) or might not understand why Sandy was excited to go. Similarly, even if Claudia didn't know Sandy was a fan of Alexander Wang before she received the snap, it in of itself is something that would inform future communication between the two.

This exchange could also prove meaningful in their relationship. Fashion week carries a cultural significance; one that Sandy was engaging with both by attending the event and by sharing the event with Claudia. This might inform Sandy's understanding of the fashion trends that will be hitting stores in the coming months and helps Sandy's reputation as a fashionista to Claudia and the rest of their friendship group. If Sandy is constantly reading *Vogue* and *Elle*, and always knows the best places to shop, these help to maintain Sandy's status. On a larger scale, the various fashion weeks are understood to be influential because everyone—from designers to sponsors to the media covering the shows—treat it as such. Claudia's feedback that she was "so jealous!" helps to communicate the desirability of fashion week attendance to Sandy. If Claudia had responded with "LOL—who still likes Alexander Wang?" the interpretation and meaning made between the friends would be vastly different.

However, imagine for a minute that Claudia had sent the message, "LOL—who still likes Alexander Wang?" in response to Sandy's original snap. How would Sandy read it? Much of it might come down to the relationship between Sandy and Claudia and their previous experiences. Perhaps Sandy would understand it as a joke since Claudia is also a big fan of the designer? Or perhaps Sandy would think Claudia is making fun of them and respond in turn? Many different factors would go into how Sandy might interpret that feedback—including their past experiences, Sandy's mood, perhaps even whether Claudia capitalized the "LOL." All of these factors contribute to the context communication happens in, but also makes the communication process, especially the *human* communication process, infinitely complex.

Communication and/as Rhetoric

Perhaps that's why people have been studying communication for more than two millenia—*literally*. The study of rhetoric, which in many ways is a precursor to studying communication, was introduced by the ancient Greek philosopher Aristotle more than 2,300 years ago.[21] Rhetoric, as it's being used here, doesn't have the negative conntations that the word *might* have in today's world; rhetoric is, essentially, an interest in understanding how communicators (generally, public speakers) can persuade an audience. Broadly, here, Artistole thought persusasive arguments could be understood from three intertwined pieces: logic of the argument (logos), the character of the communicator (ethos) and the emotional appeal of the message (pathos).[22] Ethos, or the character of the speaker, is perhaps the most direct way clothing plays into this communication. Politicans are generally "dressed up" when giving a public speech, as are newscasters and talk show hosts. Largely, we assume that the way we dress implies something about our character and those who look well put together are more likely to know what they're talking about. (This is *not* always the case.)

Unsurprisingly, there have been developments and challenges to the idea of rhetoric since Aristotle's time. For example, Sonja Foss and Cindy Griffin pointed out that rhetoric, as traditionally understood, suffers from a patriarchical bias in that it sees communication as a means of persuasion and, as such, is combative and seeks to dominate others.[23] Drawing off of feminist values of "equality, immanent value and self-determination," they lay out an invitational rhetoric where the goal is relationship building and shared meaning.[24] In this way, rhetoric is not *just* about convincing people using logic and argumentation, but also about helping people understand each other. The tenets of rhetoric have also been applied outside of pure arguments: *visual* rhetoric pays particular attention to the power of images, including in mediums like photography, film and advertising.[25]

Regardless of whether we apply rhetorical principles to spoken, written or visual communication, it's important to remember that communication helps us create reality.[26] What this means is that forms of logic and knowledge become so routinized that we forget or can't imagine different arguments or ways of doing things; exploring communication—even through clothing— using a rhetorical lens allows us to question all forms of communication and expose the underlying logic therein. While we won't be explicitly applying rhetoric through the book, the ideas of rhetoric—especially its communicative ability to construct reality—can be applied to both individual communication and messages from the mass media.

Verbal and Nonverbal Communication

Beyond the divisions between spoken and visual rhetoric, we can also see communication divided between verbal and nonverbal components. When we talk about "verbal communication," we're really talking about anything that relies on language as a means of communication. Language is a structured system of symbols that help us pass information to each other.[27] Often times this is understood to be spoken; however, any communication that relies on language can be considered verbal communication. Text messages, handwritten letters and even this book are examples of verbal communication.

Contrast that to nonverbal communication, which includes any messages that do *not* rely on a structured system. Perhaps most commonly, this is understood as communicating through body movements and facial expressions. Think about what Claudia might be "saying" if she rolled her eyes at Sandy or what Claudia might be communicating to someone else while she keeps checking her phone for Sandy's messages; both are examples of nonverbal communication. Since there is no specific system we're communicating with, nonverbal communication is often more context-dependent and open to interpretation; as such, Claudia rolling her eyes might be seen as a light-hearted joke rather than an insult or Claudia checking her phone might be better understood if we know she's waiting for an important call.

Beyond the body movement, material goods, inanimate objects and yes—clothing—can also be used to communicate. Often, we refer to this as communication with objects or artifacts.[28] The things we own, use and put on our body help us communicate to ourselves and to others[29] and have the ability to express a variety of traits and even emotions. However, these meanings are constantly in flux, which makes understanding them highly complex and always open to interpretation. This has led some to question whether or not we can see clothing as a medium of communication at all.[30] (*Spoiler alert: We can.*) Still, the constant changes make it more complex and less direct than a lot of other communication.

Clothing and Fashion

However, before we can address the way clothing communicates, we need to better define what we're talking about because terms such as clothing, fashion, dress and style are used interchangeably to refer to the same (or similar) things.[31] Many times, even setting out these definitions is problematic because these terms are often defined in relation to one another and vary from one work to the next.[32]

Adornment and Appearance

Mary Ellen Roach and Joanne Eicher noted that while everyone adorns themselves in some way, not everyone wears fabrics or materials that protect the skin.[33] As such, they used the term "personal adornment" and noted that the way we present ourselves varies based on the society and culture we're in. Their definition worked to cut across cultures and helped us understand how we use our aesthetic appearances to a variety of ends. While adornment uses reflexivity and describes things placed on the body,[34] terms as such the "presentation of self"[35] and "appearances" look outward toward what is being projected to others.[36] As Gregory P. Stone has noted, our appearance helps to create our identities, which, in turn, shapes the way we communicate.[37]

Fashion

However, our appearances are often shaped by fashion—a much contested (and often derided) term.[38] Fashion is an immaterial system of meaning created and applied to a variety of things, primarially consumable, material goods.[39] The idea is that "fashion" is really an ever-changing system that alters society's tastes. Theorists like Georg Simmel, Herbert Blumer, Grant McCracken and Gilles Lipovetsky all see fashion as a system of cultural change.[40] While each of the aforementioned theorists have come to different conclusions and understandings about how fashion works (and this will be discussed in Chapter 4), right now it is just important to note that fashion is the *system* of change which impacts the meaning and the way we see clothing and other material goods.[41]

As such, it is easy to see how clothing is not synonymous with fashion, even if it is a part of it. Think about it: what else goes in and out of fashion? Other products and objects that we use to personally adorn ourselves (think: hairstyles or makeup trends), cars, cell phones and home décor. If you've ever seen olive green appliances and thought they looked dated—it's because they, too, are part of the fashion system! Open up any home magazine today and it's clear the trend in kitchens is black, white or (preferably) stainless steel.

Clothing

In comparison, Ingrid Brenninkmeyer notes that clothing is a "raw material" used in the creation of the fashion system.[42] As such, we can understand clothing as the fabric-based garments—shirts, pants, dresses—that we wear every day. Clothing can be part of the fashion system as cuts, washes and designs change from one season to the next, even if the overall categorization of the garment doesn't (see: jeans).[43]

Accessories

If we see clothing as the fabric objects with which we generally adorn ourselves, the accessories we wear can be seen as pieces which accentuate or add to the clothing we have selected. Generally speaking, accessories—things like shoes, jewelry, glasses and jackets—are usually made of sturdier material than "clothing" and can be worn multiple times without needing to be cleaned.

Dress

At various times, the term "dress" has been used as a stand-in for clothing and/ or personal adornment. However, here it will be used in one of two ways: (1) as a noun to refer to a dress—the article of clothing that is usually worn over the shoulders or upper body and has a single opening at the bottom for the wearer's legs, or (2) as a verb describing a process of getting ready (e.g. "to get dressed"). Generally, "getting dressed" can include doing your hair, putting on a fragrance, clothing and accessories.[44]

Costume

Like dress, the term "costume" has been used for refer to ways of placing clothing on the body. Again, to avoid confusion, the word costume will be used in opposition to fashion—the unchanging and traditional attire worn for special occasions. This use of costume has often been chalked up alternatively to antifashion[45] or nonfashion[46] since it does not change as rapidly. Alternatively, costume may refer to an ensemble of clothing and accessories worn by performers within a specific visual medium to convey a specific image and/or turn the individual into someone else.

Style

Finally, style will be used to describe the way something is made or put together to achieve a desired aesthetic. For example, a cable-knit sweater might be said to be created in a "preppy" style or someone may be wearing that sweater tied around their waist to express a relaxed or casual style. This use of style overlaps somewhat with appearance, but appearance will be used for the overall aesthetics where style is more specific. If someone is wearing a sweater over their shoulders, it may exude a preppy style; however, if the sweater is wrinkled or not properly tied around the neck, the wearer might appear merely disheveled or messy.

Clothing in Modernity and Postmodernity

Clothing, as a material and consumable item, has an intrical relationship with the time in which it was created, and this has also influenced some of the ways clothing has been approached as a form of communication. You might have heard the adjective "modern" used in a way that implies something is "new" and "of the moment;" however, that is a colloquial use of the term. More specifically, modernity refers to a period of history that is intertwined with social, cultural and economic considerations. As there have been volumes written about this, we aren't even skimming the surface of the topic. However, as some of the discussion throughout this book will return to these ideas in various senses, it is important to have a basic understanding of these terms now.

Generally speaking, modernism is considered as a period of time that started in the mid-1850s and went hand-in-hand with industrialization, the rise of urban areas and objective scientific developments.[47] For the most part, during modernity, society was understood to be highly structured and relatively stable. Categorizations like class and religion permeated society and personal identities were understood to be stable and unchanging. The overarching belief was that, through scientific reason, societies progressed toward better ends.

Comparatively, in postmodernity, researchers and philosophers began to interrogate modernity itself and question whether its tenets were true. To be fair, there are a lot of theorizations and uses of the term "postmodern," and this summation is hardly exhaustive. However, among the developments of postmodernism was an increased focus on communication through the mass media and the question of whether society was always working toward something better.[48] The acknowledgment of subjective experiences came to question the dominance of an "objective" reality and rather than see society as a stable, structured system, ideas like community and identity were understood to be more fluid than were previously believed—with individuality being prized over group membership.

According to Erfat Tseëlon, each era—premodern, modern and postmodern—brought with it a different relation to fashion.[49] In premodern times, fashion was marked by scarcity; items like dyes or fabrics were not available to everyone, so only the wealthiest were able to stay in fashion. In modernity, thanks to industrialization, the production of clothing was made easier and, ultimately, fashion was democratized so more people could participate in it. While there were still distinctions within clothing, fashion was generally understood to be a stable system that changed at regular intervals. And, the understanding of what is "in fashion" was generally understood and accepted by all. As society moved toward postmodernity, clothing and style became more of a individualized expression. Moreover, the fashion system began to interpret and reinvent its previous styles, becoming a self-referential system.

Communicatively, these changes also altered our understanding of clothing as well. In premodern times, it was easy to see the connection between clothing and its wearer as scarcity made the display of wealth through clothing apparent. The democratization of fashion in modernity removed the obvious links between clothing and status and made fashion a matter of social taste (e.g. knowing what's in fashion) as much as how much was spent on the clothing and accessories. Finally, in postmodernity, the links between clothing and wearer became a matter of individual taste and our understanding of what clothing is communicating became even more complex and difficult to surmise. We're going to come back to these ideas when we talk about identity in Chapter 2, the fashion system in Chapter 4 and branding in Chapter 7.

Communicating Clothing

However, we can also see how modernity and postmodernity shape our understanding of how clothing communicates. Now, when we're discussing communication, we are ultimately discussing meaning: how people understand the world and what interpretation is gleaned from messages and actions.[50] Specifically in regard to how clothing communicates, various models and understandings have been suggested, however, many of these understandings come back to the idea of semiotics[51]—or that our clothing works as a sign system. Semiotics, in brief, comes to the idea that something signifies something else. It was widely seen as a foundation of language[52] and verbal communication (as noted above), but has also been applied to visual communication and clothing. Perhaps the most famous and extensive work in this vein was Roland Barthes' *The Fashion System*, which turned to fashion magazines to tease out how specific uses of clothing might mean "sporty" or "dressy," among other things.[53] Barthes' construction was largely rooted in a modernist and structured semiotic system that was unchanging and could be clearly delinated. (Barthes' other work would be far less structured than his work in *The Fashion System*.) There have been others who have proposed this understanding to varying degrees,[54] however this view has been criticized for taking the metaphor or "language of clothing" too literally, and isn't dynamic enough to fully grasp how clothing and appearance communicates.

Fred Davis suggested that clothing cannot be a full language, but can represent something of a quasi-code of understanding. In this understanding, not every choice we make can be structured into some set of rules and while some things might be encoded in our clothing—not everything can be.[55] Colin Campbell took this a step farther and argued that even a quasi-code is too much to expect from our clothing. The problem, as Campbell sees it, is that in order for something to be classified as communication, the receiver must get the same message as the encoder.[56] However, Campbell's understanding that only *accurate* communication is communication misses several developments in communication theories and rests largely on the transmission model of communication. However, we are always communicating—whether we intend to or not.[57] As such, we have to accept that clothing is communicating in some sense, whether or not the "correct" messages are being read.

In this vein, Malcolm Barnard was rather successful in explaining how clothing communicates. For Barnard, the messages within clothing cannot be seen before or after its use and, therefore, its expressiveness is always in flux. In this way, we can see Barnard's understand of clothing is more in line with the circular model of communication and postmodernity since understanding and interpetations are more subjective. Barnard acknowledges that the meaning of clothing might be held together by our demographic and/or cultural groups,[58] something that has been suggested by others as well.[59] As such, clothing must be seen contextually: *what* is worn matters, but it also matters *where, when* and *how* it is being worn.[60]

Equally important to the context is *who* is working to create the meaning. Semiotic approaches largely suggest meaning can either be found within the things we use to adorn ourselves or attached to the objects from outside sources like the designer of a garment or a fashion critic.[61] Instead, if we see communication as a process between two or more individuals, we can see that the meaning is created *within* the exchange. To invoke Sandy and Claudia one more time, consider this hypothetical exchange.

Sandy shows up for a lunch with Claudia and their less fashionable friend, Jane, with the latest (and most expensive) bag from Alexander Wang. Claudia, who realizes what the bag is and how much it costs, is impressed that Sandy was able to purchase it. However, since Jane is neither aware of the brand nor how much money the bag cost, she's likely to evaluate it on other factors: perhaps practicality, color or design. Sandy and Claudia could take the time to explain why Sandy's new bag is a status symbol, but that would also run the risk of making them look materialistic or bragging about the money they were able to spend. Alternatively, if Claudia knows that Sandy used their rent money to purchase the bag—or worse, now doesn't have money for her own lunch— she might be less impressed with the purchase or will understand the purchase and its consumption within the larger relationship she has with Sandy.

Some have suggested the idea of interpreting the objects we purchase and use for adornment is a relatively new development that is steeped in consumerism.[62] However, the extended fascination with clothing and appearances from both the general public and academic researchers suggests interpretations like these have been made for centuries (at least), and likely much longer. In Chapter 2, we'll look at some of the internal motivations for selecting the things that we wear, while Chapter 3 will better explore how clothing can be used as a means of communication within groups.

Further Reading

There are a plethora of textbooks out there which help shape up the communication landscape from both a human communication perspective and from a mediated communication perspective. Sarah Trenholm's *Thinking Through Communication* (Routledge, 2020) is one of the best to discuss both individual communication and the mass media. For a more thorough introduction to the mass media, *Mass Communication: Living in Media World* by Ralph E. Hanson (Sage, 2018) covers history, theory and practice. *Communication Models for the Study of Mass Communication* by Denis McQuail and Sven Windahl (Longman, 1993) provides a more thorough discussion of the models mentioned in this chapter and *A First Look at Communication Theory* by Em Griffin, Andrew Ledbetter and Glen Sparks (McGraw-Hill, 2019) covers an impressive variety of theories.

From the fashion side, *Fashion-ology* by Yuniya Kawamura (Bloomsbury, 2018) is a good introduction to the landscape of fashion studies, as is *Fashion: The Key Concepts* by Jennifer Craik (Bloomsbury, 2009). Several volumes offer a variety of readings that can help people get into fashion studies, including *Fashion Theory: A Reader* by Malcolm Barnard (Routledge, 2020) and *Dress and Identity* by Mary Ellen Roach-Higgins and Joanne Eicher (Fairchild, 1995). Meanwhile, two books are especially useful for understanding the intersection of clothing and communication. The first, *The Social Psychology of Clothing: Symbolic Appearances in Context* by Susan B. Kaiser (Fairchild, 1996) looks at how clothing can be understood from various interactionist perspectives. The second, *Fashion as Communication*, also by Barnard (Routledge, 2002), approaches clothing from a semiotics and cultural perspective.

1   Trenholm, Sarah (2020). *Thinking Through Communication: An Introduction to the Study of Human Communication.* New York: Pearson.

2   Hanson, Ralph E. (2018). *Mass Communication: Living in a Media World,* Sixth Edition. Los Angeles: Sage.

3   McQuail, Denis and Sven Windahl (1993). *Communication Models for the Study of Mass Communication.* New York: Longman.

4   Griffin, Em, Andrew Ledbetter and Glen Sparks (2019). *A First Look at Communication Theory.* New York: McGraw-Hill.

5   Kawamura, Yuniya (2018). *Fashion-ology: An Introduction to Fashion Studies.* New York: Bloomsbury.

6   Craik, Jennifer (2009). *Fashion: The Key Concepts.* New York: Bloomsbury.

7   Barnard, Malcolm (2020). *Fashion Theory: A Reader.* New York: Routledge.

8   Roach-Higgins, Mary Ellen and Joanne Eicher (1995). *Dress and Identity.* New York: Fairchild.

9   Kaiser, Susan B. (1997). *The Social Psychology of Clothing: Symbolic Appearances in Context.* New York: Fairchild.

10   Barnard, Malcolm (2002). *Fashion as Communication.* New York: Routledge.

Figure 2.1 *Does She Care? Melania Trump raised eyebrows with her jacket as she traveled to visit immigrant children at the US border. © Chip Somodevilla via Getty Images.*

2

Clothing as Intra- and Interpersonal Communication

"I REALLY DON'T CARE. DO U?" Those words that appeared on US First Lady Melania Trump's back set the political (and fashion) worlds ablaze in 2018.

The firestorm erupted following the Trump administration's decision to separate migrant families being held at the US–Mexico border.[1] The controversial policy meant to stymie undocumented immigration had been considered for some time, but gained national attention in June 2018, as former first ladies—notably Laura Bush, but also Rosalynn Carter, Hillary Clinton and Michelle Obama—began to speak against the policy.[2] Political observers even postulated that Melania Trump was in agreement with the former first ladies and was against the policy.[3] Then, came the jacket.

Taking a "surprise trip" to visit migrant children being held at the border, Melania Trump was photographed wearing an olive green jacket with the phrase on its back in faux-paint. The photo set off a parlor game of reading into the First Lady's fashion choices while her office denied there was a hidden message in the clothing.[4] Despite the statement, the President took to Twitter to suggest it was an attack on the news media.[5] Observers debated whether or not something should be read into the $39 jacket made by Zara, with most dismissing the explanation from the First Lady's office.[6] Taking the statement literally, Robin Givhan of *The Washington Post* suggested that, if it was just a jacket, then the First Lady's clothing decisions will never matter again.[7] Meanwhile, *The New York Times* Fashion Director and Chief Critic Vanessa Friedman agreed with the First Lady's office that there wasn't a *hidden* message. "It wasn't hidden," Friedman wrote. "It was literally written on the first lady's back. The question is: Who was the intended audience?"[8]

It would take months for Melania Trump to weigh in on the debate, finally telling a reporter in October 2018 that it was a message for the news media—and not the children. "It's obvious I didn't wear the jacket for the children," she said, "I wore the jacket to go on the plane and off the plane."[9] She would go on to criticize the press's coverage of her fashion choices saying she would sooner media pay attention to her actions, rather than what she wears.[10]

First ladies have long used fashion and material goods as a way to support their husbands and the nation at large. Early on, Dolley Madison used implicit references to Classic Antiquity to help establish the United States as a global force. More recently, Jackie Kennedy was well-known for using both clothing and the media to create and share the "Camelot" mystique around the Kennedy administration in the 1960s,[11] and Michelle Obama gained attention for slipping out of the White House to shop at Target.[12]

Still, the brouhaha around Melania Trump's jacket raises two important facets of our clothing: Who do we dress for and how will people understand it? While few will understand the intense scrutiny of being the First Lady (or any trendsetter for that matter), our clothing choices are constantly being read and understood by others—whether or not they are intended to be. Moreover, our clothing always has the power to be read in ways we might not have intended it to; Melania's jacket was widely seen to be a comment on the migrant children, but she later said she intended it to be a comment to the media.[13]

Clothing works on various levels to identify wearers and individuals, but also helps us fit into various social and cultural contents. Sociologist Diana Crane dubbed this fashion's "social agenda,"[14] as clothing helps us communicate (and identify) things like gender, class, region and nationality, while also allowing us to maintain our own individuality, through our selection, wearing and styling of garments. Our identities and sense of self, however, start developing long before we are able to make decisions for ourselves and can be wrapped up in the decisions our parents and caregivers made for us. Communication scholars generally see our identities developing through communication with others, our association with groups, the roles we take on, and our self-labels.[15] As will be discussed in the rest of this chapter, clothing and the material goods we surround ourselves with are intricately bound up within these processes—both helping to shape our identities and allowing us to express ourselves.

Why Do We Wear Clothing?

Before we get into how clothing helps shape our identity and allows us to communicate with others, it might be useful to discuss a bit about *why* we wear clothing. It might not be something you've given much thought to; after all, wearing clothing is likely something you've done since birth so it comes as second nature. However, the idea that we need to be "covered up" before we go out in public is assumed in nearly every culture.

Psychologist J.C. Flügel proposed three reasons that we wear clothing.[16] The first, and probably the most important, is protection. Clothing and accessories help to protect us from the elements, whether it is a down jacket keeping us warm during a cold Canadian winter or a sunhat protecting us from harmful sunrays. The second reason cited by Flügel was modesty—the idea that we didn't want to show off all of our "wobbly bits" to the world. This idea has deep roots in the Judeo-Christian world: the story of creation involves Adam learning he's naked and trying to cover up. The third idea is for adornment or ornamentation; here, clothing and accessories help to display various parts of our body, whether that's by wearing a tank-top that shows off our shoulders or an expensive necklace that shows off our wealth.

Some garments were once practical but have moved from protection to adornment. Take, for example, academic regalia—the type you might have seen professors wearing during convocation and the type you'll wear at your graduation—was once used to keep people warm in drafty, unheated buildings in the twelfth and thirteenth centuries. However, by the late 1400s, caps and gowns had become more ornamental than worn out of necessity. Today, most colleges adhere to the Intercollegiate Code of Academic Costume, first published in 1895, which designates the shapes and colors of gowns based on types of degree and disciplines.[17]

While it is true that clothing is a practical item that protects us, today we largely see it as much (or more of) a cultural force than just for protection. Theorists have explored this in various ways. For example, Erving Goffman wrote that people use their appearances for "impression management"[18] or communicating *something* to those who they interacted with. In a similar vein, Fred Davis argued that both clothing and the fashion system work in tandem to help us develop and communicate our identities.[19] Meanwhile, Joanne Entwistle adds that the way we understand our body and, subsequently, the way we dress, is developed through our cultural understandings.[20] In short, we wear clothing because that's what we're taught to do and it is what is expected of us.[21]

Clothing, Our "Self" and Our Subjective Positions

From the moment we're born (and sometimes even before!) we are assigned various identities. Take, for example, gender reveal parties where expectant parents find out the sex of their baby, usually while surrounded by friends, family members and cameras. Couples cut into cakes, pop balloons and set off fireworks to reveal pink or blue colors indicating a boy or girl. Some versions of this newfound tradition have drawn further distinctions including "touchdowns or tutus," "tractors or tiaras" and "pistols or pearls." Regardless of the specific framing, there are embedded assumptions in all of these connections. Party planners are assuming baby boys will like blue, as well as football, farming and guns, and that girls will like pink, ballet, princesses and jewelry thereby helping to ritualize gender identities and performances.[22]

However, as dress historian Jo Paoletti has shown, the correlation between pink and girls and blue and boys has been a relatively recent development. Babies were frequently dressed in gender-neutral clothing through the early 1900s and the alignment of pink for girls and blues for boys took substantially longer. Paoletti notes that it was only in the 1980s that the prevalence of prenatal testing ultimately led to the color-gender alignment common in the US today.[23] Researchers have noticed that we communicate differently with babies from the time they are born—for instance using different adjectives to describe boys and girls[24]—therefore the fact that clothing and material consumption follows similar patterns should come as no surprise. Moreover, it makes all the more sense that toys have become something of a touchpoint for gender debates, especially as preschoolers have been shown to recognize gender stereotypes.[25]

Gregory P. Stone noted that appearances, which, for him included "gestures, grooming, clothing, location and the like," can be identified by others and placed into social categorizations.[26] The identities we place on others (as well as ourselves) fit within contemporary social structures. Luckily, clothing is one of the spaces where our individual agency is able to interact with and alter the meanings held by sociocultural structures at large.[27] There are several complex systems at work that help to create particular clothes and material goods, as well as the meaning that plays into them.

As Susan B. Kaiser notes, our clothing and style interacts with several different social elements including (Figure 2.2):

(a) our subjective positions (i.e. the way we understand ourselves such as our gender, race and nationality);

(b) the things we consume;

(c) how these goods are produced;

(d) how they are distributed; and

(e) how they are regulated.[28]

In today's globalized world, these various facets have grown in complexity and importance—some of which are obstructed (intentionally or unintentionally) from public view.

To illustrate how this might work, let's discuss the hypothetical situation of Chris, a 19-year-old football player attending college in Philadelphia. Chris grew up in a middle-class household in rural Ohio before moving East. From a young age, Chris developed a sense of himself as a white, straight, cisgender

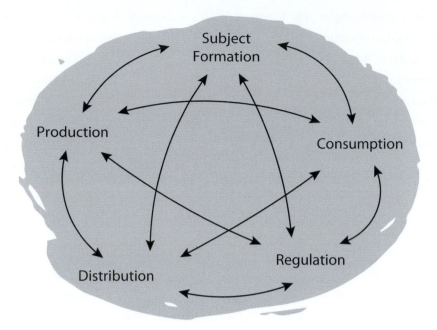

Figure 2.2 *Kaiser's Circuit of Culture. This Circuit of Culture, applied to clothing by Susan B. Kaiser, illustrates the various concepts which impact the fashion system.*

male, who lives in the United States. This has shaped the activities he's taken part in (e.g. football), but also the things he buys (i.e. men's garments as opposed to women's). When Chris decides to buy a pair of Nike running sneakers, the shoes were already shaped by production (the design, sourcing of materials and construction of the shoes), most of which was done in a different country and shipped to the United States.[29] Chris' ability to purchase the shoes depends on the distribution of materials to the factories, and then the distribution of the goods to the store (or, if purchased online, to Chris himself). This is all regulated by various organizations. The governments of respective countries regulate trade and (ideally) protect consumers and workers from being taken advantage of or harmed by the goods. All these elements factor into the things Chris *can* buy; some of which might not be available to a 19-year-old living in a different nation. And, all of these facets come into play before Chris *can even buy the shoes!* Once he buys them, then he can wear (i.e. consume) them.

However, Chris' actual consumption comes down to a question of what he *wants* to buy.[30] Chris has the ability to decide whether he wants to spend his money on a pair of Nikes or if he'd rather purchase a pair of Adidas shoes or a less notable brand. Maybe it comes down to color choice: Chris really likes black shoes and the Nikes he likes only come in white. Or maybe Chris is skeptical of Nike's labor practices—which have been highly criticized in the past[31]—and prefers to go with a more socially conscientious shoe brand. Finally, every day Chris needs to wake up and decide that this is what he *wants* to wear or the shoes become something forgotten in the back of Chris' closet. This is a complicated process that starts and ends with Chris, as a person.

Getting to Know Ourselves

Largely, social psychologists and communication scholars think we develop our sense of self through four different aspects, according to Steven A. Beebe, Susan J. Beebe and Diana K. Ivy. These include: communication with others, roles we assume, group membership and self-labels. Each one of these interact with our clothing and appearance. Think about it: A man wearing a T-shirt with the slogan "This is what a feminist looks like" is clearly self-labeling, while uniforms worn by nurses and firefighters clearly identify their roles.

Communicating with Others

Perhaps the most important factor in how we come to know ourselves is through our communication with others. Charles Horton Cooley once dubbed this process the "reflected" or "looking glass" self, suggesting that we develop our identities through how others interact with us.[32] Importantly, when we talk about communication in this context, we're referring to both our verbal and nonverbal communication. (And, some of it isn't even intentional!)

Imagine, if you would, that you're shopping with a friend and they come out of the fitting room in an outfit that looks completely unflattering on them. Perhaps you don't even have to say anything, but the expression on your face tells them you don't approve. If, instead, your friend decides to buy the outfit anyway and gets looks from various strangers, the idea is that they'll eventually internalize these communications and wear something else. To be clear, that's not to say that you should let your friend wear unflattering clothing nor that it's morally sound to judge people on what they wear. The process is just one part of symbolic interactionism—the social-psychological view that believes the self is developed and any changes are due to everyday interactions.[33]

Assumed Roles

Every day we act out any number of roles. Right now, reading this, you might be enacting the role of student. The roles we take on can vary widely from familial and personal (friend, significant other, child, parent) to professional (bartender, cashier, barista) to social (sports fan, gamer, groupie). These roles help us understand our expectations and decide how we want to present ourselves. For each of these roles, we're likely to select different clothing and appear differently. If you've ever run into one of your teachers or even a professor in a social setting, you likely noticed they looked different than they did in the classroom. This is an example of professors using clothing to demonstrate their roles: instructor in the classroom or everyday person outside of it. Likewise, you might show your "school spirit" during the homecoming parade, but would wear something nicer when you and your friends are going out. The way we dress for these roles varies and might be dictated by explicit or implicit expectations. We'll return to this idea later on.

Group Membership

Another way we understand who we are is from the groups we're part of. Like many parts of our identity, some of these may been assigned while we might have chosen to be part of others. As mentioned above, gender is something we're often grouped in before we're even born. However, something like a collegiate student body is something you choose to be part of. Some memberships are more malleable than others: the racial and ethnic groups we see ourselves as are largely constructed by others (Google: "Rachel Dolezal" if you're suspicious), and religious groups might have requirements that must be met for group membership. Both of these examples are groups with significant identities that help shape our understanding of ourselves and the world around us. At the other end of the spectrum, social clubs, sports teams and class membership are things that we easily join and leave. Often, the groups that are most important to us—family, faith communities—are considered primary groups while the groups we socialize in are considered secondary groups.[34] We'll talk more about these in the next chapter.

Self-labels

The final way we come to know ourselves is from the way we label ourselves. Think about how you might describe yourself in a Tinder profile: "Smart, fun-loving guy looking for a good time" or "Part-time student, full-time football fan." Smart, fun-loving, and football fan are all qualities you can label yourself as. These labels may come about from your communication with others—maybe people keep telling you how smart you are—or from your own experiences. For example, maybe you know you've decided you're not a great painter, but that you have killer math skills. Or maybe you've decided you want to be "open to new experiences" and follow through by trying new foods and going on road trips. In all of these situations you're labeling specific traits about yourself. Some of these might play into your appearance, like if you're a self-described fashionista, while others might not. Still, these labels help us understand ourselves, our decisions and our communication.

Performances, Identity and Ambivalence

Goffman—like Kenneth Burke before him—took the phrase famously attributed to Shakespeare literally: "All the world's a stage, and all the men and women merely players."[35] Understood as dramaturgy, Goffman argued that each of us have several different areas and scenes in which we act out our lives, including front stage, back stage and off stage.[36] Front stage is where we perform for others and back stage is where we prepare for those performances. Off stage is when we aren't performing and, more than likely, are in a space alone.

To explain this, let's take the television comedy *Superstore* (2015–). For those unfamiliar with it, the show follows the staff of the fictional Cloud 9 superstore throughout their lives as employees of the company. The show follows Amy (America Ferrera), Jonah (Ben Feldman) and the rest of the employees as they interact with various customers on the sales floor; this includes helping them find items, answer questions and apply makeup. These interactions would be the "front stage" for the Cloud 9 staff. However, *Superstore* frequently shows staff meetings in the lunchroom where management instructs associates on company happenings and what they should be doing on the sales floor. These scenes are clearly the "back stage" activities as the employees are preparing to work on the sales floor. Like in real stores, Cloud 9 employees wear blue vests and name badges—things that would be arranged back stage and out of view of customers. Yet, even when back stage, Cloud 9 employees are interacting and performing for each other to show their enthusiasm (or lack thereof) for the job and in their other interactions with each other. Finally, in rare circumstances, some of the characters in *Superstore* have been shown "off stage" meaning when they are alone or expecting to be. For example, one character who took up residence in the store, was caught walking around in his underwear when other staff members were at the store late. In this case, the character didn't anticipate anyone would be around; as such, he was caught off guard when he wasn't expecting to be "performing" for anyone.

Face vs Facework

Closely related to the idea of performances is Goffman's compatible idea of a "face" and "facework." In this case, a face is a favorable impression that one is hoping to portray within an individual performance. Facework includes all the actions that help shape our interactions with each other. Again, it's not hard to imagine clothing fitting into these performances and our facework. Think about it: What do you wear when you want to look studious for a professor? Is that the same thing you'd wear if you want to look attractive and desirable for a night out? Hopefully not! Still, what you wear helps present an image to others.

At various times, there might be threats to our face or something that might make us appear differently than what we'd like. In these cases, William

R. Cupach and Sandra Metts suggest there are two different types of facework we engage in: preventive and corrective.[37] Preventive are the actions we take *prior to* breaking our face (i.e. doing something out of our desired character). If you've ever said something like, "I normally wouldn't wear this, but it's a special occasion," you've engaged in preventive facework. Meanwhile, corrective facework is done after something happens to damage the image you're presenting. A somewhat common trope is when someone loses a swimsuit, leading to significant embarrassment and some actions to try and protect themselves from embarrassment and save face.

Changing Faces

It must be remembered that our identities—as expressed by our performances, our facework and felt by ourselves—are neither fixed nor stagnant. The way we see ourselves and the way we react to things around us evolves over time and, likewise, we might seek to portray different qualities or identities strategically to help us in various situations. The idea that we can take on different identities is often seen as something of a "postmodern" understanding, as we have become less tied to traditional social structures, such as class.[38] Even with some social structures and categorizations, the way we see and understand ourselves constantly changes when we interact with new people, take on new roles, join new groups or begin to label ourselves differently. This is an ongoing process of making sense of ourselves and the world around us,[39] and these changes can play out in the way we dress and present ourselves. This is often understood to be ambivalence—or the changing (and possibly contradictory) views of ourselves and our clothing.

Ambivalence and ambiguity are frequently seen as instrumental to fashion and how we present ourselves. Recently, Maria Mackinney-Valentin has expanded on this idea by exploring how other categories within fashion, like age, class and authenticity, are also open to ambivalence. For example, she argues that "granny chic" works to upend fashion's focus on youth, instead sartorially playing with the age and looks traditionally assigned to older women.[40] This is an example of fashion's constant need for the new—something that we'll expand on in Chapter 4.

Intra- and Interpersonal Communication

Now, when talking about clothing on a personal level there are really two different aspects at play: how we interpret the dress and appearance of others, and how we use clothing and style to express ourselves to others.[41] To put this into the communication models discussed in Chapter 1, in the first case we are the receivers of the messages whereas in the second, we are the senders. This is an ongoing process where we interpret the messages (or the case of clothing looks and garments) around us, internalize them and attempt to use them for our own ends. This is sometimes called "micro social processes,"[42] but might more commonly be called intrapersonal communication and interpersonal communication. Intrapersonal communication is when you're communicating to yourself, whether aloud or internally. Think back to getting dressed this morning. Maybe you tried on an outfit, decided it wasn't appropriate for the weather and changed. Or maybe you checked yourself out in the mirror, realized you looked great and headed out for the day. In either case, you engaged in intrapersonal communication, where you saw and recognized your reflection and made judgements about your appearance—to yourself.

In comparison, interpersonal communication refers to the messages sent between you and other people. Communication scholars, however, believe there are a few distinguishing characteristics of interpersonal communication: largely that we see the other person as an individual and/or that our communication speaks to our relationship with that other person.[43] In the past, scholars considered it imperative that interpersonal communication take place *in person* since verbal *and* nonverbal messages are important, but today we largely acknowledge that interpersonal communication can also take place through various media, such as FaceTime Skype and Zoom.[44] For our purposes here, we just need to keep in mind that interpersonal communication involves seeing a person individually and not as an anonymous group.

Before we can get into the specific ways clothing plays into interpersonal communication, we need to talk a bit about relationships, or the connections we have with others.[45] These connections largely influence the context of our communication, including how our clothing choices will be interpreted.[46] The relationships we have vary greatly and may be short, sweet and forgotten or long-lasting and meaningful. Generally, the longer we interact with someone the more we're willing to share with them and vice versa. However, these relationships need to start somewhere.

The very first step in any relationship is the pre-interaction awareness stage.[47] This is where you might first notice someone, but have yet to truly interact with them. For example, say you walk into your favorite coffee shop and there is a new, alluring stranger sitting in the corner near your usual seat. You know they are there, but order your coffee and wait for it at the bar. As you glance in his general direction, you might notice he's wearing a blue knit cardigan over a worn T-shirt, with tortoise shell rimmed glasses. Or maybe he's wearing a common white T-shirt and dark blue jeans while a black leather jacket is draped over the back of his chair. The clothing and accessories around him will help you determine if, and possibly how, you initiate a relationship with him. Here relationship doesn't mean dating or even more than a casual conversation with this stranger, it simply means interacting with him. Maybe the James Dean-style guys aren't your type and you decide to sit elsewhere today. Or maybe you like the thoughtful, book-smart guys and decide to take your usual seat. In both cases, clothing helped to make that judgement call.

On the flip side of that, think about what you're wearing in the coffee shop. Maybe you woke up late and tossed on a pair of sweats and sneakers. Or maybe you're headed to an interview later and got dressed up in a professional-looking outfit. The way this stranger will respond—or not!—to you, is also framed by your clothing selection. This is why you might dress one way for class and differently when you're going out with your friends. Just consider the face you're trying to create in these various situations.

Largely, checking out someone's clothing in this way can be understood as a form of uncertainty reduction—a process where we seek out information to better predict how an interaction will go.[48] Moreover, let's think about how we dress around our friends and family—and what they wear around us. Maybe we know our friend is a jeans-and-T-shirt type of a gal and rarely wears anything else. So, if you went to class and see her in a sleek, black dress, you're going to assume something is different. Unless you have a baseline understanding of what someone wears on a regular basis, you're not going to know if something has changed. But, as our relationships develop and we get to know people better, we can tell when they dress up (or down) and will interpret and respond to those actions in various ways.

Finally, there are other ways clothing plays into relationships. Maybe you've slept in your boyfriend's shirt or borrowed a pair of shoes from a friend. Both the willingness to share speaks to your relationship with that person, and—if you wear it out—might send a message to others. For example, past generations of high school girls donned their boyfriend's varsity jackets. Moreover, if a family member or significant other buys you an article of clothing, you might feel obligated to wear it to show your appreciation. Here, there's a few layers of interpretation, where the giver decides the clothing is something you might like—or should have—as well as your interpretation of the gift. It may not fit your preferred style, but maybe you wear it to show you value the gift or the giver. And, especially in the case of children, they might be forced to wear what was given to them.[49]

Insight: Tinker-*ing with Appearance*

Clothing has long been used for political purposes, including by women's suffragists, political candidates and activists. In the US, buttons and T-shirts have long been a staple of political campaigns, while Donald Trump turned red baseball caps that read "Make America Great Again" into a cultural flashpoint. Often times, these items do double duty by raising revenue for candidates or advocacy groups from the Human Rights Campaign to People for the Ethical Treatment of Animals, as well as advocating for a specific policy position. Moreover, the US Supreme Court has determined clothing is a communicative medium protected by the First Amendment.

This largely stems from a case in the 1960s called *Tinker v Des Moines*, which revolved around a student protest of the Vietnam War. Mary Beth Tinker, who was 13 at the time, along with her brother, John, their friend, Christopher Eckhardt, and two other students decided to wear black armbands to school on December 16, 1965 to mourn those who were killed during the war and to support a proposed truce that would end the war.[50] However, school officials caught wind of the students' plan and preemptively banned the protest. John and Christopher refused to remove their armbands and were suspended; Mary Beth removed her armband but was still suspended for violating the prohibition. After snaking its way up through the courts, the Supreme Court ruled that the school students were free to express themselves under the First Amendment of the US Constitution—as long as the protest wasn't disruptive.[51]

School dress codes remain a source of contention across the US, as proponents say it helps learning by fostering community while opponents say it stifles free expression[52]—issues we'll touch upon in Chapter 3. However, the outcome of *Tinker v Des Moines* speaks to the acknowledgment that accessories—in this case a simple black armband— can truly be a mode of self-expression. Unlike shirts printed with words or slogans, the US Supreme Court recognized the ability of material goods to communicate, purely through aesthetics.

Meaningful and Meaningless Clothing

Of course, using clothing to express our individuality implies that clothing can be expressive in some form. As noted in the previous chapter, theorists have argued over if and how clothing is expressive for decades now, by frequently taking phrases like "The Language of Clothing" a bit too literally.[53] However, it cannot be ignored that some clothing is intended as a specific communication (i.e. meaningful) while other clothing is used without much thought (i.e. meaningless). Now, before we get into understanding the difference, we need to talk a bit about "meaning."

Meaning is largely how something is interpreted,[54] or what we take away from communication. As mentioned earlier in the chapter, we can use clothing to encode meanings for others to understand *or* we can take meaning from what others are wearing. Early scholars believed that both individuals needed to come to the same meaning for communication to occur[55] (as does some criticism of "clothing as communication"[56]), but we now accept that meaning creation is an ongoing process that has a ton of potential to go awry. When discussing verbal communication (i.e. communication using language), we break meaning into denotative—the dictionary's definition—and connotative, which can neither be neatly summarized nor defined.[57] The problem for clothing is that its communication is largely through connotative meanings and, even when it uses linguistic elements, they are still open to interpretation—just ask Melania Trump!

Instead, we can discuss clothing that is meaning*ful* and meaning*less*.[58] Meaningful clothing are garments we're using to communicate a message to others. For example, let's say your professor is making you give a presentation to the class, but to show them you really don't care about it, you show up in a pair of pajama pants and an oversized hooded sweatshirt. In this case, you're making those garments meaningful, by sending a nonverbal message to your professor. Your professor may or may not recognize this fact (and may or may not react to it), but that meaning is still being encoded by you, even you're unsure if it's being received. This is what happens when we use clothing and our appearance as a way to protest (see this Chapter's Insight Box) or as a way to support political candidates, sports teams or any variety of things. Using clothing as a form of nonverbal communication has long roots and has been used for generations as signs of self-expression.[59]

On the flip side, sometimes we don't give much thought to what we put on our bodies, or attempt to wear something simply because it isn't very expressive. The latter is what Daniel Miller and Sophie Woodward found when they asked Londoners about wearing blue jeans. While blue jeans were once heavily associated with the US and the American West, more specifically, the garments have become something almost post-semiotic, or essentially meaning*less*, since they are so commonplace.[60] While that may be true to some extent, as we learned in the previous chapter, just because we aren't intending to communicate with our clothing does not mean others know we are not communicating. We may not think a lot about the jeans we're putting on, but things like color (dark blue or stone-washed), fit (loose or baggy), and style (ordinary, distressed or boot-cut) will be interpreted by others. And, as will be discussed in Chapter 7, immaterial elements such as designers and brand names will also be interpreted by those with whom we come into contact. In this way, our clothing is never devoid of meaning, even if we don't recognize, acknowledge or intentionally use it.

Truthfully, the meaningful and meaningless aspects is one of the important discussions around clothing as communication. Fashion—and in conjunction, clothing consumption—is often derided as being too superficial to worry about. This often leads to people not paying attention to what they wear (or at the very least not admitting that they pay attention). And, they may do that by wearing mismatching socks, clashing colors or some other clothing that seems out of place on them or within their environment. However, in doing so, people are showing their hand. By wearing clothing that goes against social expectations, they reinforce the same aspects of clothing. To return to Miller and Woodward's findings around blue jeans, they found that people in London do not assign meanings to the jeans they wear. However, if the same individuals wore jeans to a conservative country like Saudi Arabia or to a remote part of Asia, the jeans would identify the wearers as members of Western culture, if nothing else. In Chapter 3, we'll dive deeper into how clothing, style and appearance work as social cues for those in various cultural, subcultural and taste groups.

Power, Conformity and Individuality

Finally, the ability to influence another person's behavior is referred to as interpersonal influence or power.[61] While power can come in several different forms, it is frequently discussed in one of five ways: legitimate, referent, expert, reward and coercive. Briefly, these types of power are as follows:

- *Legitimate*: Comes from positions of authority (President; parents).
- *Referent*: Comes from being well-liked (celebrities; friends).
- *Expert*: Comes from having authority or knowledge (professors; stylists; consultants).
- *Reward*: Comes from having the ability to give gifts (billionaires; Oprah).
- *Coercive*: Comes from having the ability to punish (parents; government authorities).

Again, clothing and power can work in at least two different ways. First, our clothing can express the power we have; second, clothing can be used as a tool of those in power. For example, police officers have an element of legitimate power and usually wear a uniform to show that authority.[62] On the flip side of that, lawmakers have some power to decide appropriate attire to be worn in public. While sumptuary laws that forbid the specific fashion are largely a thing of the past,[63] lawmakers and those with legitimate power still maintain laws against public nudity. Likewise, the "No shoes, No shirt, No service" signs you might have seen could be a local ordinance or the owner of an establishment exerting her legitimate power over customers.

In contrast, there are few formal indications of referent power via clothing, but it's possible to think about this power from those who aren't afraid to take risks. Consider the power of celebrities on the red carpet—from Jennifer Lopez's Versace dress to Rihanna's massive train she wore to the Met Gala—we largely allow them to push the envelope with little backlash because they are well-liked. Likewise, this could lead us to attempt to imitate celebrity styles in an effort to be like them.

Now, if legitimate power can be manifested in clothing and referent power cannot, expert power fits somewhere in the middle. The word "expert" likely conjures up some images—maybe of a doctor with a white lab coat or a CEO in a business suit. These markings of expert power play into larger social ideas of who we expect to be an authority and how they display that authority. Issues of this representation, which will be discussed in Chapters 5 and 6, have largely defaulted to old, white men and what they wear. Moreover, there is a large number of people who wield expert power when it comes to the way we dress. Some names might be well-known, like Tim Gunn (of *Project Runway* fame) and Stacy London (of the US's *What Not to Wear*), while celebrities and politicians alike employ a host of style consultants.[64] While we'll talk more about taste authorities in Chapter 5, fashion writers like Robin Givhan of *The Washington Post,* *Vogue* editor Anna Wintour, and designer Victoria Beckham might all be considered to have expert power when it comes to clothing and style.

Finally, while it's incredibly rare that someone could use reward power (and even rarer to use coercive power) in regard to clothing, promotions by brands, radio stations or even a costume contest might fit the bill. However, more frequently we'd discuss these forms of power within a broader understanding of social power.[65] In these cases, the reward or punishment is not clearly stated or even obvious, but are things we internalize nonetheless. For example, when we think of a successful businessperson, we likely imagine someone in a well-tailored outfit matched with wingtips or designer heels. If you're interviewing for a job at a banking firm and don't adhere to the standard of dress during the interview—either because of choice or lack of resources—you're less likely to get the job. Here there isn't a clear "reward" or "punishment," but an implied understanding of the expectations. You might have experienced a version of this in school where you wore clothing in an attempt to fit in with the "cool kids."

While this social power is exerted in a variety of situations workplaces, from retail establishments to office spaces, generally have more finite rules on what can and can't be worn.[66] While this is sometimes done for safety reasons, branding purposes or legal protection, there is often some give-and-take so employees can express their own individuality. For example, workers at a chain restaurant may require workers in all of their stores to wear black, non-slip shoes, black pants and black button-ups, but the individual styles can vary from person to person. Servers at TGI Fridays were once known for wearing red-and-black striped shirts that they decorated with their own unique "flair."[67] In comparison, clothing stores might have a less restrictive dress code, but still require employees to embody the look of the store.[68] In these cases, the workers can form their own identities through what is in stock—or similar garments that might be sold elsewhere.[69] (Stores often offer employee discounts to encourage their workers to wear the clothes they are selling, both while working and outside of the store.) Where there are less formal dress codes, employees are generally expected to figure out appropriate attire and dress accordingly. As will be discussed in the next chapter, conforming to group norms can be beneficial on a number of fronts, but people still like to have some sense of individuality and self-expression.

Further Reading

Various works address the intersection of communication, appearance and clothing. Erving Goffman's *The Presentation of Self in Everyday Life* (Anchor, 1959) might be one of the most influential books on the topic, while Gregory P. Stone's chapter "Appearance and the Self" and *Fashion, Culture and Identity* by Fred Davis (University of Chicago Press, 1992) are also quite foundational. *The Psychology of Fashion*, edited by Michael R. Solomon (Lexington, 1985), is now somewhat dated, but provides a nice variety on both clothing and fashion. Additionally, both Joanne Finklestein's *The Fashioned Self* (Temple University Press, 1991) and Joanne Entwistle's *The Fashioned Body* (Polity, 2015) are insightful for understanding the relationship between cultural forces and the physical body. Daniel Miller's various works offer an anthropological and material culture perspective on clothing and material goods including *Stuff* (Polity, 2009) and his book with Sophie Woodward, *Blue Jeans: The Art of the Ordinary* (University of California Press, 2012).

Some more recent books that push identity issues forward include *Fashioning Identity* by Maria Mackinney-Valentin (Bloomsbury, 2017) and *Identities Through Fashion: A Multidisciplinary Approach* edited by Ana Marta González and Laura Bovone (Berg, 2012). Meanwhile, a themed-issue of the journal *Critical Studies in Fashion and Beauty* offers some insightful critiques of the relationship between clothing and identity, including "Is identity a useful critical tool?" by Efrat Tseëlon, "Fashioned identity and the unreliable image", by Joanne Finkelstein, and "Digital identity management: Old wine in new bottles?" by Michael R. Solomon.

1　Goffman, Erving (1959). *The Presentation of Self in Everyday Life*. New York: Anchor.

2　Stone, Gregory P. (1995), "Appearance and the Self", in M. E. Roach-Higgins, J. B. Eicher and K. K. P. Johnson (eds.), *Dress and Identity,* 19–39, New York: Fairchild.

3　Solomon, Michael R. (1985). *The Psychology of Fashion*. Lexington, MA: Lexington Books.

4　Finklestein, Joanne (1991).*The Fashioned Self*. Philadelphia: Temple University Press.

5　Entwistle, Joanne (2015). *The Fashioned Body: Fashion, Dress and Modern Social Theory,* 2nd edition. Malden, MA: Polity.

6　Miller, Daniel (2010). *Stuff*. Malden, MA: Polity.

7　Miller, Daniel and Sophia Woodward (2012). *Blue Jeans: The Art of the Ordinary*. Los Angeles: University of California Press.

8   Mackinney-Valentin, Maria (2017). *Fashioning Identity: Status Ambivalence in Contemporary Fashion.* New York: Bloomsbury.

9   González, Ana Marta and Laura Bovone, eds. (2012). *Identities through Fashion: A Multidisciplinary Approach.* New York: Berg.

10 Tseëlon, Erfat, ed. (2012). *Critical Studies in Fashion and Beauty,* Volume 1.2.

Figure 3.1 *Dressing Up. In* Crazy Rich Asians (2018), *dir. Jon M. Chu, Warner Bros. Pictures, Rachel (Constance Wu) gets a makeover from her friend Goh Peik Lin (Awkwafina) before she meets her boyfriend's family.*

3

Clothing Dynamics in Groups and Cultures

Meeting the family of a significant other is stressful. Beyond the usual stress of meeting new people, these are people you want to impress—unless you don't like your significant other that is! When planning for this, you'll likely want to put your best face forward: getting your hair done and wearing a nice outfit. In *Crazy Rich Asians* (2018), this is what Rachel Chu (Constance Wu) faced when she accompanied her boyfriend, Nick Young (Henry Golding), to a wedding in Singapore. Rachel, who grew up in a poor immigrant household in the US, but was now doing all right for herself as a professor, is unaware that Nick is part of an incredibly wealthy Singaporean family.

Luckily, she had her old college friend Peik Lin (Awkwafina) and her family to clue her in.

"The Youngs are like royalty," Peik Lin tells Rachel, reinforcing her father's declaration that the Young family are some of the most prominent real-estate developers in the country. When Rachel explains that she's not quite sure because she hasn't met Nick's family yet, but will be visiting his grandmother's house that night, she is met with disbelief.

"You're going to Nick grandma's house wearing this?" Peik Lin asks gesturing to Rachel's simple red dress. "Wearing *that?*" Peik Lin continues eliciting chuckles from her family.

In the following scene as Peik Lin digs through her walk-in closet she explains the situation to her friend, "Rachel, these people aren't just rich, they're crazy rich." Peik Lin explains how most of the wealth in Asia is "new money," but that the Young family are "old money rich," as they had moved to Singapore and helped it become a modern city. Clearly, the simple red dress that makes Rachel seem like "Sebastian from *The Little Mermaid*" (in Peik Lin's words) would not do.

This part of the film speaks toward how our clothing helps us fit in within groups and meet social expectations. Rachel, living in the US and being unaware of Nick's family's wealth, aimed to wear something simple but nice in order to be respectful. In fact, she even chose a red dress because it symbolized luck and prosperity. However, showing up in a simple dress to meet Nick's wealthy family would also show that Rachel certainly did not fit in. Instead, she needed something more flamboyant or flashy to be accepted. Even though Peik Lin gives Rachel a more appropriate dress for the evening, the disparity between Rachel's status as an American professor and Nick's status as a rich scion animates the rest of the film.

In the last chapter, we discussed how group membership helps us develop our sense of self and how we use our clothing to both fit in with and distinguish ourselves from certain groups. This chapter will look more specifically at how clothing and appearance is dictated by social and cultural groups both large and small. Factors including our culture, the region we live in and our religion might influence the way we dress, as do more personal factors like age and occupation. Clothing in this context can become a marker of group identification and an element of social power by identifying in-group members and praising or reprimanding those who don't follow the groups' rules.

Groups, Clothing and Perspectives

We'll talk a bit more about this in Chapter 4, but it's important to note some fundamental differences between the way researchers have approached clothing and, as such, approached how it interacts with groups. Many researchers have approached clothing from a cultural and anthropological perspective. This approach sees the clothes we wear and how we wear them as being ingrained in the communities we live in; that part of our appearance gives meaning and value to us. In comparison, from a psychological point of view, researchers see clothing as a manifestation of our inner selves which communicates or shares something intrinsic about us. Still, sociological research considers the social classifications, grouping and power dynamics at play across society and, in relation, as they play out through clothing.[1] This chapter draws off of these various strands of research, however it will be doing so to somewhat different ends.

As discussed in Chapter 2, the way we dress and attempt to style ourselves is a learned process: we are taught how to dress and look (intentionally or not), and then we are able to selectively use that knowledge to communicate and share information about ourselves toward various goals. This isn't *all* about meaning, social dynamics or an intrinsic desire to express our identity, but rather more of a performance in which we selectively deploy this knowledge in order to influence various social situations. For example, we realize that if we want to work at a particular place, we need to fit into their formal dress code. Likewise, we may think that if we want to fit into a certain group of people, we need to dress and act the part.

At the same time, it is important to reiterate that clothing and our style communicates to us and to others. Therefore, we might make assumptions about who belongs to a particular group because of their clothing and, likewise, we might be categorized by others because of our clothing. The external communication becomes a bit more complex here because we are communicating with various sets of other people. To return to the work example, a server might wear a well-pressed uniform to show his boss that he takes the job seriously and to communicate to others that he is a part of the team. Meanwhile, the outfit is also identifying them to customers as an employee of the establishment, but might also imply a particular class status or position within the corporate hierarchy.

Moreover, the various cultural and social groupings that we might join change over time, as does our desire to fit into those groups. In high school, it might be all important to fit in with the "cool kids," the jocks or, to refer to the movie *Mean Girls*, the Plastics. In *Mean Girls* (2004), The Plastics—initially made up of Regina (Rachel McAdams), Gretchen (Lacey Chabert) and Karen (Amanda Seyfried)—are the most popular and feared girls at their high school. The trio invites new student Cady (Lindsay Lohan) to sit with them at lunch, and soon she is attempting to become part of the group. Eventually, Cady undertakes a sabotage scheme with two other non-Plastic friends changing and ultimately breaking up the group. As *Mean Girls* illustrates, when someone new joins a group they also shape its ideas and its ethos moving forward. Perhaps that is upsetting the power dynamic or simply molding some of the groups' ideals and beliefs. While some groups are more structured and restrictive than others, nearly all morph and change over time.

Uniforms among Cultures and Groups

As noted in the previous chapter, the clothing we wear often has an embedded element of power within it. Sometimes, superiors, say bosses or teachers, dictate what we can and can't wear, whereas at other times, we learn from less clearly defined social power. Uniforms can generally be understood as a particular set of clothing for a group of people.[2] Uniforms, overall, work to denote authority, prestige or admiration on those who wear them well, due to the knowledge it takes to do so. Moreover they can be traced back to the military uniforms of Western Europe and sumptuary laws around the globe.[3] Jennifer Craik suggests the idea of "uniforms" and "uniformity" can be understood more broadly and in three distinct ways: formal proscribed uniforms, quasi-uniforms and informal uniforms.[4] If not clear from their names, these categories are generally defined by their rigidness and structure.

"Formal proscribed uniforms" are likely what you think about when you hear the word uniform: those worn by police and members of the military. Uniforms in this category are clearly structured in what and how they are worn and can largely be traced back to France in the 1600s. Originally, uniforms were created to easily identify opposing sides in battle; however, military leaders also recognized that uniforms helped to train soldiers and promoted discipline. During the Napoleonic era, uniforms across Europe became more standardized although nations kept some identity in their colors, such as red for Great Britain and blue for France. As it was recognized that overly decorative uniforms were not useful in battle, military uniforms were simplified and eventually three different types would be created: dress uniforms for formal occasions, active service uniforms for fighting, and barracks uniforms for other times.[5]

Again, while the military is par excellence for formal proscribed uniforms, they have also been adopted by other parts of civilian society. Police in Germany and parts of Europe have long resembled the dress of the military through tactical uniforms and SWAT gear, even as some countries, like Great Britain, sought to distance the civilian service from the military.[6] Other entities, like the Salvation Army, a Christian church that deems its converts "soldiers"[7] and groups, like the Boy Scouts, specifically use uniforms to hark back to their military tradition. Still, these uniforms denote a hierarchy or rank and are believed to inspire group loyalty, like military uniforms.[8]

Most uniforms worn by schoolchildren would fit into this group, as would work uniforms that we briefly touched upon in Chapter 2. School uniforms have, at times, become a flashpoint for larger social debates about fashion and adornment. Craik suggested that school uniforms were used as part of a particular way of teaching; this was why not all schools required them since they worked to discipline the body and train it in particular ways.[9] As such, school uniforms have been common in many European countries and their former colonies, while other countries, especially those of Scandinavia and North America have traditionally shied away from them. Where they are used, school uniforms are linked to "nation construction" and prepare students to fit within larger social and corporate expectations. Likewise, it wouldn't be hard to see school uniforms as a patriarchal tool—as they dictate and delineate gender lines and have been steeped in masculine ideals—and could easily be seen as supporting colonialism.[10]

The US provides an interesting case study of school uniforms, as the adoption of uniforms there came much later than in other nations. While some private schools in the United States required uniforms, the government only began promoting uniforms for US public schools in the 1990s. (For comparison, New Zealand had broadly adopted school uniforms by the 1940s while France adopted them in the 1870s—and England even earlier![11]) Then-US President Bill Clinton praised school uniforms in two State of the Union addresses to Congress, suggesting they improve safety and discipline.[12] Critics have suggested that the implementation of school uniforms limits free expression, creates a false sense of nostalgia and can marginalize poor students;[13] despite these arguments more than a quarter of US schools required them by 2016. Further, despite fears that uniforms limit self-expression, research from other countries, such as Japan, suggests that students will still find a way to express their individuality.[14] At the same time, uniforms in the United States continue to imply a monied or upper-class status; most schools that require uniforms are private and thus reserved for those who can pay.

Like school uniforms, those used within the labor force generally offer some degree of individuality, but may require workers to conform to some sort of overall look. Those who work directly with the public frequently have some sort of uniform, such as those who work in retail and food service. Notably, the airline industry, especially flight attendants, have been the subject of some of the most notorious work uniforms and looks standards—at one time flight attendants were forced to meet height and weight requirements.[15] Airlines continue to push stylish uniforms for their attendants and have even enlisted the help of fashion designers: in the past few years, Virgin Atlantic debuted uniforms by Vivienne Westwood, Delta worked with Zac Posen and United got help from Brooks Brothers. Beyond the outfits, many airlines still have restrictions on jewelry, makeup and hairstyles—although some of these restrictions have been loosened in recent years.[16] Uniforms for workplaces are sometimes in place for practicality and safety. Hardhats and steel-toed boots on a construction site or soccer players' shin guards help protect them from injury, while vests and specifically colored shirts help identify retail workers in a sea of customers.

Some work uniforms aren't imposed by an outside structure; instead they have essentially been socially agreed upon. These are quasi-uniforms since they aren't a *requirement*, per se, but are an expectation. People like lawyers and financial advisers might be expected to wear suits in order to communicate their professionalism and gain the trust of their clients. Likewise, doctors and nurses might wear scrubs for sanity reasons, but also to identify themselves as medical professionals—providing credibility and authority to patients. Other examples of quasi-uniforms include those involving significant social expectations, like wearing black to a funeral. In earlier times, such as the Victorian era and parts of the twentieth century, there were far greater quasi-uniforms for periods of mourning, even what to wear at different times of the day, but many of those social expectations have been dropped in recent decades.[17]

Finally, informal uniforms are those which are used by the general population, not unlike the culture-wide designations mentioned above. In the US and much of the Western world, jeans and a T-shirt create something of an informal uniform or, at the very least, a pair of pants and a separate top. Informal uniforms generally follow fashion trends, and can include beachwear or winter wear.[18] Restrictions on informal uniforms aren't spelled out and may be managed through social power, such as gossip in everyday settings, while celebrities and those in the public eye might be guided by tabloid headlines and even social media messages. And, within the informal uniforms adopted across a culture, there remain smaller groups who may adopt, alter or challenge the dominant clothing styles.

Grouping Groups

As you might remember from Chapter 1, communication scholars generally see a difference in the way we communicate interpersonally and within groups. Small group communication is usually understood to be when three or more people interact at the same time.[19] Generally, small groups cease to be well, *small groups*, at about fifteen or so members, since not everyone can participate in a group of that size. At that point, if the group remains intact and focused on one conversation, the communication becomes somewhat more presentational, where one person is communicating to the rest, or separate, as groups within that group hold their own conversations. We can see this difference in our lives: a professor speaking to everyone is presentational (even if the class is the size of a small group) whereas a house party is likely to break into more intimate conversations of fewer people. These types of small groups are common in a variety of places such as classrooms, workplaces and social events; however, they usually aren't the most common nor usually the most influential groups we belong to.

The groups which help form our identities are usually referred to as "primary" and "secondary" groups.[20] Primary groups are those which help with the basics—food, shelter and socializing. We often refer to this group as a family, whether that is biologically, adoptively or just emotionally. In comparison, secondary groups are those formed with a specific purpose or goal in mind. These might include study groups, book clubs or fantasy sports leagues. Broadly speaking, these groups have a series of dynamics, including roles, rules, norms and power but, in all cases, remember that it is key that individuals see themselves as part of the group and have the ability to influence each other within it.

Once we get beyond these primary and secondary groups the boundaries become a bit less definite and, as such, are generally discussed in different ways. Specifically, we can see larger groupings of people as communities (of various sizes) and even as nations. We can attribute much of this to Benedict Anderson's idea of an "imagined community." For Anderson, the idea of a nation was developed through the creation of the mass media, which informed people that (a) they were part of a given community, and (b) what qualities members of said community had in common.[21] This was something more than simply geography, for Anderson, and it took on more importance through self-identification. This is important because even though most people in these imagined communities won't interact which each other, the mass media—newspapers, originally, but also broadcasting and now the internet—help create shared meaning, communal rituals and mutual obligations. As such, self-identified members of that community have an idea of the rest of the community from the clothes they wear to the activities they engage in.

The norms, values and beliefs of community can be considered its culture. Culture, in this sense, includes how we interact with one another, what we eat and wear, what and how we celebrate and how we see the world. Geert Hofstede suggests there are six dimensions by which cultures can be classified:

1   Power distances, such as social mobility or access to forms of power.

2   Uncertainty avoidance—how a culture deals with the future.

3   Individualism—Collectivism, or how independent members of the culture feel.

4   Masculinity—Femininity, or how emotional labor is distributed amongst members.

5   Long-term—Short-term orientation, regarding how members understand and react to time.

6   Indulgence—Restraint, or how members look at gratification.[22]

However, not everyone within a nation or culture follows the same norms, values and beliefs. Some smaller groups of people within a larger culture develop unique elements that frequently interact with the larger culture. We often call this a "subculture" or a "co-culture" to denote the interaction between the smaller group's norms, values and beliefs and that of the larger culture. Generally, we use the term co-culture to suggest neither group is dominant and acknowledge that people can be parts of equal cultures simultaneously, whereas a subculture is generally understood to be a niche group within a larger culture or even actively attempting to subvert or undermine the culture.[23]

Some notable subcultures or co-cultures might include hippies and punks—both of whom developed distinctive tastes within clothing, music and lifestyle. Punks have remained an active group in both the US and Europe, while hippies have largely faded as a cultural group. The amount that a subcultural or a co-cultural group shares the values of the dominant culture varies. The Amish, an Anabaptist-based religious sect found in various parts of the United States, share little with the rest of American culture as they shun technology and focus on plain dress and simple living. In comparison, the lesbian, gay, bisexual, and transgender (LGBT+) community in many parts of the world largely share the cultural values of the dominant culture, from things like dress to marriage, even as some elements—like drag shows, gay bars and LGBT-specific publications—are unique to those within the co-culture.

Theories of Groups and Clothing

As the aforementioned dynamics of clothing generally communicate on a cultural level, clothing can work on smaller scales to help people feel part of a co-culture or other group. As Lauren Keblusek and Howard Giles delineate, several theories dictate how people use clothing to interact with groups and subcultures. Among these are (1) social identity theory, (2) self-categorization theory, (3) identity management theories, and (4) optimal distinctiveness theories.[24] While each of these theories understand the group-individual dynamics in slightly different ways, the idea of each is that members will come toward the same conclusions on clothing choices. Researchers believe that group membership is important to both our identity (as discussed in Chapter 2), to feel a sense of a belonging and to promote our self-esteem. To see themselves as part of the group, people will start to adapt group norms, including the style of dress.

Social Identity Theory

Originally outlined by Henri Tajfel and John Turner, social identity theory argues that group membership is important to self-identity and clothing and appearance are key in helping form that membership. There are several ways clothing can work within the scope of Social Identity Theory. Ingroup members may praise others within the group and mock or otherwise derogate others. To return briefly to *Mean Girls*, the most popular girls were referred to as "The Plastics" because of their looks and it was clear throughout the movie that they were the highest status group in the school. Clothing can also be used to help promote social mobility and/or reinforce group boundaries.

Self-Categorization Theory

In comparison to Social Identity Theory, Self-Categorization Theory suggests that people see themselves as part of various groups with varying levels of abstraction. As such, we might see ourselves as "humans" broadly, but also as part of various social groupings—such as age, class and gender, as mentioned above—but also within various other groups, such as a member of a specific religion and group of worshippers, a student of a school or a fan of a particular sports team. (Really, this chapter is organized in much in the same way, with the abstract being discussed on the previous pages and more concrete groups upcoming.) Here various grouping and beliefs intersect: in the US, for example, jeans and T-shirts are commonplace, but someone might wear a shirt with the slogan "Black Lives Matter" to show their support for social justice. As such, what we wear is at the intersection of these various groups and different clothing can highlight different group membership at different times.

Identity Management Theories

People generally like stability, especially when it comes to their sense of self. As such, theories of identity management suggest that clothing can help stabilize or control our identities and how others see them. This isn't all that different than Erving Goffman's ideas of dramaturgy and performances from Chapter 2. Beyond the way we understand ourselves, these theories suggest we might also look for clues in an attempt to make sense of others and better anticipate communication with them. For an extreme example, we might be put off from interacting with someone prominently wearing Nazi insignia, or, on a positive note, might freely strike up a conversation with someone wearing our favorite football team's jersey.

Optimal Distinctiveness Theory

As has been discussed throughout this chapter, clothing provides a way for us both to fit in with larger groups and also construct ourselves as unique individuals. Optimal Distinctiveness Theory, as explained by Marilynn B. Brewer, argues that we each have a level of similarity and difference from other members of the group and we are constantly balancing these extremes. If we are too different than others in the group *or* if we are too *alike* to the others in the group, our identity can be threatened by feeling like we're not a group member (in the former) or like we're not an individual (in the latter). The amount of similarity and difference varies based on the group: larger groups might require more individualization than smaller groups, although this also depends upon the status of the various groups.[25]

Clothing Within a Culture

As mentioned in the last chapter, our clothing choices are constantly made in dialogue with larger groups that we're part of: this is the fashion paradox of fitting in while standing out. However, it is still useful to think about how clothing and appearance works on both a cultural scale, but also how it constructs various culture-wide groupings of people. The following pages examine clothing and appearance and it helps to distinguish among age, gender and class within a "Western" or Euro-centric perspective. It's important to note that the way clothing and appearance communicates varies by culture and does not have a fixed meaning.[26] As such, while some of this speaks to cultural processes writ large, they may play out differently—or not at all!—within different cultures.

Clothing and Age

Clothing's connotations of age has collapsed considerably over the past few decades, however, it still helps to break down some relevant categories. Generally, today, we can divide clothing of children from that of teens and from that of adults, not to mention that much of this is relevant upon gender, religious and class-based issues as well. However, Jo Paoletti notes that until the 1900s, clothing for children under six was generally seen as unisex and used both colors and fabrics that would be understood as "feminine" today. The move away from white dress for children younger than six was gradual, and didn't fully disappear until the 1940s.[27]

Eventually, children's clothing moved into darker colors to show less dirt[28] and would later get to the contemporary gender dynamics we see today. Further, as Daniel Thomas Cook points out, there was a shift in the 1930s where retailers started to turn away from appealing to parents, turning instead to children. The agency afforded to children is a contested space, both in theory and in practice, although knowing how to properly consume is key to growing up.[29] Still, it is probably unsurprising that the way children look is understood to be a reflection on parents. This idea was espoused as early as 1831, where magazines suggested that children's appearances reflected their mothers' qualities.[30] As such, an unkempt child might imply a mother was unwilling or unable to care for her child. While such assumptions remain today, we might suggest this reflects on both the mother *and the father.*

Children of all ages provide a unique situation because while they are not fully independent and cannot make their own clothing choices, they can certainly influence what their parents buy and put on them. Moreover, this can include a cast of "hand-me-downs" that start with one child and can be passed onto the next.[31] Still, as children grow up, they develop more of their own tastes and by high school can usually spend some of their own money. Decades ago, *Seventeen* magazine was founded on the premise that teen girls needed to be guided into proper ways of consumption, and, along with advertising firms,[32] it helped to build the entire consumer category of the teenager. Teen culture, as an US phenomenon, was an outgrowth of the post-Second World War baby boom, and helped define high school hallmarks like proms and football games.[33] It also produced teen clothing styles, including now-dated traditions like the sharing of letterman jackets. Advertising was also instrumental in the acknowledgment of teenagers, and brands would later help expand and create a "tween" market for those just shy of their teen years.[34]

At the opposite end of the spectrum, Pamela Church Gibson notes that many older women often wear similar clothing that is different in style, but not practice, from teenagers.[35] These older women—in their 40s and 50s—pay attention to fashion, but felt excluded by clothing that was youth driven. In the years since, older women have been included in a mass market fashion campaign for American Apparel and there has been the rise of "granny chic," as Maria Mackinney-Valentin calls the attention given to style influencers like Iris Apfel.[36]

Difference in age-appropriate dress for men is somewhat less pronounced given a semblance of uniforms in various settings.[37] Still, there are some variances where younger men will be more likely to experiment with different styles, even if they largely conform to the hegemonic dress standards as they age. Recently, a new type of retailer has emerged on the fashion scene: the brotailer, as coined by journalist Sam Grobart.[38] Brotailers are thought to target younger men—those beyond high school and possibly even college—but who aren't ready to join the fully adult world of marriage, home and children. While there is the potential to develop a market which will have lasting implications for menswear, it is too soon to tell where this retail trend will end up.

Clothing, Gender and Sexuality

While clothing does connote various elements, gender is perhaps the largest distinction; most garments are classified as being either for men or women. Much of this differentiation can be traced back to what J.C. Flügel has called "The Great Masculine Renunciation," where men began to turn away from bright colors and ornamentation in their clothing, instead preferring more somber colors and less extravagant styles. (Art historian Anne Hollander has suggested this has roots as far back as the late 1600s.) While there were certainly some individuals who stood out from the crowd—Beau Brummel kept up his "dandy" appearance—this was often done in opposition to the dominant view of men's clothing and appearance, which was that such things are too frivolous for men to worry about.[39]

The result of this "renunciation" was that the fashion system became a primarily female domain, even though most prominent designers are men, and that various styles of dress, fabrics and even colors are associated with gender performances. Men's clothing and fashion aim to seem effortless and simple, but women's clothing took on a more molded and deliberate air. The clothing of men and women has changed in relation to one another, at various times working toward greater contrast, while other periods have seen more similar styles.[40]

Some women have used clothing to nonverbally subvert clothing trends: what Diana Crane calls "alternative dress." This style of dressing involved women using men's clothing—or masculine-coded garments— to challenge stereotypes and gender divisions. An early (and ongoing) example of this was the use of men's ties, which can be traced back to the Victorian era.[41] While the early adopters wore men's ties with bodices and skirts, this evolved into the more widespread use of men's clothing styles. For example, actress Blake Lively gained attention in 2018 for wearing well-fitted suits to various events during the promotion of the film *A Simple Favor*. Lively's outfits were inspired by her character and done in homage to the film's director, Paul Feig, who is known

Figure 3.2 *Dressing Masculine. Star of the television show* Pose *and the Broadway musical* Kinky Boots *Billy Porter played with gender expectations when he wore a Christian Siriano gown to the Academy Award Ceremony in 2019. © Mark Ralston via Getty Images.*

for his suits. Comparatively, in a more obvious form of protest, Lady Gaga wore an oversized suit to a ceremony declaring, "I decided today I wanted to take the power back. Today, I wear the pants."[42]

Moreover, besides women appropriating men's clothing and looks, some clothing producers offer products such as "boyfriend jeans," which are designed for women, using men's cuts. Usually, the assumption is that women will borrow or otherwise use clothing originally intended for men, but not the other way around. While there are some practical reasons for this dynamic (i.e. generally, men are physically larger, thus making it possible for clothing to only be shared unidirectionally), there is frequently an underlying misogyny which implies that feminine garments and associations are less desirable and shouldn't be adopted by men. Garments and even colors that are associated with women are generally seen as having more powerful connotations[43] and, given the common bipolar understanding of gender, men wearing women's clothing poses a more series threat to traditional ideas of a masculinity. The reverse (women wearing men's clothing) is not nearly as powerful and doesn't threaten femininity in the same way.

Because of fashion's close association with femininity, men who were interested and engaged in this realm were frequently thought to be gay. Moreover, as gay men have been excluded from the norms of heterosexual society, they were more attuned to appearances and how they could manage their identities within society. Martin Levine noted that gay men generally adopted one of three strategies for dealing with their identities: "passing, minstrelization and capitulation." Passing is where someone is not recognized as being from a minority group—this can also be seen within racial and ethnic communities as well—whereas minstrelization is where a member plays up their difference for comic ends. As Levine points out, many gay men adopted the "clone" culture, where they followed the dress and styling of blue collar workers, but did so to a level of perfection that was practically camp.[44] (The Village People provided something of an archetype for this.)

Insight: What's "Business Casual" Anyhow?

Some work places have a standard dress code, while some others don't. If you're a retail associate, you might have a uniform vest to wear (think: Walmart) or you might be required to dress in certain colors (think: Target). Likewise, if you're at the pinnacle of a profession, say a CEO or company president, you might dress formally in a suit or a dress. However, within the large gulf between the service workers and corporate leaders stands a large field of dress known as *business casual*.

The term itself is only a few decades old and is indebted to Dockers. The khaki brand set out a brochure in 1992 about business casual style and, still publishes advice on "business casual" on its website.[50] Suits have had a relatively long life, but the market has been shrinking as more companies turn toward business casual.[51] While tech CEOs like Mark Zuckerberg of Facebook, Steve Jobs of Apple, and even Meg Whitman of eBay have dressed down at the office,[52] it has taken the financial world a bit longer to catch onto the trend. However, what is business casual anyway?

Usually, it seems, the idea is to dress to fit in: Goldman Sachs noted that many of their clients had "more casual" environments and that workers should dress to the client's expectations. The same basic rules have applied at smaller accounting firms.[53] However, the move to a more unwritten style of dress does not come without risks: as reported in *Elle*, a tech firm without clear rules technically couldn't rule out a bikini,[54] even though many human resources professionals disapproved of casual garments like shorts, tank-tops and flip-flops.

More than the human resources angle, business casual applies somewhat better to men: khakis or well-fitting, conservative style jeans, a button-down (maybe a polo) and a decent pair of shoes. However, that doesn't translate to womenswear,[55] and has become an impediment since expectations are unclear. The unwritten rules rely on a form of knowledge or cultural capital to be able to fit in and those from disadvantaged groups likely have a steeper climb to acculturate themselves into these environments and may not have the financial means to fit in. More cynically, replacing official dress codes with more flexible and less finite expectations can have the effect of "othering" workers who are not part of the dominant group.

Camp, as described by Susan Sontag, involves playing up or exaggerating the artificiality of our appearances.[45] Often, this has been attributed to drag queens, but the aesthetic has been garnering more mainstream attention from the prominence of the reality competition *RuPaul's Drag Race* to a 2019 exhibition at the Costume Institute of The Metropolitan Museum of Art.[46] Moreover, this speaks to a larger trend of acceptance of homosexuality and queer culture in general. Two high-profile examples of gender-bending include Jaden Smith, who wore a skirt in a 2016 Louis Vuitton campaign,[47] and Billy Porter, the actor known for the musical *Kinky Boots*, who wore a Christian Siriano "tux ball gown" to the Oscars in 2019 (Figure 3.2).[48] As we acknowledge the complexity of gender beyond the male–female binary, unisex and more gender-fluid clothing is increasingly important. And, while there does not seem to be a large-scale adoption of skirts for men, having high-profile celebrities play with gender performance in this way is a step in the direction of more mainstream adoption. One day, Smith and Porter may be looked back at as trendsetters in the way Marlene Dietrich and Katharine Hepburn are for making pants acceptable for women.[49]

Clothing and Class

Largely, we can thank the likes of Thorstein Veblen and Georg Simmel for the understanding that clothing and the fashion system work as a class-based system. We'll get more into each of these ideas in Chapter 4 but, in related ways, both saw the upper class as the trendsetters that everyone else sought to emulate. Veblen, especially, introduced the concept of "conspicuous consumption," or the idea that our consumption is carried out for others to see. As such, driving a Mercedes is a more obvious sign of wealth than driving a Honda. For Simmel, the upper classes were always the people "in fashion" and everyone else was hopelessly emulating them.

However, before we can really think about how clothing and consumption interacts with class, we need to first understand how "class" systems work. Frequently, class and wealth are intricately linked, however, class involves aspects outside of income or financial capital. Things like career (regardless of the compensation), education, cultural knowledge, and social connections also play into our understanding of class. This is what sociologist Pierre Bourdieu called "cultural capital."[56] And, recently, Elizabeth Currid-Halkett has noted how inconspicuous consumption—that which is not immediately visible, like paying for private school or the neighborhood one lives in—leads to economic differences.[57]

Given clothing's visible nature, it is usually an element of conspicuous consumption. However, it is not only the value of particular garments that communicates class and, as such, we can see this as a form of conspicuous and less-than-conspicuous consumption. The key to conspicuous consumption is that the expense of the goods is *obvious*. Something like an engagement ring is generally prized for the size of the stone, since it is commonly known that the larger the diamond the more expensive it is. This can also be seen in a variety of branded products: we might recognize the logos of Chanel or Louis Vuitton as directly correlating to the value of the products (whether or not someone paid full price for it). In this way, Sharon Zukin has suggested Americans, at least, have become a society of shoppers as they are constantly examining goods being sold and consumed to make sense of how much items cost.[58]

Comparatively, there are ways our clothing and accessories do not directly connote the expense of the products, but speak to other elements of class. Consider the following examples. Ted, a university administrator, purchased an expensive suit to impress his co-workers. However, he does not remove the label sewed onto the sleeve and doesn't remove the stitching of the pockets nor from the vents of the jacket. While the suit itself might be a substantial investment, it is clear that Ted didn't have the cultural knowledge of suits to realize the label and stitching on the vents should be removed. As such, despite the amount of money Ted spent, the details show his unfamiliarity with suits and, likely, a lower-class upbringing.

Likewise, the US magazine *The New Yorker* caused a sensation when they gave new subscribers a canvas tote bag, which prominently displayed its logo. While technically free with the price of subscription, the tote bags became a symbol of status and class given *The New Yorker*'s highbrow reputation. Currid-Halkett called the bag "cultural currency" and noted, "Reading *The New Yorker* implies possession of a rarified knowledge, cultural awareness and refinement of taste that is beyond simply reading about world happenings."[59] In this way, the bag symbolizes something intangible that its owner is clued into, and others might not be.

Clothing and Religion

For the most part, religious dress would be considered something of a quasi-uniform since it is frequently invested with social value and understanding, but is not strictly dictated from a cultural authority nor does it change with widespread trends. In a more extreme example than some other ways of dressing, religious clothing set believers apart from others and may help to express their beliefs. At the same time, religious dress has the potential to be a form of social control exerting its power over members of the religion and seemingly more so over women within these groups.[60]

Clothing among Amish and Mennonite communities works in both ways. These communities—common to Southeastern Pennsylvania, Eastern Ohio and Northern California—are generally referred to as "Plain people"[61] due to their shunning of ornate clothing and hairstyles. This clearly sets these individuals apart from those outside of the community. Members see their outward appearance as a "manifestation of inner attitudes"[62] and follow the guidelines set out by local churches to show modesty and honor God.[63] Adherents dress similarly to stay in the good graces of the group; too much individuality implies the wearer is rejecting group norms and beliefs. Those who step out of line might be gossiped about and, if it continues, they might have something of an intervention by friends and family. Eventually, there might be a formal reprimand from local leaders.[64]

In comparison, worshippers at Black churches within the US have been known to dress ornately and in vibrant colors. As Gwendolyn S. O'Neal explains, the Black church historically performed three functions for its members: it allowed an expression of religious life, supported members who were in a subordinate racial class, and differentiated them from the dominant (and domineering) culture through unique rituals. And, it is not just women who dress up, but men as well, allowing them to use creativity and to play with aesthetics in an avenue not as frequently allotted to men.[65]

While perhaps not as explicit, religion has recently become a force in other fashion aspects as well, especially when it comes to Muslim women. More conservative followers of Islam—as well as the most conservative members of Judaism and Christianity—dress in non-revealing clothing and cover their hair with a hijab or headscarf. This has led to the rise in what is deemed "modest fashion," which frequently includes loose fitting clothing and headscarves as part of the collections. This has been helped along by both modest fashion blogs and designers like Hana Tajima, who created a collection with mass retailer Uniqlo.[66] At the same time, some countries and locations have moved to ban burqas (the most conservative dress for Muslim women, which are all usually black and only show one's eyes) and burkinis—full body swimsuits that fit with Islamic values.[67] While these types of bans have been expanded in parts of Europe, they are widely seen to be xenophobic and anti-Muslim. The burkini (or burqini), in fact, was developed by Aheda Zanetti in an effort to connect Muslim Australians after tensions arose; it allowed Muslim women to act as lifeguards on Australia's beaches.[68]

Clothing and Race

Like the aforementioned categories, race and ethnicity are constructed categories and a working of the dominant group, but these categories are frequently defined by the material body (e.g. skin pigmentation or hair color) and heredity or biological lineage. As such, there isn't a way for dress to denote "race" or "ethnicity," *per se*, although styles of dress can vary from the dominant culture, and clothing and appearance can be used in different ways. Some of the earliest studies of subcultures took into account how Black Britons dressed in comparison to the broader culture.[69]

We should take a slight detour here to note that what is generally understood to be the "fashion system"—like much of the dominant culture at large—is heavily influenced by a Western or Euro-centric perspective. So, while all people wear clothing or adorn the body to some extent, the social hierarchy embedded within fashion and the qualities that have been traditionally valorized come from a Western European point of view. In fact, as Sabrina Strings points out, the contemporary promotion of thinness has historically racist roots as fatness has long been linked to Black bodies and racial inferiority.[70] In a different way, Asians have also been excluded from the global fashion industry, being seen as laborers rather than consumers.[71] Undoubtedly, representation and input has expanded as more fashion centers have grown outside of Paris, London, New York and Milan,[72] but there is still a long way to go.

That said, in relation to race, ethnicity and clothing we can discuss it in two different ways: costume and fashion. As explained in Chapter 1, costume refers to the clothing that is unchanging and thus outside the fashion system. (This is different from *costumes* used in artistic productions.) Costume, in this sense, can refer to a variety of items from the kimonos worn by geishas, to Scottish kilts and Native American headdresses. While there may be some changes over time, these garments and the way they are used remain relatively steady and can harken back to the past as a means of shared identity and group membership.

Comparatively, ordinary clothing, or clothing that isn't intended to share one's heritage, is significantly more complex when it comes to race and ethnicity. Within the US, Black Americans' clothing and appearance is formed in tension with the dominant, white culture. Modes of dressing often highlight individual style and use appearance as a form of cultural capital.[73] Carol Tulloch suggests that the "Style-Fashion-Dress" circuit allows meaning change with individuals and over time. She points out that clothing and imagery can both create differences from the dominant culture, but can also work to diversify it, thereby giving previously excluded groups more power.[74]

Subcultural and Style Tribes

As dress and uniforms can be seen as something of a totalizing force that requires people to fit into the system, researchers have demonstrated the ways in which people carve out niche identities and appearances. Perhaps the best-known work in this vein is Dick Hebdige's *Subculture: The Meaning of Style*, in which he documents how particular groups set themselves apart from mainstream society through their clothing and appearance. Hebdige argued groups that had been marginalized from the mainstream culture would eventually begin to define themselves in opposition to the culture in style and appearance.[75] In some cases, these new looks would attempt to mold class signifiers from the dominant culture. Safety pins which were adopted by punks—and used by the designers Vivienne Westwood and Malcolm McLaren—are perhaps the best example of this; an everyday household item was repurposed into something menacing.

As identities have become more flexible in recent decades, some have questioned whether or not subculture is an apt description at all. Instead, some have turned to alternative understandings such as tribes, lifestyles and scenes in an attempt to better explain how these various social formations as traditional demarcations like gender, class and profession have become more fluid.[76] Lifestyle, in particular, has been seen as having close ties to consumption,[77] while all of the conceptualizations point toward less social cohesion. For our purposes, it's important to note that our identity and the groupings we belong to are also fluid, whether we call them a subculture or a style tribe and, as such, we might look and dress one way at one point in our lives and vastly differently in another.

Ted Polhemus extends this idea when he suggests those in contemporary Western society can now "style surf" by wearing different clothing and changing their appearance from one day to the next.[78] Again, this is *possible,* however, the slightest reflection suggests it's not *probable* or at least not done frequently. Instead, we change our style of dress over time, as we change our other material goods and as we take on different roles and interact with new people.[79] Our identity and clothing choices are not stagnant, but neither do they alternate widely.

It is here that Sarah Thornton's idea of subcultural capital comes into play. Whereas Bourdieu argued that social and cultural capital works across a community, subcultural capital is used by those who identify with a particular group of people.[80] The status symbols that help someone build cultural capital at large, say, knowledge of classical music and "proper" wine pairings, might mean little to the contemporary punk subculture which prioritizes the frequency of concert attendance and the collection of band T-shirts. In this way, subcultures are mediated and not all that removed from the aforementioned community-building functions of the wider media.

Groups vary by size and scale and are largely amorphous and open to change. Some of these have structured hierarchies that can establish and perpetuate rules while others are held together by a loose sense of belonging and desire to fit in. Others just imply broad social categorizations that work to identify us in various ways. In the following chapters, we will better explore how fashion as a system is created, and maintained through various mediated means.

Further Reading

The intersection of fashion and its role in group formations is usually interrogated within individual groups or subcultures and not across cultures as a whole. Still, there are some interesting works that speak to broader concerns. *Fashion and Cultural Studies* by Susan B. Kaiser (Berg, 2012) works across cultures with specific chapters looking at race, class, gender and sexuality. And, Jennifer Craik's *Uniforms Exposed: From Conformity to Transgression* (Berg, 2005) interrogates the uniform across various cultures and contexts. Meanwhile, subcultures have been discussed in various books and articles, but *Subculture: The Meaning of Style* by Dick Hebdige (Routledge, 1979) and *Club Cultures: Music, Media and Subcultural Capital* by Sarah Thornton (Wesleyan University Press, 1996) are perhaps the most important foundations. Meanwhile Andy Bennett's article, "The Post-Subcultural Turn: Some Reflections 10 Years On" offers a nice overview of the various debates within this field, although not all of it relates to clothing.

More specifically, books can be found that deal with gender, race and age within cultural contexts. There are several books that deal constructively with gender in a Western sense: Jo Paoletti's *Pink and Blue: Telling the Boys from the Girls in America* (Indiana University Press, 2012) and *Sex and Unisex: Fashion, Feminism and the Sexual Revolution* (Indiana University Press, 2015) deal with changing gender dynamics within the US, while the books *Buttoned Up: Clothing, Conformity and White-Collar Masculinity* by Erynn Masi de Casanova (ILR Press, 2015) and *Why Women Wear What They Wear* by Sophie Woodward (Bloomsbury, 2007) explore middle-class men in the US and women in the UK, respectively. Carol Tulloch's *The Birth of Cool: Style Narratives of the African Diaspora* (Bloomsbury, 2016) is an insightful look at how dress informs Black identities within Western contexts, while Tanisha C. Ford's *Liberated Threads: Black Women, Style and the Global Politics of Soul* (University of North Carolina Press, 2015) explores how style has been merged with activism. Meanwhile, *The Beautiful Generation: Asian Americans and the Cultural Economy of Fashion* by Thuy Linh Nguyen Tu (Duke University Press, 2010) and Minh-Ha T. Pham's *Asian Wear Clothes on the Internet* (Duke University Press, 2015) explore the intersection of Asian identity and fashion. Finally, Julia Twigg's *Fashion and Age: Dress, the Body and Later Life* (Bloomsbury, 2013) and *Music, Style, and Aging: Growing Old Disgracefully?* by Andy Bennett (Temple University Press, 2013) explore age's impact on our choices of clothing and personal appearance.

1   Kaiser, Susan B. (2012). *Fashion and Cultural Studies.* New York: Berg.

2   Craik, Jennifer (2005). *Uniforms Exposed: From Conformity to Transgression.* New York: Berg.

3   Hebdige, Dick (1979). *Subculture: The Meaning of Style.* New York: Routledge.

4   Thornton, Sarah (1996). *Club Cultures: Music, Media and Subcultural Capital.* Hanover, NH: Wesleyan University Press.

5   Bennett, Andy (2011). "The Post-Subcultural Turn: Some Reflections 10 Years On." *Journal of Youth Studies,* 14(5): 493–506.

6   Paoletti, Jo (2012). *Pink and Blue: Telling the Boys from the Girls in America.* Bloomington, IN: Indiana University Press.

7   Paoletti, Jo (2012). *Sex and Unisex: Fashion, Feminism and the Sexual Revolution.* Bloomington, IN: Indiana University Press.

8   De Casanova, Erynn Masi (2015). *Buttoned Up: Clothing, Conformity and White-Collar Masculinity.* Ithaca, NY: Cornell University Press.

9   Woodward, Sophie (2005). *Why Women Wear What They Wear?* New York: Bloomsbury.

10   Tulloch, Carol (2016). *The Birth of Cool: Style Narratives of the African Diaspora.* New York: Bloomsbury.

11   Ford, Tanisha C. (2015). *Liberated Threads: Black Women, Style, and the Global Politics of Soul.* Chapel Hill, NC: University of North Carolina Press.

12   Tu, Thuy Linh Nguyen (2010). *The Beautiful Generation: Asian Americans and the Cultural Economy of Fashion.* Durham, NC: Duke University Press.

13   Pham, Minh-Ha T. (2015). *Asians Wear Clothes on the Internet.* Durham, NC: Duke University Press.

14   Twigg, Julia (2013). *Fashion and Age: Dress, the Body and Later Life.* New York: Bloomsbury.

15   Bennett, Andy (2013). *Music, Style, and Aging: Growing Old Disgracefully?* Philadelphia: Temple University Press.

Figure 4.1 *Dior's Success. Dubbed the "New Look" by editor Carmel Snow, the feminine look by Christian Dior appealed to the public after the Second World War.* © Roger Viollet via Getty Images.

4

Fashion: Systems, Meaning, and Time

The years of the Second World War were a difficult time in the fashion industry. Up until June 1940, when Paris fell to the Nazis, French designers were the world leaders of fashion—so much so that American magazine editors were willing to risk the war to travel to Parisian shows.[1] After the center of fashion was cut off from much of the world, British and American designers were forced to go their own way. The materials to produce clothing were highly rationed, including fabrics, like wool, cotton, linen and silk, dyes and cheap metals so resulting in styles were simple with slim, shorter skirts.[2]

After the war ended, French couturiers set out to reaffirm Paris' place as the pinnacle of the fashion world. This effort included the Théâtre de la Mode— 200 intricately designed outfits made for wire mannequins to promote the latest French styles in 1945 and 1946.[3] The success of this endeavor, along with the help of the US and British fashion press helped propel Paris back to the forefront of fashion and set the stage for an iconic design that would stand the test of time: the New Look.

The first collection by designer Christian Dior, the "New Look" harkened back to the days before the war. Dior, who had worked with various designers before opening his own house in 1946, produced the style in 1947 which featured a tighter-fitting jacket, a slim waist and full skirt that was nearly a foot longer than the prevalent trends of the time. US magazine editors were taken by the look and *Harper's Bazaar* editor Carmel Snow is credited with giving the "New Look" its name.[4] Timing is believed to have played a role in the design's success: without some nostalgia for the 1930s and the ending of war rations, Dior's iconic look would not have been possible.

However, the return to more fabric and longer skirts in the period after the war was met with some resistance as it seemed somewhat unpatriotic. A housewife in Dallas, Texas founded the "Little Below the Knee Club," which spread across the US. The original club paraded through department store Neiman Marcus to protest the lower hemlines. In England, the backlash took on a more classist tone, as the New Look was seen as being promoted and instituted by the whims of the upper class. Despite such protests, longer skirts were eventually adopted by women of all classes, even if lower-end styles couldn't replicate Dior's master designs.[5]

The New Look illustrates the trickle-down movement from an haute couture design for upper class clientele to middle class and finally working class. And, while there are other touchstone styles—such as Paul Poiret's tunic dress or the miniskirt alternatively attributed to Mary Quant and André Courrèges[6]— that had such a huge impact, Dior's iconic look remains a flashpoint for fashion change after a monumental world event. This chapter will explore the contemporary flow of fashion combined with the rise of advertising and marketing, and the overall fragmentation of the media and cultural landscape, which may make it impossible for a single style to hold as much sway again.

Fashion as a System

As we discussed in Chapter 1, "fashion" and "clothing" are often used interchangeably, but they really refer to two different things. "Clothing" refers to the garments constructed to put on our bodies. It can be made of natural or synthetic materials and is largely used to protect us from the elements, cover up our private parts and show us off in various ways. In comparison, "fashion" is a broader sociocultural system which gives our clothes—and other consumable goods—meaning. For example, cars, furniture, music styles, exercise routines and certain foods are all subject to changes in fashion.

That said, practically speaking, when we refer to the "fashion system" we are generally referring to a wide range of jobs, people and products that come together to create, distribute and give meaning to clothing and other consumer goods. Yuniya Kawamura argues that fashion is an institutionalized system that helps to create and sustain myths around the goods we buy.[7] Clothing and other consumer goods straddle a line where they are created by various systems—think about Kaiser's Circuit of Culture we discussed in Chapter 2— but are also used on an individual level. Researchers have approached and theorized the system from a variety of different perspectives, working within disciplines such as anthropology, sociology, psychology and economics but, coming from different disciplines, these discussions frequently have different start and end points. For example, an anthropologist might be looking at meaning within a culture while business researchers are more interested in how to sell something.

The discussion here will largely be grounded in sociology and anthropology, but will run in two directions. First, we'll explore fashion as a system, or, more specifically, how and why the fashion system changes. The theorization of why fashion changes can be traced back more than a century and, while there have been challenges and reimagining, the classic understanding still holds some weight. After we understand the system of fashion change, we can look at how *meaning* gets embedded into particular garments and styles of dress, at both a communal and individual level. As several theorists have noted, there is a dialogue between how fashion functions as a system and how people give meaning to garments, but these are disparate questions.

Before we jump into this, let's cut some arguments off at the pass here. You've likely heard some criticisms of fashion, whether that it is vain and superficial or helps create unrealistic beauty expectations. A Marxist take is that fashion helps to perpetuate the capitalistic system that redistributes wealth upward. Relatedly, fashion—especially the relatively recent development of fast fashion—has perpetuated unsafe working conditions for some of the most vulnerable people in the world *and* created inordinate amounts of waste by changing styles frequently and selling cheap garments that are not made to last. And, yes, fashion is largely created to be an exclusionary practice, whether people are excluded due to financial means or body type. These criticisms, frankly, aren't wrong—but they also aren't the full story.

Gilles Lipovetsky offers a substantial defense of fashion by noting that such a system can only develop in places of relative stability.[8] If people are concerned about more basic needs—say food or shelter—fashion isn't going to be a top concern. However, in a time and place where basic needs are met, the system of fashion offers a social process that can act as a form of art, entertainment and even social mobility. Moreover, in the contemporary age, how we dress and the things we consume help us to construct fulfilling identities and create meaningful lives. Ultimately, a fashion system always has benefits and drawbacks. And, while there are major hurdles that the clothing industry needs to overcome—pollution and environmental concerns chief among them—that should not negate the value of the entire system.

Simmel's Trickle-down Fashion

Georg Simmel was one of the first writers to tackle the idea of fashion and his idea of "trickle-down fashion" remains a largely dominant understanding of the fashion system. For Simmel, fashion is reliant on a class-based social structure whereby the "lower classes" will see and imitate those at the top of the social hierarchy. However, once the highest class sees those from lesser classes wearing the same garments or otherwise copying them, they change the fashion in order to create difference between themselves and those on the lower rungs of society. Within this view, fashion change is driven by the need of the highest class to differentiate itself and the system largely creates status symbols out of clothing and particular styles of dress.[9] In this way, Simmel's argument isn't all that different from an earlier writer, Thorstein Veblen, who outlined a similar social structure in *The Theory of the Leisure Class*.[10]

Perhaps the best way to think about Simmel's explanation of fashion would be an image of a royal court from The Middle Ages. The royals—the king or queen, especially—would hold the highest social position and would always be trying to distinguish themselves from everyone else. Their styles would trickle down to the royal court, to the dukes and duchesses, onto lords and ladies and finally to the commoners. Whenever the king, queen and those on the royal court saw others dressing like them, they found new ways to distinguish themselves from everyone else. Obviously, during the high days of royal courts, elements of clothing and accessories such as fabrics, dyes and gems were rare and more difficult to copy, thereby extending the life of styles. However, mass production and increased globalization has altered these patterns dramatically.

One important part of Simmel's understanding is the notion of class mobility (e.g. the ability to change classes or at least *appear* to be of a different class). Simmel believed that fashion cannot take place in societies with a strict social structure, since there's either no ability to, or no point in, imitating the better off.[11] Sumptuary laws—the laws that regulate clothing choices—often tried to solidify these class distinctions, although they didn't always work.[12]

In contrast, democratic societies without a definitive social hierarchy also seem to pose a problem for Simmel's understanding of the fashion system. In the US, for example, which has never had a system of nobility, who exactly would be the highest class? The president and politicians? The top 1% of earners? Actors or other well-known celebrities? Part of this certainly plays into ideas of interpersonal power (as discussed in Chapter 2), but part of this also hints at a larger issue within Simmel's understanding. Who do *you* want to imitate? The answer varies for every individual and cannot always be chalked up to those with power or capital. Not to mention, there has always been an undercurrent of rebellion within what we wear—wearing particular clothing or styles to "stick it to the man" has been a trend that can be traced from Amelia Bloomer's pants to Zoot suits of the 1930s and 1940s and the punk aesthetics of Vivienne Westwood in the 1970s.

Alternative Understandings of Fashion

While Simmel's foundational understanding of the fashion system has influenced much of the field, several articles and propositions have been pitched in opposition to his top-down, elite approach to fashion, including Herbert Blumer's "Collective Selection Model" and Ted Polhemus' "Bubble Up Fashion." Meanwhile, the fashion life cycle has attempted to integrate competing understandings of the fashion, as has the application of symbolic interactionism.

Blumer's Collective Selection

One of the main challenges to Simmel's model was Blumer's Collective Selection model of fashion.[13] Blumer spent time with buyers in Paris in an effort to understand how specific styles and fashions are adopted and distributed. One of his principal observations was that while fashion buyers were presented with hundreds of styles and designs to choose from, most came to similar conclusions and only a handful of the designs would be chosen. Thus, while buyers could select radically different styles and fashion could thus take vastly different forms, fashions competed with one another for dominance with one usually winning out.

For Blumer, new fashions were largely decided within a process of what he deemed "collective selection"—that is a process whereby the decision makers are in frequent communication with each other. This communication helps to shape the buyers' worldview and, ultimately, their decision-making processes. As such, the selection of certain styles wasn't purely based on one person's taste or judgement, but rather relied on all the other people they communicated with and—in the cases of buyers—all the other fashion buyers' tastes, judgements and criticisms which had been shared in various forms.

To see this in personal terms, think about how you communicate with a close group of friends. How often is it that you have vastly different opinions when it comes to something like music? You may not like the exact same songs, but chances are you like the same genre of music or, at the very least, have a working knowledge of the same songs and artists. This is the same situation within professions; you are constantly comparing notes with others and reshaping your observations, judgements and actions accordingly.

Blumer's conceptualization is important in a few ways. First, he argued that the fashion system was more than just clothing and could be applied to any number of fields—some of which have been mentioned—but fashion also applies to things like philosophy, science and technology.[14] The changes within these fields can be considered in fashion if they are at the forefront of current thought, whether or not we acknowledge them as "fashion." With this reconceptualization, it implies people and ideas can be in and out of fashion. As such, fashion isn't *everything*—like not all clothing is in fashion—but rather a subset of clothing items (and thereby the wearers) are understood to be fashionable at a particular time. Finally, Blumer's contention was that fashion change is an orderly process and not completely random. Within Simmel's telling, the upper classes are changing in whatever ways they can to distinguish themselves, but collective selection leads to more incremental changes. Fred Davis would later add to this that new fashions are in a relationship with the current, dominant style and that any changes must address what already exists.[15] As such, we don't have change for the sake of change, but change toward something people see as better than the current style.

Polhemus's Bubble-up Fashion

While Simmel saw the top of the social structure as being able to make change, Polhemus's understanding of the fashion system focuses on the lowest rungs of the social hierachy. Polhemus argues that the authority of the fashion system has been reworked and it is now individuals at the lower levels of the fashion system—or those in opposition to the dominant fashion trends—who are those making changes. In this understanding, there's an innovation within "streetstyle"—or, what people are wearing everyday—that gets picked up in the media and by others lower on the fashion totem pole before influencing high-end designers and becoming part of their collections.[16] This is the "bubbling up" as the style emerges outside of the fashion system, but is ultimately coopted by it.

An example of this can be Dapper Dan's Guccy styles of the 1980s and 1990s. Initially, his styles were in contrast to Gucci's designs, although they later took on a life of their own—becoming high-priced fashion in their own right. Decades later, the Gucci brand would collaborate with Dapper Dan showing that his initial designs had bubbled up to the top of the fashion trends. While this movement took quite a while to fully bubble up, the trajectory here is clear.

There were a few changes across society that would allow fashion to move from trickle down to bottom up. First, there was the development of the "Supermarket of Style," to use Polhemus's phrase,[17] which allows the purchase of clothing from various trends and subcultures at any time. No longer are consumers held to what is available that season, but rather everything is available to be found. While Polhemus's writing on this was during the early days of the internet, online shopping has made this process even more pronounced. The second was a shift from fashion to style as the dominant force.[18] While style has long been important in fashion (hence the term *fashion victim* to describe someone who doesn't successfully complete a look), *how* items are worn and what image is projected has been increasingly important.

Fashion Life Cycle

Outside of the sociocultural explanations, George B. Sporles started from an economic point of view but ultimately drew in a variety of theorizations to create a unified conceptual framework or what we can call a "life cycle" model. For Sporles, fashion works in a five-step model. In order, they are: (1) invention; (2) dissemination; (3) social prominence; (4) social saturation; and, (5) decline. Within Sporles's telling, new fashions are invented and introduced through the business and production systems. From there, they move onto what Sporles calls "fashion leadership" as in "prestigious consumers" and "creative individuals who experiment with new aesthetic objects."[19] Social prominence occurs once the mass media pick up on the trend and communicate it to a wide audience. Finally, the fashion becomes overused and the novelty wears off forcing the fashion leadership to experiment with new looks and styles.

This model gives a more complete picture than simply chalking fashion change up to differentiation. Moreover, Sporles took pains to include a multitude of fashion understandings within each of the stages.[20] The idea that fashion and consumption patterns are part of a life cycle has been used in other situations. Roman Meinhold suggested that fashions are always in the process of being killed in order to be replaced.[21] Meanwhile, business researchers have suggested that brands, which, like fashion, have both economic and cultural elements, can also been seen as steps within a life cycle or evolution.[22]

Insight: Allbirds, Uniqlo and Fashionable Developments

In many ways, fashion and technology may not seem to be natural bedfellows. However, innovations have long driven fashion trends. For example, Madeline Vionnet's development of the bias-cut, where she began to cut fabric against its woven direction, helped propel her and her designs to the forefront of fashion, while Coco Chanel's innovative use of jersey and the development of synthetic fabrics like rayon also helped to advance specific fashions and styles. In recent years, the idea of developing new materials and, in turn, creating "better" garments has taken hold. For example, Uniqlo, the Japan-based retailer, has branded much of its clothing as Lifewear, including two specific lines: Heattech and Airism. Uniqlo's marketing materials attribute new weaving and threads to developments, that allows the brand's Heattech line to keep the wearers warm in cold weather without being bulky or sweaty, while its Airism line helps wick sweat away to keep people cool in the summer.[23]

Uniqlo, however, is hardly alone in this endeavor. Men's shirt brand Mizzen + Main uses fabrics that are moisture-wicking and wrinkle-free for men's dress shirts. Founder and former CEO Kevin Lavelle said he was inspired after seeing a government staffer sweating through a traditional button down and thought performance fabrics might be the answer. As such, Mizzen + Main shirts look like traditional button downs, but use fabrics that had previously been used for athletic apparel to be more flexible and utilitarian.[24]

Some up-and-coming brands have merged technological innovations with design to create products that are not only fashionable, but also comfortable *and*, in some cases, eco-friendly. For example, shoe brand Allbirds was started in 2016 by athlete Tim Brown and engineer Joey Zwillinger. The shoes initially came as a simple running sneaker made of wool and other sustainable materials, like wood pulp, caster bean oil and even recycled bottles. The brand, which aims for comfort along with eco-consciousness, hasn't been seen as the most stylish or fashion-forward, but has quietly converted many in the tech industry and won over doubters in other industries as well. Similar to Allbirds, women's shoe brand Rothy's uses material made of recycled water bottles and other recycled and eco-friendly materials for their shoes, although their shoes tend to be more fashion-forward.[25]

And, working somewhat from the opposite direction, 4ocean was inspired by eco-consciousness, specifically cleaning up the world's oceans. By selling bracelets made from recycled materials, the firm seeks to help worldwide ocean cleanup, and claims to have collected more than 5 million tons of trash from the ocean.[26] All in all, these innovations in technology have the ability both to drive fashion change and—if recent developments are any indication—support eco-consciousness.

Fashion, Appearance and Symbolic Interactionism

We touched upon symbolic interactionism briefly in Chapter 2, but to revisit, it's a vein of sociology that holds that people act toward people and things in line with the meaning it has for them. Works by Herbert Blumer and Gregory P. Stone form the foundation of symbolic interactionism's engagement with fashion and appearance. Stone's work argues that appearance is important to all social engagements and helps to frame individuals and their communication with one another.[27] Susan B. Kaiser, Richard H. Nagasawa and Sandra S. Hutton attempted to bridge the earlier works arguing that people change their style and appearance in an attempt to finding meaning in their lives. As such, small changes by individuals help to drive larger fashion changes forward by being picked up by more and more individuals until the look becomes a bona fide trend.[28]

In some sense, not all of these theorizations are incompatible with one another; both Sporles' life-cycle model and Kaiser, Nagasawa and Hutton specifically attempted to blend or connect different models. Moreover, each is anchored in a historical moment, and, as such, there is something to be said for that context. Yet, these explanations are largely looking at how the fashion system works as a whole, rather than dealing with the specific *meanings* of fashion.

Meaning, Clothing and the Fashion System

In comparison, others have looked specifically at how meaning is created, distributed and interacts with consumer goods on both general and specific levels. There is a bit of nuance here as the "fashion system" can largely be seen as *part* of meaning creation and distribution. As we discussed in Chapters 1 and 2, we each understand and assign unique meanings to people and things based on our experience with them and our communication about them. In this way, the mere act of a particular garment being *in fashion* can be a meaning in and of itself—providing we know that (and care). As we've discussed in previous chapters, meaning that is communicated through clothing is somewhat dependent upon the intentions of the wearer, but also on the perceptions and knowledge of the observer. Anthropologist Grant McCracken was particularly interested in the meaning of our consumable goods, including clothing. He argues that meaning is always in transit, flowing between collective and individual efforts.[29]

In McCracken's telling, meaning resides in three different places (Figure 4.2). The first place meaning resides is in the "culturally constituted world" or, to put it a bit more simply, in the culture. As such, a majority of people in the US will have similar ideas of concepts such as athleticism or success. Drawing off the cultural meanings, processes like advertising and the fashion system help to give goods particular meanings. Consider athleisure wear: garments made largely of synthetic fabrics that can be used for working out, but can also easily transition to other situations. Leggings, a key staple of athleisure wear, have been around for decades, but rose to prominence again when Lululemon made them a staple of their brand. For its part, Lululemon built its brand around its association with yoga and all things athletic and wellness, and helped to establish a niche clothing market that would be followed by the likes of Gap-owned Athleta and Kate Hudson's Fabletics. Drawing from the "culturally constituted world" advertising—and the "fashion system" of magazine editors and the like—helped give these garments an air of fitness and athleticism (heck, even the name *athleisure wear* implies the physicality that goes with the clothing).

Figure 4.2 *McCracken's Model of Meaning Transfer. McCracken theorized that meaning exists at both a cultural level and a individual level.*

Now these garments, leggings and the like, have a cultural meaning that people can literally buy into. This sets up the second stage of McCracken's model where these goods can be imbued with individual meaning. Specifically, McCracken used a number of rituals—possession, exchange, grooming and divestment—that give meaning to consumers.[30] For example, it might mean something just to "own it"; Lululemon is somewhat expensive so the mere idea of buying and owning it might be meaningful (possession). Likewise, you might be gifted a workout top from a significant other that becomes meaningful (exchange), or after wearing the garments during your weekly workout, the clothing helps you get in the mindset to work out (grooming). Finally, you might be on the giving end of a gift or, like Marie Kondo, find joy in getting rid of clothing you no longer need, thus finding meaning in the action (divestment). The reasons we engage in these rituals are infinite, but McCracken sees these processes as a way to give our lived experiences meaning.

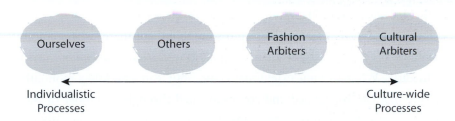

Figure 4.3 *Hamilton's Macro-Micro Model. Hamilton saw the meaning of clothing move from culture-wide creation to more individualistic interpretations.*

In comparison, fashion scholar Jean A. Hamilton offered a somewhat similar setup to McCracken, although it differs in significant ways. For Hamilton, the meaning of clothing and appearance always occurred on a spectrum of micro to macro forces (Figure 4.3). On the micro end, clothing and our appearance interacts with us, first and foremost, and then with those around us. Hamilton, who was writing in response to Kaiser, Nagasawa and Hutton (who we discussed above) saw her construction in line with the micro applications of symbolic interactionism[31]—much like Chapters 2 and 3 of this book. At the other end of the spectrum, Hamilton saw cultural-system arbiters as having the widest reach and fashion-system arbiters as a step between groups and the cultural arbiters. Despite her model suggesting there is a distinction between fashion and cultural arbiters, Hamilton lumps her examples together, which includes everything from designers and product developers to retailers to elections, economics and movements within music, film and "the arts."[32]

While both McCracken and Hamilton's models are useful for bridging the gap between cultural and individual processes, neither are quite dynamic enough to fully grasp how we develop, understand and deploy meanings within clothing, appearance and the fashion system at large. Admittedly, some of the issues are due to the time when they were writing: McCracken in the 1980s and Hamilton in the 1990s. McCracken's model is largely unidirectional and doesn't make room for reflectiveness within the model, not to mention that rituals are not the only way to develop "meaning." Second, there's little to no reason to see meaning as a positive association. Undoubtedly there are things—clothing styles, brands, various products— we individually don't like and that's meaning as well! Finally, a problem for both McCracken and Hamilton—and this is where timing of their writing comes into play—is that they lean into something "out there" where cultural meanings are produced and then this gets transferred or *communicated* to individuals. While to some extent that's true, both lean a bit into a monolithic culture that can be defined and communicated through a number of ways. However, thanks to media fragmentation which began in the 1980s, a monolithic culture hasn't existed within the US and many nations for some time (if it ever did). More recently, the rise of the internet and social media has made the "culturally constructed world" or the "macro arbiters" that much harder to pin down.

There's one final practical, yet crucial, point about meaning, which largely underpins this entire book (see Chapter 1) and stands in contrast to the way both McCracken, Hamilton and various other researchers approach the subject within clothing, consumer goods and the fashion system. *Meaning*, as understood from a communication perspective, is a micro or individual level process that takes place within each of us. As such, we need to be receivers of messages from *somewhere* and will make sense of them with the way we understand the world. Meaning only comes from our own lived experiences; if we don't receive or interpret those messages, they are literally meaning*less*.

For example, the opening vignette discussed Dior's New Look and how it influenced fashion once it was released. The design of the New Look meant something at the time because it was created by Dior and signaled a change from the austerity of the Second World War. The design was picked up and distributed widely throughout the Western world inspiring stores to carry it, some women to wear it and some women to revolt against it. However, for those living in semi-reclusive societies—say those living with the Inuit or in Samoa—this fashion could have happened and they never would have known. While that's an extreme example (and can be chalked up to different cultural contexts), consider someone who is blind. Does Dior's New Look mean something to you if you can't see it?

The point of the previous example is not to be glib, but to demonstrate that this is all based on receiving messages of some sort. If you don't know a fashion trend is happening, don't recognize a designer or know how much something costs, it simply doesn't have that meaning for you. In this way, it's nearly impossible to know what we don't know, but also speaks to levels of knowledge and other forms of cultural capital.

Now Trending . . .

To reiterate, *fashion* is largely a constructed system that dictates when various garments, styles, looks and even brands are "in" and "out." However, one of the most practical ways fashion gets developed is through that of trend forecasting—a business of professionals who tell those within the fashion industry what *might* be popular soon. Before we get into what trend forecasting is and how it works within fashion, it's important to make a brief note. Some researchers have attempted to distinguish between a few competing concepts: fashion, trends, fads and innovation.[33] This argument suggests that *fashion* changes at regular intervals and is otherwise stable in its changes, while fads and trends are less predictable. While such a distinction might have been useful at one point, today it would be severely limiting to what we considered "fashion" to runway shows and related products. From the rise of fast fashion to the development of blogs and social media influencers, styles can change more rapidly and frequently are not in sync with the fashion calendar of yore. As such, for our purposes here, fashion and trends will be looked at as one and the same, lasting for indeterminate amounts of time. In this way, trends are something of a social construction whereby we agree that there are trends and that something may be in or out of fashion at a given time.[34]

Fashion forecasters can be traced back to France in the 1600s where a magazine offered up the first report on trends. During the same century, textile manufactures began circulating samples of fabrics and colors available to designers. In the late 1700s and early 1800s, these offerings became more professionalized as business people would collect fabric samples and sell them to dressmakers and rival mills. Eventually, Victor Jean-Claude and his brother, François, began selling trend information to manufacturers, schools and associations of designers and created perhaps the earliest trend forecasting agency.[35] While France led the way in color and fabric forecasting, the Textile

Color Card Association in the US, and the British Colour Council in the UK followed suit in the early 1900s.[36]

Through the circulation of these predictions, it became clear that there was a practical value in predicting trends in colors and materials, and that they also worked as a propaganda tool for various industries.[37] As such, trend forecasting was (and remains) not just about accurately predicting what would come next, but selling the trends to the public. This was also seen in the work of American fashion forecaster, Tobé Coller Davis, who began her own fashion forecasting and consulting firm in 1927, selling her insights to major department stores. Davis' insights were assembled in the publication *Fashion Reports from Tobé*, which survived the Great Depression and was read by stores in the US, the UK, Canada and Australia by 1939. During the Second World War, the reports pushed patriotic goods and would later help promote the new Parisian fashion collections after the war ended.[38]

Today, the best-known names include Pantone and WGSN. Pantone, a firm started in 1963 to help standardize colors within the graphic arts, has been naming a "color of the year" for roughly two decades.[39] (Fun fact: Pantone's first-ever color of the year was Cerulean Blue.) While Pantone remains the leader in the color prediction, other companies have joined the fray, from various paint companies to WGSN.[40] However, UK-based WGSN predicts much more than just colors. Started in 1998, WGSN utilized the web to make more frequent and nuanced trend predictions, and offers insights not just into fashion, but also to hospitality, financial services and the automotive industry.[41]

And while there may be some sort of art or skill to predicting the next trends and fashions, it remains a social construction (i.e. something intangible a group of people accept as real) and closely linked to power and promotion. Pantone remains the epitome of color forecasting largely because its predictions are written about by the likes of *The New York Times*,[42] CNN[43] and *Adweek*.[44] As researcher Jenny Lantz has noted, many of these predictions become self-fulfilling prophecies almost willing the trend into existence. Still, these predictions run up against other tastemakers, such as fashion editors, bloggers and retail buyers,[45] so there is a bit of a legitimization process. We'll dig deeper into this dynamic of cultural intermediation in

Chapter 5, but suffice to say that part of WGSN's success—and that of any other forecaster, for that matter—comes from having a close relationship with publications.

About Time

Whether we're calling these changes in clothing and appearance, fashion, trends or fads, the one thing they have in common is time. Fashion works to help us mark time (such as time of day, time of year or historical moments) and is equally influenced by time. It was historian James Laver who delineated the relationship between fashion and time. Laver connected styles or ways of dressing with particular moments, holding that our uses and views of clothing change with time periods. Laver believed that ways of dress that are "ahead of their time" are viewed as "indecent" while those past their prime might be considered "hideous" and "ridiculous" before being praised again as the look moves into antiquity.[46] Laver, here, was buying into a modernist and linear notion of time that is constantly progressing toward something better rather than drawing on and reinterpreting the past.

Comparatively, Walter Benjamin saw fashion as key to the progression of time, insomuch that its changes help to signify different cultural moments.[47] Still, the changes in the fashion system always draw off the past with an eye toward the future or what *will* be happening. In the case of the aforementioned forecasters, they are attempting to predict what will be happening with clothing and personal adornment, but can only do so based off on what has happened before. Will a movie introduce a new fashion? Or, a political movement? By using the past as a reference point, it is possible to infer what might happen in the future. Similarly, designs and styles of dress frequently draw on the past as well, as was the case when US First Lady Dolley Madison emphasized "classical" dress and designs in order to give authority to the early US government.[48] Elsewhere, Karl Lagerfeld's long run at Chanel frequently channeled the namesake's designs, just using them in new ways. In these ways, time can be seen as folding back upon itself, coming close to the past, but never repeating it exactly.[49]

As Laver indirectly pointed out, one of the most pronounced aspects of the fashion–time relationship is how clothing and style are viewed differently within different temporal contexts. What is seen as fashionable *today* may look very different next month, next year or next decade. Susan B. Kaiser makes the case that fashion and appearance cannot be disconnected from contexts—both time and space.[50] What we choose to wear and how we choose to present our bodies are wrapped up in our own sense of time and how we are experiencing it through age or generations.[51]

Fashion is frequently understood to be a dividing line of time, delineating the past from the future. When turning toward the fashionable clothing of previous times, clothing can help create memories or even nostalgia for the time. In this way, clothing acts as a form of memory where the tactical dimensions of clothing help to remind people of the past. Moreover, it is within these ideas of the past that people frequently feel some sort of "truth" or authenticity in the people or times that came before it.[52] And, even as clothing can signify the past and what came before, fashion can also help to drive time forward. The temporality of the fashion system is not a given, rather, it is the end result of modern organizations. Timelines and even the seasons work to structure time and encourage new fashion and consumption.

The End of Fashion?

It's been more than two decades since journalist Teri Agins declared *The End of Fashion* in her book of the same name. While the title of the book might have been a tad hyperbolic, Agins certainly wasn't wrong in her understanding of how the fashion system changed in the late 1900s. According to Agins, the haute couture driven, Paris-to-the-world fashion system faded through the last decades of the twentieth century and was supplanted by marketing, advertising and business considerations. Financial upheaval—first in the US in the 1980s and then Asia in the 1990s—considerably hurt haute couture as there were fewer people willing to splurge on impractical clothing. Moreover, as fashion houses increased licensing agreements to keep their lines afloat, brands often moved down market and into product categories that might not fit with the overall image of a couture line.[53]

At the same time, as Agins explains, various social trends all but ensured there would never be another fashion with the impact of Dior's New Look. First, most people stopped buying and wearing formalwear. As women moved more prominently into the workforce of the 1980s, their styles started to emulate menswear, which had long been more somber and formulaic. Then, by the early 1990s, offices turned to business casual—as discussed in Chapter 3— which meant that people needed less clothing overall since what they wore to the office they could also wear outside of work. A second contributor to this change was the outsourcing of production and the cheapening of labor which lowered the quality of luxury clothing and thus undermined a central proposition of fashion houses. If clothing wasn't better quality than cheaper versions, why would someone spend the money? A final trend was the development of lifestyle marketing, pioneered by Ralph Lauren. We'll tackle this more in Chapter 7, but simply, Lauren built his preppy American brand as one that was steeped in more traditional class connotations than the latest designs. With this move, clothing moved from being less about specific trends and moved more into the meaning created not only by designers, but also through marketers, advertising and brand managers overall.[54]

To be clear, Agins wasn't the last person to declare the "end of fashion"— scholars Adam Geczy and Vicki Karaminas would release a scholarly volume of the same title nearly two decades later. Rather than proclaiming an end to the system, Geczy, Karaminas and their contributors were more interested in the ways the fashion system was changing in light of digitalization and changes in media production. As both works demonstrate, *fashion* is a system that classifies clothing and consumer goods, but does so in ways that keep up with the times. Runway shows, luxury labels, modeling and even haute couture continue to exist; however, today much of it is used to drive lines of ready-to-wear clothing and brand opportunities for perfumes, accessories and even household goods.[55]

That being said, it is important to note that the decline in the influence of couture houses did open the floodgates for other styles of dress to rise to prominence. The aforementioned "bubble up" theory of fashion that Polhemus documented likely wouldn't have happened if couture houses had retained their grip on authority and fashion change. At the same time, many of the issues fashion theorists have been wrestling with would look very different without the decline of the couture houses. Geczy and Karaminas argue that fashion has become a means of self-expression and akin to art (more on *that* in Chapter 9), but the range of options and meanings clothing offers people is something that simply couldn't exist without the overlay of advertising and branding. As noted in Chapter 1, clothing and material goods don't have the range of communicative capabilities that language does and, as such, without the help of media its signification would be much more limited. In fact, we could argue that some of the simplistic understandings of the fashion system— namely Simmel's, but Blumer's research as well—are a product of the fashion system *before* its communicative turn. In the next several chapters, we'll address how various media (print, film and television and the internet) and cultural institutions (the advertising industry and the art world) help identify and create fashion trends which, in turn, are used for communicative purposes by individuals.

Further Reading

While the chapter summarized both of these, the articles "Fashion" by Georg Simmel and "Fashion: From Class Differentiation to Collective Selection" by Herbert Blumer are key readings on how fashion works. Outside of those, Tim Edwards' *Fashion in Focus: Concepts, Practices and Politics* (Routledge, 2011) dedicates an entire chapter to delineating fashion perspectives by discipline and the chapter "Fashion as an Institutionalized System" in Yuniya Kawamura's *Fashion-ology* (Bloomsbury, 2018) provides a nice overview and more nuanced discussion of how specific jobs and industries create and support the immaterial fashion mythologies. Likewise, Grant McCracken's *Culture and Consumption* (Indiana University Press, 1988) details how he understands meaning flow from an anthropological perspective. The book also extends or "rehabilitates" (McCracken's word) Simmel's Trickle-down Theory in response to various criticisms.

In recent years, three works have tackled trend forecasting. *The Trendmakers* (Bloomsbury, 2016) by Jenny Lantz is a deep dive into forecasting firms while the edited volume *The Fashion Forecasters* (Bloomsbury, 2018) from Regina Lee Blaszczyk and Ben Wubs provides a more historical analysis on how the industry reached this point. *On Trend* (University of Illinois Press, 2019) by Devon Powers looks at forecasting as a cultural process beyond just the fashion world and pays particular attention to its orientation to the future. Finally, while a bit dated, *The End of Fashion: How Marketing Changed the Clothing Business Forever* (William Marrow, 2000) by Teri Agins is still an interesting read if looked at from a historic perspective, while *The End of Fashion: Clothing and Dress in the Age of Globalization* (Bloomsbury, 2018) by Adam Geczy and Vicki Karaminas provides a great foundation for how we understand fashion moving forward.

1   Simmel, Georg (1904/1957). "Fashion." *The American Journal of Sociology*, 62(6): 541–558.

2   Blumer, Herbert (1969). "Fashion: From Class Differentiation to Collective Selection." *The Sociological Quarterly*, 10(3): 275–291.

3   Kawamura, Yuniya (2018). *Fashion-ology: An Introduction to Fashion Studies.* New York: Bloomsbury.

4   McCracken, Grant (1988). *Culture and Consumption: New Approaches to the Symbolic Character of Consumer Goods and Activities.* Bloomington, IN: Indiana University Press.

5   Lantz, Jenny (2016). *The Trendmakers: Behind the Scenes of the Global Fashion Industry.* New York: Bloomsbury.

6   Blaszczyk, Regina Lee and Ben Wubs (2018). *The Fashion Forecasters: A Hidden History of Color and Trend Prediction.* New York: Bloomsbury.

7 Powers, Devon (2019). *On Trend: The Business of Forecasting the Future.* Chicago: University of Illinois Press.

8 Agins, Teri (2000). *The End of Fashion: How Marketing Changed the Clothing Business Forever.* New York: William Marrow.

9 Geczy, Adam and Vicki Karaminas (2019). *The End of Fashion: Clothing and Dress in the Age of Globalization.* New York: Bloomsbury.

Figure 5.1 *Vreeland as Editor. Diana Vreeland, left, and Carmel Snow work in the* Harper's Bazaar *offices in 1952. © Walter Sanders via Getty Images.*

5

Clothing, News, and Tastemaking

Why don't you . . .

- Rinse your blond child's hair in dead champagne to keep it gold, as they do in France?
- Paint a map of the world on all four walls of your boys' nursery so they won't grow up with a provincial point of view?
- Have two pairs of shoes exactly alike except that one pair has thin rubber soles for damp days? Any cobbler can put these on.[1]

These were just some of the pieces of impractical advice doled out by Diana Vreeland in the pages of *Harper's Bazaar*. Vreeland, a socialite, who was married to a wealthy banker, started writing the "Why don't you . . .?" column in 1936. The column offered over-the-top advice that was largely impractical after the Great Depression, but it has become legendary. Over the course of her long career, Vreeland became a leading taste arbiter, first as fashion editor of *Harper's Bazaar* and then as editor-in-chief of *Vogue*.[2]

While parodies of fashion editors have become a staple of popular culture—from *Funny Face* (which was based partially on Vreeland) to *Ugly Betty* and *The Devil Wears Prada*—their influence on what we wear is undeniable. Vreeland, for instance, is credited with popularizing the bikini and making blue jeans fashionable.[3] Still, relatively few people have led fashion magazines. Since its inception in 1892, only seven people have helmed *Vogue*, including

Edna Woolman Chase, who was editor for 38 years (1914–1952), Vreeland and Anna Wintour, who has led the magazine since 1988. Fashion competitor *Harper's Bazaar* has more of a turnover with seventeen different editors-in-chief, notably Carmel Snow, who oversaw the magazine for twenty-three years (1934–1957), Glenda Bailey, who ran the magazine for nearly twenty years (2001–2020) and Samir Nasr, who become the publication's first editor-in-chief of color in 2020. While magazines are certainly a product of the entire editorial staff—and people like André Leon Talley and Grace Coddington have been influential without becoming editor-in-chief—it's striking how few people have led these publications. For comparison, *The New York Times* has had seven executive editors since 1977.[4]

This chapter takes a broad view of clothing and fashion, and how it interacts with print media, namely magazines and newspapers, as well as the news media at large. While magazines have long been a prime source for fashion scholars, the implications for other media research have been less interrogated. As such, these following pages connect the foundations of the fashion and lifestyle press before delving into media theory. First, we'll explore how the media can help to develop specific communities, whether they are based on demographics, geography or simply interest. Then, we can begin to see how mass media theory can be applied to fashion and the mass media, namely theories of agenda-setting and framing. Finally, we can turn our attention toward the tastemaking functions of the media and how it confers status on certain individuals and preferred tastes.

A (Very) Brief History of Journalism, Fashion and Clothing

Although "news" has likely spread through all of human history, it wasn't until the development of the printing press that "modern" styles of journalism began to take hold. While China had forms of printing dating to around 800 CE, Western printing is largely chalked up to the workings of Johannes Gutenberg in the mid-1400s. It's been stated that Gutenberg debuted his printing press in 1454, but some Gutenberg Bibles have been dated to the 1440s. News pamphlets began circulating in the early 1500s and, while there is some debate about the exact timing of the first newspaper (largely because the definition of a "newspaper" varies), it is safe to say newspapers appeared by the early 1600s.[5]

Moreover, illustrated fashion publications began to take shape starting in the 1640s. Early examples include *Ornatus Muliebris Anglicanus*, which included "costume plates," or depictions of what was worn to specific events, and *La Gallerie des Modes,* published in the 1770s. *Le Cabinet des Modes,* published between 1785 and 1786, was likely the first intended fashion magazine; the publication went through several names during its history, including *Le Magazine des Modes Nouvelles Françaises et Anglaises* and *Le Journal de la Mode et du Goût.* The magazine aimed to provide fashion for women and men, and included information about carriages, furniture and home décor. Other notable publications from the era, include *Le Monument du Costume, The Lady's Magazine* and *The Gallery of Fashion.*[6] Fashion magazines truly came into their own in the nineteenth century, as lithography helped make color illustrations cheaper, even though the cheapest publications remained in black and white.[7]

While the earliest fashion magazines were published in Europe, *Harper's Bazaar* became the United States' first fashion magazine in 1867.[8] *Vogue* began publishing—first as a weekly society newspaper and later as the fashion magazine we know today—in 1892. *Vogue* was purchased by *the* Condé Nast in 1909, and Nast also went on to purchase the upstart *Dress*, which he later merged with another purchase, *Vanity Fair,* in 1913. While not usually distinguished as "fashion magazines," women's "service" publications—namely the "Seven Sisters" of *Ladies Home Journal, Good Housekeeping, Better Homes and Gardens, Redbook, Family Circle, Women's Day* and *McCall's*—also wrote about clothing. (*Good Housekeeping, Better Homes and Gardens* and *Women's Day* are the only magazines remaining today, with *Redbook* as a digital property.) Often focusing on the domestic side of women's lives, these publications printed dress patterns—as did the early editions of *Harper's Bazaar* and *Vogue.*[9] Dress patterns are no longer in demand; however, coverage of fashion and clothing has remained vital to women's magazines of all stripes, from newer fashion magazines like *Elle* and *InStyle* to more general-interest women's magazines like *Real Simple.*[10]

The story of *Seventeen* largely highlights the influence and importance of magazines. The magazine, which launched in 1944, aimed to be a fashion and service magazine for teen girls. At the time, magazines either skewed younger or older, but founding editor Helen Valentine believed there was a market for the in-between; as did famed publisher Walter Annenberg, who would hire Valentine to launch *Seventeen*. While Annenberg wanted the magazine to be "wholesome"—he banned advertisements for alcohol, cigarettes and hotels—Valentine sought to help young women become active citizens, as well as good consumers. As such, *Seventeen* included pieces on highbrow arts and serious topics as well as the now common-fare of fashion, beauty and advice pieces. As the magazine grew, it worked to help guide teens toward "idealized feminine adulthood," and all of the consumer products, including the clothing, beauty aids and household goods, that went with it.[11]

Community Building Through the Media

While the term "teen-ager" didn't even come into existence until 1904—and the term didn't hit the popular lexicon until the late 1930s and early 1940s[12]— *Seventeen* magazine helps to illustrate a key use of the media: community building. As mentioned in Chapter 3, Benedict Anderson argued that the media help people see themselves as part of "imagined communities"—groups of individuals who share some commonality, but don't know each other and likely never will.[13] Anderson suggested that the printing press and newspapers helped to create nations, but it's possible to see this dynamic at work elsewhere. Geographically, we distinguish Philadelphia from New York City, and this is reinforced by the media—e.g. reading *The Philadelphia Inquirer* or the *Philadelphia Daily News* rather than *The New York Times*, the *New York Post* or the *New York Daily News*.

However, the media doesn't simply work to create a community within an entire country, city or geographic area. As was the case with *Seventeen*, the media helps create smaller groups—say a subculture—within a larger community that may have its own practices and values.[14] For *Seventeen*, this helped to delineate teenagers as a useful demographic, but also taught teen girls what was socially acceptable—whether through direct advice columns or through other published articles. *Seventeen*, along with the post-Second World War economic prosperity in the US, helped to create teenagers as a durable demographic group. A clear link can be made between the publishing and advertising aimed at teens and other youth-driven phenomena, like Beatle-mania and the rise of MTV.

Both across the social landscape and within specific subgroups, the media work in several different ways to help keep society moving: it allows us to know what's going on, to coordinate different elements and activities, and to transmit important cultural traditions and ideas.[15] To give a concrete example: *Seventeen* sought to teach teens what they should be doing during high school, including how to interact with their peers and parents. This helped impart values onto teen girls, including framing domestic work as fun and instilling traditional views of marriage and gender relationships. Once *Seventeen* developed the market, teens were able to grab the reigns to challenge the status quo.[16] This set up a give-and-take dynamic between media outlets, such as *Seventeen* and (years later) the likes of MTV and teen culture, where the media both created and helped reflect teen values.[17]

Media's Influence: Theories of Agenda-Setting and Framing

However, often times, the media gets a bad rap and is blamed for social ills; historic examples include the radio reading of *War of the Worlds* (supposedly) leading New Jersey listeners to kill themselves, and Marilyn Manson being blamed for the Columbine High School shooting.[18] This misunderstanding often comes from the direct effects of the media, or what is colorfully referred to as the "magic bullet" theory. These types of theories and research largely grew from psychology and held that everyone experienced media in the same way; once a particular type of media was consumed the message was "shot" into the reader's or viewer's brain.[19] While there might be some semblance of truth here in the ways we learn and remember (think about children's shows like *Sesame Street, Blue's Clues* and *Dora the Explorer*), media more often works at a less conscious level to help construct our expectations and worldviews.

Theories and research within this later perspective are more often understood as critical cultural perspectives on the media and are more interested in the views the media helps to create, rather than finding direct connections between specific products and human actions. While the next chapter will delve more into ideas of representation within popular media, this chapter aims to address a few theories from the perspective of the news media or the printed work, and explain how they apply to the clothing and the fashion systems. Often times, these theories have largely been developed for and applied to what journalists referred to as "hard news"— political stories, international and/or business affairs and the like—but, these also work within soft news, such as fashion. The following theories of agenda-setting and framing largely fall within the scope of media effects research; however, unlike the aforementioned direct effects theories, they acknowledge the media is limited in its influence. Instead, these theories turn toward what draws our attention and how the media helps us make sense of what is happening.

Agenda-Setting

Maxwell McCombs and Donald L. Shaw initially set out what would become agenda-setting research in *The Public Opinion Quarterly* in 1972. In it, they interviewed voters during the 1968 presidential contest between Richard Nixon, Hubert Humphrey and George Wallace. Their study followed voters in Chapel Hill, North Carolina, and compared what they believed to be the important issues facing the electorate with the news media they claimed to consume. The findings supported the proposition that the issues covered within the mass media led the voters to believe those were important issues— and not that the media was covering what voters were interested in. Short-handedly, agenda-setting has been chalked up to the idea that "the media doesn't tell us what to think, but what to think about."[20]

Even though agenda-setting is often summarized with a pithy shorthand, significant nuance has been given to the theory. For instance, the ability to set the agenda hinges on the relevance of the topic to the audience and how much the audience already knows about it. As such, if people have decided a topic doesn't affect them or they already know about it, they will be less likely to further engage. Further, McCombs and Shaw suggest that framing—as will be discussed later in this chapter—falls within agenda-setting's domain as do concepts like status conferral and stereotyping through media.[21]

Take, for example, the story of fashion blogger Tavi Gevinson. Back in 2008, she was toiling away on her blog, Style Rookie, when the then-eleven-year-old Gevinson was mentioned in two different posts by *New York* magazine's *The Cut*[22]—one of which questioned whether the stylish tween was who she

Seven Names to Know in Print Fashion

Edna Woolman Chase (1877–1957)—Instrumental in *Vogue*'s early success, she promoted the magazine when it was in danger of closing in the early 1900s. Eventually, she would be named managing editor in 1911 and editor-in-chief in 1914, a position she held for 38 years until retiring in 1954. Chase helped to stage the first American fashion show in 1914 and later served on a government committee to redesign female uniforms during the Second World War.[1]

Carmel Snow (1887–1961)—Editor-in-chief of *Harper's Bazaar* from 1934 through 1958. Snow started as a fashion editor under Edna Woolman Chase at *Vogue* before moving to *Harper's Bazaar*, where she revitalized the publication with the help of art director Alexey Brodovitch, fashion editor Diana Vreeland and photographers Martin Munkácsi, Louise Dahl-Wolfe and Richard Avedon.[2]

Diana Vreeland (1903–1989)—First drafted by Snow to write for *Harper's Bazaar*, where she became fashion editor before becoming editor-in-chief of *Vogue* in 1962. She highlighted models' unique features and created fantasy within photoshoots.[3]

Anna Wintour (born 1949)—One of the most influential voices in fashion, Wintour became editor-in-chief of *Vogue* in 1988 and eventually became artistic director for publisher Condé Nast. She helped *Vogue* dominate fashion media by establishing supermodels in the 1980s and 1990s and later turning toward celebrities on the magazine's pages.[4] Wintour's profile was raised by the book (and later film) *The Devil Wears Prada*, which was a fictional account of working for her and she later appeared in the documentaries *The September Issue* and *The First Monday in May*.

André Leon Talley (born 1949)—Legendary creative director of *Vogue*, Leon Talley made a name for himself with his deep knowledge of fashion, despite facing discrimination in the fashion world. Talley worked closely with Vreeland at The Metropolitan Museum of Art and Wintour at *Vogue*.[5] He has appeared in various fashion documentaries, including one about his life, *The Gospel According to André*.

Samira Nasr (born 1964)—After 153 years, Nasr took over as the US editor of *Harper's Bazaar* in 2020 and became the first woman of color to head the magazine. Born in Canada to Lebanese and Trinidadian parents, Nasr was a stylist and worked at some storied publications like *Vanity Fair* and *Elle* before taking the reins at *Bazaar*.[6]

Elaine Welteroth (born 1986)—Something of a Renaissance woman, Welteroth worked at *Ebony* and *Glamour* before becoming the editor-in-chief of *Teen Vogue* at twenty-nine—the youngest person ever to hold the title at Condé Nast. After *Teen Vogue* folded in 2017, Welteroth became a judge on reality show *Project Runway* and wrote the book *More Than Enough: Claiming Space for Who You Are (No Matter What They Say)*.[7]

claimed to be. From there, Gevinson was used as the opening anecdote in an Associated Press story about privacy within the blogosphere and was included in a profile on young bloggers for *T* magazine.[23] Before long, Gevinson was inducted as fashion royalty. By 2010, her blog was receiving nearly 30,000 views a day and in 2011 she was sitting front row, next to Anna Wintour, during Fashion Week and launching her own online magazine, *Rookie*. Gevinson, now in her twenties, has been pursuing an acting career as well as a writing career, and still gets profiled by *The New York Times*.[24]

This example is a bit meta since it is the media framing another media producer, but the agenda-setting function is clear. Gevinson's work was first picked up by *T* magazine, and *The Cut*'s posts were in anticipation of that piece. The Associated Press story grew out of *The Cut*'s writing and also mentioned the upcoming magazine piece. The news media helped to set the agenda by celebrating Gevinson as an up-and-coming fashionista and someone to be known. By being featured by *The New York Times* and talked about by *The Cut*, Gevinson could be seen by audiences as a blogger to watch (if they cared about fashion or bloggers). These stories were unable to tell readers *how* to think about Gevinson—which is exemplified by *The Cut* questioning her real age—but they still pushed her into the public consciousness as *someone* to think about. Moreover, there are likely other "agendas" that helped lead to this—such as a focus on online safety as in the Associated Press story—and the prominence of fashion blogs (some of which will be covered more in Chapter 8).

A more clear-cut example of agenda-setting, however, might be that of a "vintage" Kent State sweatshirt being sold by Urban Outfitters. First reported on by Buzzfeed, the sweatshirt was a "faded" pink with bright red blotches, if we're being generous, or faux blood splatter, if we're not. The sweatshirt was quickly pulled from Urban Outfitters online store and the company offered what some called a "non-apology" that claimed the brand did not mean to reference the 1970 Kent State massacre and the offering was part of the brand's "sun-faded" collection.[25] While this topic was initially discussed on Twitter, Buzzfeed's reporting elevated the prominence of the shirt and, thus, helped set the agenda that this is something the audience should care about.

In both the case of Gevinson and of Urban Outfitters, the media was able to place a spotlight on a particular person, event or issue. Individual audience members may agree that the story is important or not based on their feelings toward fashion, bloggers or mass market brands. Likewise, they might have already read Gevinson's blog and be a fan or not, or already have determined that Urban Outfitters was simply looking for free publicity; in either case the reader, even if they determined the topic is important, might already have developed feelings about it.

Framing

Meanwhile, not only what is talked about, but also the *way* something is talked about or "framed" is also important. The concept of framing has been set out and influenced by several theorists, notably Erving Goffman, Robert Entman and Stephen D. Reese. Goffman, who was mentioned in Chapter 2 for his work on performances, also believed that we frame our lived experiences in particular ways. This framing helps us make sense of what has happened (or is happening) and draws on our previous experiences to help us understand. However, while Goffman's work was published in 1974 and spurred various research thereafter, Entman's influential article in 1993 helped to "reframe" the process, if you will.

Entman noted that despite the work in this area, there was no understanding of how frames actually become embedded in society or how they reproduced. Entman set out the following definition:

> To frame is to *select some aspects of a perceived reality and make them more salient in a communicating text, in such a way as to promote a particular problem definition, causal interpretation, moral evaluation, and/or treatment recommendation* for the item described.[26]

These frames, which again help us make sense and communicate about particular problems, events and issues, exist simultaneously in several places. Frames reside within the head of the journalist, editor or media producer, who is communicating about the event; they exist within the text—say the magazine article or fashion spread; and they exist within the audience who understands the frame presented within a media and internalizes it.

To return to the examples of Tavi Gevinson and Urban Outfitters above, each could be understood as a particular representation. Initially, there was a question around Gevinson's self-produced fashion commentary because there was disbelief that an eleven-year-old could be so stylish. (The salient characteristics being her youth and the ability to be deceptive via online communication.) Meanwhile, as Gevinson's profile was rising, the Associated Press article framed her as a tween blogger at risk of being bullied or worse. (This was also highlighting her youth and the risks of the internet.) Finally, as Gevinson grew up, expanded her reach and was welcomed into fashion's fold, the stories began to frame her as a trendsetter and question what she was going to do next. (Now, her relevant characteristics were that she was a fashion wunderkind and someone who was pushing the envelope.) The moral evaluations were that Gevinson was at first, possibly deceptive, second, possibly at physical risk and, third, should be lauded and/or followed because of her fashion prowess.

In comparison, the Urban Outfitters debacle did not last as long, but was framed as a company disrespecting a national tragedy. The framing here involved as much of the experience—knowing the history of the Kent State massacre and understanding what a blood splatter would look like—as well as significant cynicism on the role of fashion brands. The telling of the story was largely seen not as a faux pas, but something intentionally done to be provocative and get Urban Outfitters' name in the press. Here, the problem was that the brand was acting tastelessly which sparked moral outrage and, while not directly stated, this led to the brand pulling the item from its store.

While Entman's delineation went a long way toward explaining how framing works, Stephen D. Reese offered an important addition: power.[27] Reese acknowledged that those in power—by and large those who control and produce the media—play a large role in how we see events and their possible solutions. For Reese, this isn't an objective fact, but the ways of understanding a particular topic are relative and dependent upon who tells the story and how they do so. This remains part of the reason why diversity in the media is so important.

For example, when Elaine Welteroth took over as the editor-in-chief of *Teen Vogue* in April 2016, she was something of an anomaly at publisher Condé Nast: she was the youngest person to hold that title and only the second Black person to be an editor-in-chief at the company. (Welteroth followed Keija Minor who had taken over *Brides* in 2012.[28]) Under Welteroth's leadership, *Teen Vogue* followed the 2016 US Presidential election extensively and continued its political advocacy in addition to its fashion coverage. Covering both politics and softer news had long been a feature of men's magazines like *Esquire* and *GQ,* but this new direction from *Teen Vogue* was groundbreaking and largely attributed to Welteroth's pioneering leadership. Writers heralded Welteroth with orchestrating *Teen Vogue*'s "socially concious bent"[29] and pointed out the magazine was "drawing explicitly from a rich tradition of aggressive, opinionated, adversarial coverage of sexist white men."[30] Welteroth and her writers were able to cover the topics they felt were important and frame them through their experience; this was largely possible because the editor was a young woman of color who chose to highlight topics and people who weren't getting coverage.[31]

Tastemakers in the Media

Going hand-in-hand with the agenda-setting and framing functions of the mass media, those working in the media also have a hand in dictating taste and appropriateness. Taste, the judgements we make about aesthetic qualities, has a long, long history. As Peter McNeil and Sanda Miller point out, beauty, as an aesthetic quality, was considered paramount in the eighteenth century. However, seeing that aesthetic judgements are subjective, soon the "critic" and the "qualified observer" were introduced as people who could objectively judge such qualities and, as such, taste. Critics, it was understood, maintain a safe distance from the subject and have the experience and practice to make these judgement calls.[32]

More recently, people in these roles have been classified in a variety of ways, including cultural intermediaries, members of the petit bourgeois, honest brokers or just more generally "tastemakers."[33] While each term has its own specific connotation and definition, the role of each has largely been the same—to determine what is "good" and "not good." Many of these judgements came from the idea that aesthetic qualities like beauty and taste are unchanging and remain the same over time. In doing so, these cultural intermediaries were often people in the upper middle class (or bourgeois) who then disseminated their values. Russell Lynes suggests that this role took on more prominence in the early 1800s when US consumers were beginning to distinguish themselves from European influences.[34] Meanwhile, Sharon Zukin suggests that the role of the "honest broker" developed in the 1960s in an effort to objectify subjective understandings of consumer goods. For Zukin, the *Good Housekeeping* Seal of Approval is the epitome of an "honest broker," which also includes taste judgements like restaurant critics.[35] The 1960s were an especially prominent time for such criticism, as *The Village Voice* was also pushing popular music criticism in new directions about the same time.[36]

What largely came out of these cultural intermediaries are taste assessments like "highbrow" and "lowbrow," or the idea of "good" and "bad" cultural products. For example, activities such as going to the ballet, dining at a fine restaurant and listening to classical music would generally be seen as highbrow activities, while watching television, eating fast food and listening to rock or rap music would be considered lowbrow. Of course, something like film might be considered middlebrow—since it appeals to a large variety of people—and also because it can be highbrow (an art house film) or lowbrow (a slasher flick). Again, these classifications can change over time. Television shows, which were once considered lowbrow, are today considered much more artistically significant and therefore highbrow, since we've moved away from things like the three-camera sitcom and laugh tracks.

While today few academics would say that terms like highbrow and lowbrow are finite assessments,[37] these terms live on in the popular imagination. Have you ever declared that something was your "guilty pleasure"? If so, you've made an assessment based on taste. Largely, the idea of having "good taste" is a way to build cultural capital, which you can generally turn into financial capital via a job and, maybe, a fashion magazine.

While much has been written about cultural capital and cultural intermediaries, we can largely thank French sociologist Pierre Bourdieu for both terms. Cultural capital comes from knowing "legitimate" culture and having those tastes in consumption, i.e. being able to judge fine art or knowing the best music.[38] These decisions, which seem natural, are guided by external forces, frequently class-based functions, such as familial upbringing and level of education. For Bourdieu, the aforementioned cultural intermediaries and tastemakers were integral to the creation and substantiation of cultural capital, by translating legitimate tastes to the masses. The problem, of course, is that there isn't *one* legitimate taste, but multiple versions that compete for dominance. Moreover, tastes vary from one geographic region to another, between age groups and in various other ways. (Bourdieu, it should be noted, acknowledged this and saw the cultural intermediaries as a role that grew along with the mass media.[39]) However, as the Western mass media systems of the twentieth century began to fragment, so too did the ideas of cultural capital.

For example, as mentioned above, the rise of *Seventeen* magazine was integral in the development of a teen culture that would come to encompass a series of rituals, tastes and other hallmarks. However, as something of a subculture (as discussed in Chapter 3) developed around teens, a form of subcultural capital also developed, meaning that what is considered "cool" by teens might not translate to the rest of society. Subcultural capital, as defined by Sarah Thornton, relies on what is deemed "hip" or "cool" within a particular group. Like the broader cultural capital, this can be shown in various forms: from what bands those within the subculture listen to and what venues they frequent, to appearance and what clothing people wear. One important note is that subcultural capital is not reliant upon the class structure that contains much of cultural capital, but it still has some effect.[40] While teens are a useful example, there are any number of subcultures that can develop their own systems of capital (i.e. practices and tastes that are prized above others) and each comes with a system of cultural intermediaries who help delineate and create structures. Publications like *Essence, Out,* and even *Rolling Stone* promote niche audiences and play into creating subcultural capital structures for Black women, the LGBTQ+ community and popular music lovers, respectively.

Insight: Ashley Graham and the Coming of the "Plus" Size Model

Cultural intermediaries, those who helped construct words and images in the media, had, until relatively recently, a monopoly on the images we see in the media. Even today, they are highly influential in creating looks and images, inspiring social media influencers to craft photos in similar ways. This ranges from the clothing and accessories being sold to the bodies that are doing the selling.

Enter, Ashley Graham.

Graham, who would rather be called "curvy" or "sexylicious" than "plus-size,"[41] made history when she appeared in the 2015 *Sports Illustrated* swimsuit issue in an advertisement for the inclusive brand Swimsuits for All. She would later go on to be the first plus-size model on the cover of US *Vogue,* posing in a spread that celebrated diversity and declared that Graham—alongside Gigi Hadid, Kendall Jenner, Adwoa Aboah, Liu Wen, Vittoria Ceretti and Imaan Hammam—was "democratizing fashion." Graham would also appear in ads for retailer Lane Bryant and would become "one of the only plus-size models to get a beauty contract" when she signed with Revlon.[42]

While Diana Vreeland was known for finding and promoting women who might not be conventionally attractive like Cher, Twiggy and Barbra Streisand—and even *accentuating* what might have be perceived as "flaws"—change within *Vogue* and the modeling industry at large was slow.[43] Ashley Graham's presence remains an important point for size diversity within the fashion industry. As Amanda Czerniawski has noted, many plus-size models—which can begin at a size 10 and is still smaller than the average woman—would often be relegated to niche work rather than high fashion.[44] Instead, Graham has been seen on magazine covers *Allure* and a solo *Vogue* cover in 2019, in runway shows,[45] spearheading her own fashion collaboration and, overall representing the "curvy" among us in the fashion industry.

Fragmentation and Contemporary Tastemakers

Media fragmentation, or increased production of niche products and markets, has been happening for decades, which has led to various tastemakers and subcultures. It also means that even "popular" products no longer reach as many people as they once did; people now have more options, which leads to more individualized consumption. Journalist Chris Anderson called this development the Long Tail.[46] Where media products used to have mass appeal, contemporary products are more niche. For example, in the US, *Gone with the Wind* (1939) is still considered to be the highest grossing film (when adjusted for inflation). The other top movies include *Star Wars* (1977), *The Sound of Music* (1965), *E.T.* (1982), and *Titanic* (1997), in order to adjusted gross. Domestically in the US, it takes until the eleventh spot to get to a movie from this past decade—*Star Wars: The Force Awakens*—which was released in 2015.[47]

What this means is that there are fewer media products that are consumed by the *masses* (think: *Harry Potter*, *Twilight* or *50 Shades of Grey*), although those products help sustain a long tail of products serving smaller niche markets. For example, *To All the Boys I've Loved Before* (2018) was only released on Netflix limiting the audience that was able to see it. As such, since fewer people have seen the movies, fewer people know its stars, Lana Condor and Noah Centineo. This limits the ability of either to become a celebrity in the vein of a Reese Witherspoon or a Brad Pitt, thereby limiting their influence in a variety of realms.

Hand-in-hand with the increased media fragmentation, the rise of social media has democratized media and tastemaking. While we get more into this in a later chapter, internet platforms—from blogs to social media—have given more people a voice within the tastemaking process. Early blogs like Gevinson's Style Rookie and the streetstyle forerunner The Sartorialist, founded by Scott Schumann, helped give each a platform to inform taste; a platform that might not have been available without the internet. More recently, we've seen the rise of social media influencers—those who have a large following on Instagram, YouTube or the like. Consider people like Tyler Oakely, who turned his YouTube channel into a successful reality TV and activist career, and Arielle Charnas, who's blog Something Navy helped her become a fashion brand carried at Nordstrom. In all of these cases, these individuals did not become traditional "gatekeepers" within the media, but were able to gain a following outside of the established structure (i.e. *Vogue* and *Harper's Bazaar*) that previous experts had followed.

The result of all this is that the traditional tastemakers and cultural intermediaries no longer have the power that they once did to determine fashion and set trends. In most cases, those who work within these professions, like magazine editors and journalists, have a presence on social media to promote their work and interact with the audience. However, their authority, which was traditionally bestowed because of the positions they held and their experience in the field can be increasingly challenged by newcomers who are building their own following. We'll return to some of these issues in Chapter 8, when we discuss how the internet has transformed both personal and media communication.

A Bit on Fashion Photography

Fashion photography—like all photography really—makes a bit of a strange bedfellow when approached as a media. The roots of fashion photography can be traced back through fashion illustrations and physical printing, but because it's a visual medium, it has commonality with film and television.[48] Finally, while fashion photography has developed into an art form of its own, it was originally derided as a commercial undertaking and, even though it has been taken seriously for decades now, it still straddles a line between "editorial" production and "advertising." Indeed, some of the most memorable fashion photography has been shot for advertising campaigns—like that of Brooke Shields in Calvin Klein jeans and Mark Wahlberg in Calvin Klein underwear.

Modern fashion photography can traced to 1911 when Edward Steichen took photos of Paul Poiret designs; however, fashion illustration can dated to as early as the 1860s. Unlike the typeset word, fashion photography was dependent upon technological developments—both that of cameras and that of printing—which is why it took until the 1880s for photographs to be printed alongside text. When Carmel Snow took over *Harper's Bazaar* in 1933 she helped revolutionize both the magazine and fashion photography by welcoming color and bold images onto the pages of *Bazaar*. Snow was aided in this endeavor by art director Alexey Brodovitch, fashion editor Diana Vreeland, who we talked about at the beginning of this chapter, and photographers Martin Munkácsi, Louise Dahl-Wolfe and Richard Avedon (Figure 5.2).[49]

It was Vreeland who gave fashion photography its fanciful nature and is credited with introducing exotic locales and intricate storytelling. For Vreeland, it was about the fantasy as opposed to the reality, which helped give fashion an air of fancy and playfulness that remains today. Fashion photography— like other theoretical understanding of fashion—largely bought into colonialist notions that the system was a "European" or "Western" phenomenon; some of the resulting fashion photography then juxtaposed fashion as being Western or civilized whereas non-Western settings would be framed as less developed.[50]

Photographic images, as much as text, help contribute to the framing of people and places and helping construct them in the popular imagination.[51] Take a moment and think about New York City. Depending on how familiar you are with it, you might think it is a glamorous city that produced fashion and publishing, especially if you're drawing off popular examples like *Sex and the City*, *Gossip Girl* and *The Devil Wears Prada*. Compare that to say, Africa.

Figure 5.2 *Getting the Shot. Photographer Louise Dahl-Wolfe photographs a model for* Harper's Bazaar *in 1947. © Yale Joel via Getty Images.*

Often times, in the media, Africa is framed as a sparsely populated area of "natural" wonder, whether that is the Sahara desert or the jungles along the equator. However, Africa is a vast continent with many different climates, geographic areas and populations, including rising fashion cities like Dakar, Senegal. It is for this reason that those people taking, editing and selecting fashion photography for magazines and ad campaigns are tastemakers as much as those doing the writing—these images help us understand the world around us.

Fashion photography has come a long way since it first began and notably has taken on new dimensions with the advent of the internet and digital culture. No longer only the realm of professionals, fashion photography has been taken to the street (so to speak), as individuals have built up blogs and social media accounts featuring the latest style people are wearing in "everyday" life. Streetstyle photography, or snapshots taken and shared of everyday life have grown into a formidable genre of photography, but owes a tremendous debt to photographer Bill Cunningham. Cunningham was a roaming photographer for various publications and spent a significant amount of time at *The New York Times*, where he photographed people for the society pages. He was known throughout the New York social scene, but always saw himself as a journalist and kept a distance from the subjects he photographed.

We'll discuss more about representation in Chapter 6, but for now remember fashion photography as a visual medium confronts some of the same challenges as film, television and advertising. Who is depicted in the photographs? How are they depicted? How should the audience make sense of these images? While these images are generally more creative than in a photojournalism and catalogue content, they still have the ability to produce sexualized, violent and otherwise questionable content.

Further Reading

As mentioned earlier in the chapter, mass media theory and fashion theory have not had a lot of crossover. *Milestones in Mass Communication: Media Effects* by Shearon A. Lowery and Melvin L. DeFleur (Longman, 1995) helps to explain the trajectory of mass media research. Meanwhile, the foundational articles, "The Agenda-Setting Function of Mass Media" by Maxwell E. McCombs and Donald L. Shaw, and "Framing: Toward a Clarification of a Fractured Paradigm" by Robert M. Entman, help explain the specific theories discussed above. Further, McCombs's book, *Setting the Agenda: The Mass Media and Public Opinion* (Polity, 2014) and *Framing Public Life: Perspectives on Media and Our Understanding of the Social World* by Stephen D. Reese, Oscar H. Gandy Jr. and August E. Grant (Routledge, 2001) provide more detailed explanations of each.

Meanwhile, Sanda Miller and Peter McNeil have been at the forefront of theorizing writing from a fashion studies perspective. Their books *Fashion Writing and Criticism: History, Theory, Practice* (Bloomsbury, 2014) and *Fashion Journalism: History, Theory and Practice* (Bloomsbury, 2018) explain the development of taste and historically situate fashion within news dissemination. Further the special edition of *Journalism Practice* (Vol. 6, Issue 1) edited by Folker Hanusch offers a scholarly call to better understand lifestyle journalism. Likewise, the first section of *Fashion Media: Past and Present* (Bloomsbury, 2013), edited by Djurdja Bartlett, Shaun Cole and Agnès Rocamora also looks at the history and influence of magazines.

1   Lowery, Shearon A., and Melvin L. DeFleur (1995). *Milestones in Mass Communication Research: Media Effects,* Third edition. White Plains, NY: Longman.

2   McCombs, Maxwell E. and Donald L. Shaw (1972). "The Agenda-Setting Function of Mass Media." *The Public Opinion Quarterly,* 36(2): 176–187.

3   Entman, Robert M. (1993). "Framing: Toward a Clarification of a Fractured Paradigm." *Journal of Communication,* 43(3): 51–58.

4   McCombs, Maxwell E. (2014). *Setting the Agenda: The Mass Media and Public Opinion.* Malden, MA: Polity.

5   Reese, Stephen D., Oscar H. Handy Jr. and August E. Grant (2001). *Framing Public Life: Perspectives on Media and Our Understanding of the Social World.* New York: Routledge.

6   McNeil, Peter and Sanda Miller (2014). *Fashion Writing and Criticism: History, Theory, Practice.* New York: Bloomsbury.

7   Miller, Sanda and Peter McNeil (2018). *Fashion Journalism: History, Theory and Practice.* New York: Bloomsbury.

8   Hanusch, Folker (2012). "Broadening the Focus. The Case for Lifestyle Journal as a Field of Scholarly Inquiry." *Journalism Practice*, 6(1): 2–11.

9   Bartlett, Djurdja, Shaun Cole and Agnès Rocamora (2013). *Fashion Media: Past and Present*. New York: Bloomsbury.

Figure 6.1 *The Perfect Sponge. Singer and actress Brandy Norwood uses the Beautyblender to apply makeup.* © *Michael Stewart via Getty Images.*

6

Clothing on Film and Television

During every media revolution, those working in the industry need to find ways to adapt. The development of "talkies" posed challenges for silent film actors and music videos changed the music industry so much that the Buggles released a popular song titled, "Video Killed the Radio Star." However, not all transitions are so noticeable. Consider, the development of high-definition television. Television had been shot on a 4:3 aspect ratio and on 35mm film, which made for a blurrier picture and made it easier for imperfections to be hidden. However, high-definition television (HDTV), which debuted in the 1990s and would become standard in broadcasting by 2009, changed that, by providing clear pictures in a more rectangular 16:9 aspect ratio.[1]

"High def was this whole new world where suddenly you saw the makeup," makeup artist Rea Ann Silva told the fashion and beauty site *Racked*. "It was totally scary for directors, producers, and editors."[2]

Silva had been the makeup department head for US sitcom *Girlfriends* (2000–2008), which focused on four female friends and starred Tracee Ellis Ross, Golden Brooks, Persia White and Jill Marie Jones. *Girlfriends* was one of the first shows to be shot in high definition and, as such, the makeup needed to be literally flawless. And, Silva, who was known for airbrushing techniques, knew how to make skin look perfect and consistent in the new mode of production. Yet, airbrushing was labor-intensive and couldn't be done between takes. This was where Silva's ingenuity came in.[3]

After learning how wet sponges could help give makeup a seamless finish, Silva began experimenting with materials and shapes of sponges. Eventually, she began cutting triangle shaped sponges to make rounded sponges, which helped her apply makeup without it looking caked on. Similar techniques had been used for special effects for years, but no one had used it for beauty makeup before. After much trial and error, Silva would go on to design and produce the Beautyblender—a rounded makeup sponge that would become a makeup bag staple to ease application and contouring.[4]

This is just one example of the convergence of a medium, celebrity power and everyday life. We often think of the films, television shows and celebrities we watch as being influential to the way we dress and how we style ourselves, but the connections are not always clear-cut. For example, it's often stated that the sale of men's undershirts dropped after Clark Gable was shown without one in *It Happened One Night* (1934). However, that statistic is hard to verify, and hard to attribute specifically to the film. However, the success of Silva's Beautyblender shows a direct link from how Silva was applying makeup on actors and the product's success with the everyday person.

The following pages will look specifically at how clothing, fashion and style interact with visual media, namely film and television. The roots of these mediums are not as long as the history of print media and news but, as will be discussed, the intertwining of the two is more pronounced because clothing helps to tell the story *and* its representation within the media can be transferred off screen. From famous items like Dorothy's ruby red slippers in *The Wizard of Oz* to Audrey Hepburn's iconic look in *Breakfast at Tiffany's*, these films and their related looks can become cultural touchstones as well as style items.

Culture and Mediums

As noted back in Chapter 1, a medium is really any means by which we can communicate with one another. In this way, processes that are innate in us—say speaking or making facial expressions—can be understood as a medium since we are putting a mental thought or message into this form and passing it on to someone else. Those messages which are mass-produced and communicated (e.g. what we colloquially refer to as "the media") do have some specific dimensions to their creation, which has led them to be studied and thought about differently from more interpersonal mediums like language or even writing.

Despite the differences, as Harold Lasswell pointed out, the media largely perform the same communicative functions that we do on an individualized level. As such, the mass media help supervise the environment, coordinate different social elements and transmit cultural values between generations.[5] To consider what this looks like, let's consider each in turn. When getting dressed in the morning, we might open the curtains or the window to see what the weather is like outside. Or, we might watch the weather forecast from the local news station. Likewise, before the mass media, if we wanted to organize an event like say, a fashion show, we might have to go door-to-door to notify people about it, whereas mass media allow us to place an advertisement in a newspaper or on television letting people know it'll be held. Finally, where families and other members of society would pass parables from one generation to the next through storytelling, today the mass media helps tell the stories that give our lives value. Clothing is a really great example of this. Your parents might have taught you the value of looking "presentable" or wearing clean clothing, and maybe your friends helped socialize you into wearing similar clothing. However, these values can often be seen in film and television products, as well. The play *Pygmalion* and various films, like *She's All That* (1999) and *The Duff* (2015), interrogate appearance and social class, providing morals we may or may not agree with. We'll talk a bit more about representation and cultural values within the coming pages.

Still, the means by which we communicate has a significant impact not only on what is being communicated but also the structure of society. This understanding is fundamental to media ecology, as discussed by media theorists like Harold Innes, Marshall McLuhan, and Neil Postman. McLuhan was fond of the phrase "We don't know who discovered water, but we're pretty sure it wasn't the fish!" as a way to explain media. Since the media happens around us, it is nearly impossible for us to understand what effect it has on us; however, media ecologists have certainly tried. For example, Harold Innes noted that the development of the telegraph helped alter our understanding of time and space. Instead of taking days or months to communicate with someone through letters, telegraphs made communication nearly instantaneous. Likewise, the structure of the telegraph poles helped to connect some areas and populations ahead of others. This relay situation (e.g. how telegraph messages were passed to each other) would remain throughout radio and television broadcasting. McLuhan, meanwhile, suggested that the dominant forms of media helped shape our understanding. (This inspired his famed axiom, "The medium is the message.") For example, society's move from an oral to written and print-based culture worked to reduce the function of memory since facts and history would be saved and referred back to at a later date. Postman extended some of this discussion to the realm of television which he suggested was unserious and prohibited sustained thought given its immediacy and quickly changing topics.[6]

James W. Carey drew on some of this discussion when he argued that communication was largely a form of ritual and works to hold society together. This understanding (which has some similarities to Benedict Anderson's work mentioned in the previous chapter) suggests that the mass media helps to continually reaffirm joint meaning among members of the same community or culture.[7] At the same time, these communications often become ritualized or routinized through both time and space. In the United States, the evening news comes on at the same time every night, and television shows are (generally) shown in blocks of a half or whole hour. US television news is largely produced within New York City and Washington, DC, while films and entertainment television are largely produced in Los Angeles and New York. Taken together, these systems prioritize certain geographies and local considerations over others. Similarly, it's probably not surprising that New York and Los Angeles became the dominant fashion cities in the US given their close proximity to a multitude of media outlets.

To return to McLuhan's thought briefly, the medium in which we choose to communicate has a vast effect on what and how we communicate.[8] Considering newspapers have been around for centuries, it is only relatively recently (i.e. the past few decades) that newspapers have been able to print high-quality photographs. Thus newspapers relied on the printed word, constructed as stories with headlines and text arranged in columns to share news with readers.

In comparison, radio, which was broadcast over the airwaves and relied on sound had to describe what was happening and do so in a way that listeners immediately understood. Radio (and today, podcasts) might include ambient sound to help tell stories and rely on music to indicate transitions between stories or shows, both things newspapers can't do. Writers for newspapers and radio also write differently, using smaller words and less advanced language for radio since listeners don't have the ability to replay what they might have missed.

A Brief History of Film and Television

While paintings and photography came about before film, film was the first medium able to capture visual images and play them back in what seemed like a fluid way. While, in reality, films and television shows are created from a series of single images with slight variations that make them *look* like they are moving to the human eye, we're really looking at a series of still images. American Thomas Edison is generally credited with developing the first motion picture camera, although others like Étienne-Jules Marey and Eadweard Muybridge were also working on the project. In 1893, Edison debuted short films on the kinetoscope, a device made for a single viewer. Marey and Muybridge would open the first theater in late 1895 and the group-viewing format would be adopted around the world.[9] Films would become longer and more in-depth in the coming years, culminating with what we would call the "feature-length film"—the mode of film still dominant today. These early films were shot and displayed in black-and-white and are considered "silent" films since they didn't contain sound, but were generally accompanied by orchestras, musicians or recorded scores.[10] Film producers would eventually be able to add synchronized sound—referred to as "talkies"—and color to movies from the 1920s onward. While some of these changes would take time to adopt due to the costs involved on the production and the theater side, movies like *The Jazz Singer* (1927), *Gone With the Wind* (1939) and *The Wizard of Oz* (1939) are seen as important hallmarks for sound and color, respectively.[11]

Meanwhile, US inventor Philo T. Farnsworth would develop the processes for television in the 1920s, successfully transmitting an image in 1927. (Again, others were also working on process, but Farnsworth is generally given credit for the invention.) While television broadcasting would begin in 1939, television production would be halted due to the Second World War, thus delaying its widespread adoption until the 1940s. The first television shows were produced in black-and-white, although color would arrive on the scene in the 1950s. Broadcasters would add color to shows throughout the 1960s, but it would take until the early 1970s until all shows were produced in color.[12] Cable television would eventually be developed to help those who couldn't receive terrestrial television and would ultimately prove influential offering channels for news (CNN, Fox News), music (MTV, VH1, CMT, BET) and more (AMC, The Travel Channel, Discovery, Lifetime, Bravo).

Now, film and television diverge in many ways. For the most part, film is produced by studios, distributed to theaters (now usually theater chains) and sold directly to the public. In comparison, television is generally broadcast over the airwaves and can be viewed by anyone with an antenna and set, thus making it more publicly available. Moreover, due to the way it is distributed, television (and radio) stations have required more regulation by government entities. In the United States, the Federal Communication Commission regulates the technical aspects of broadcasting while also establishing "decency" guidelines for what can be portrayed in television shows and when. Perhaps the most famous case of these restrictions occurred during the 2004 Super Bowl when a performance by musicians Janet Jackson and Justin Timberlake ended up exposing Jackson's breast for less than a second—*literally* (Figure 6.2). As a result, CBS, who was broadcasting the Super Bowl, was fined by the FCC, but this decision was reversed.[13] In comparison, films are given ratings by the Motion Picture Association of America, which is restrictive in its own way,[14] but is not susceptible to the same legal regulations.

Additionally, television is by-and-large supported by advertising necessitating shorter blocks of time and intermittent stopping for messages from advertisers. While some networkers have remained "pay channels" (perhaps, most notably HBO), most others are advertiser-supported, including the likes of MTV and Disney—both of which started as pay channels.

Figure 6.2 *A Slip Up. Janet Jackson and Justin Timberlake's performance at the Super Bowl in 2004 would go down in history after a wardrobe malfunction. © J. Shearer via Getty Images.*

Additionally, television provides more diverse programming, including news shows which haven't been shown in theaters for some time,[15] and are generally more serialized and longer-lasting than film. The animated show *The Simpsons* is the longest-running night-time scripted series on US television airing more than 650 episodes since its debut in 1987. And it's still running. Doing quick math, if each episode runs for roughly 22 minutes (not counting commercial breaks), *The Simpsons* has run for more than 238 hours or roughly 10 full days. Talk about a marathon! And, soap operas like *Coronation Street* (1960–) and *General Hospital* (1963–) far surpass this as they air more frequently and have run for *decades*. In comparison, even the more enduring film franchises, like James Bond which has produced 23 films,[16] would be a fraction of the overall time.

Today, there are more options than ever for both movies (not necessarily on physical *film*) and television, as traditional studios, broadcast networks and cable channels compete with digital entities like Netflix, Hulu and Amazon. As mentioned in Chapter 5, this media fragmentation has made it easier for niche products to find an audience while blockbuster films and shows financially support the system.

Film, Television; Fashion, Costume

That said, there are some similarities between film and television, especially in regard to entertainment programming. Both are products of a complex network of producers and firms (with a few independent exceptions), and tell stories through audio-visual content. As such, there are a number of people who come together—from writers, actors and costume designers to producers, directors and editors—who all play a role in what we see. Sometimes these products might be historic in nature (*Marie Antoinette*; *Downton Abbey*), contemporary and realistic (*Crazy Rich Asians*; *Sex and the City*), or fantastic (*Harry Potter*; *Dr Who*). Of course, these are a fraction of the film and television genres out there, yet we can draw a broad distinction between fictional programming and documentaries, lifestyle shows, reality television and news programs. Right now, we're going to focus on fictional films and costuming and we will get into reality-based programs later in the chapter.

When we're discussing clothing within fictional accounts, what we're largely talking about are costumes—the garments, styles, and appearance provided to a performer in order to help tell their story. In short, in order to tell a story, costume designers rely on the same practices people use in everyday life to signal attributes like wealth, sexuality and power.[17] Costume designers need to take into account all aspects of how clothing looks on screen, including the material, the silhouette, and the color. Still, costume designers are dressing people, meaning that they are also dressing *bodies,* and they need to make adjustments for the actors' physicality. This can be done to accentuate or hide aspects of the performer, if need be.

Perhaps more importantly, costumes are read by the viewing audience. As Adrienne Munich writes, "Viewers quickly grasp the contemporary meanings and value conveyed by costume, even in films about earlier historical moments. Thus, fashion is an essential tool in the craft of conveying meaning through film."[18] Moreover, costumes are generally thought to add to the narrative elements of a film by putting aspects on full display. This can be seen as the visual equivalent of literary description in that it helps to set the stage and gives insight into the characters. This was especially true of costumes during the early silent films, when costuming could be used as a substitute for speech.[19]

As the motion picture industry advanced, Hollywood films would begin to attract top Parisian designers like Erté, Coco Chanel and Elsa Schiaparelli who would attempt to bring high fashion to the big screen. However, the most successful collaboration between Hollywood and the fashion industry took a uniquely American perspective in the form of department stores. Film studios partnered with stores in order to capitalize on the costumes within movies. Stores such as Macy's Cinema Style and Warner Brothers Studio, were able to sell the costumes that were being shown on screen. These stores sold clothing and cosmetics, and would make an indelible mark on fashion helping to introduce American styles to the masses. The power of fashion within film continued through the twentieth century as designers like Giorgio Armani and Ralph Lauren gained greater attention after their designs were featured in films like *American Gigolo* (1980) and *Annie Hall* (1977).[20]

As noted previously, costuming within television is similar to film in its visuality, however, there are some key differences since television is a more intimate and frequent medium. As Helen Warner explains, television and the programs seen on television were regarded as ordinary and familiar, therefore before "high fashion" could move to the small screen, it needed to be seen as a more "legitimate" medium. Part of this problem was that television was largely viewed as a *commercial* rather than an artistic medium. *Sex and the City* (1998–2004) is largely seen as a groundbreaking show because it was taken seriously and made use of fashion as a spectacle—with the help from brands like Prada and Christian Louboutin. While the earlier night-time soap opera *Dynasty* (1981–1989) was known for its fashion and even had a related licensing agreement to sell similar designs as shown on screen,[21] *Sex and the City* would elevate its fashion in a more pronounced way. Later, *Gossip Girl* (2007–2012) would pick-up on fashion-forward television where *Sex and the City* left off.[22]

Cultural Studies and Reading the Media

One of the key issues in visual media is that of representation. We largely have the British theorist Stuart Hall to thank for that. Hall, along with others at the Centre for Contemporary Cultural Studies at the University of Birmingham, UK, would help cement cultural studies as a research paradigm. Researchers including Dick Hebdige (who was mentioned in Chapter 3) and Angela McRobbie (whose work will be mentioned more in Chapter 9) studied at the center. Moreover, two of Hall's most useful works include his understanding of encoding and decoding mass media messages and his work on representation and identity.

In some ways, Hall's work on encoding and decoding reflects some of the communication models discussed back in Chapter 1. However, unlike the messages that are exchanged between people, Hall saw messages encoded within the mass media texts (e.g. the movies and television shows) that we consume. Remember the way the mass media—including films and television— communicates takes a different form because of the complex nature of the work. Hall argued that messages were encoded and decoded through products within the mass media.[23]

To understand how this works, let's revisit the movie *The Devil Wears Prada*. The film tells the story of how Andy Sachs comes to work for and (spoiler alert) ultimately *quits* working for magazine editor Miranda Priestly. The creation of the film involved knowledge, production, and technical infrastructure. Those who created the film, led by director David Frankel, created a story based on the novel of the same name, written by Lauren Weisberger. There was a good bit of technical knowledge involved both in the process of story creation and using film cameras, editing software, setting up the lighting and the like. Beyond the knowledge of how to technically do this, it also involved a relationship between all of the people who created the film— the director, actors and editors—as well as the production companies who created and then distributed the films to theaters (and later to DVDs, television stations and streaming services). Once *The Devil Wears Prada* was created and distributed, it became a film to be watched, consumed and analyzed. Viewers were able to broadly make sense of the movie because they were working within the same framework as those who created the film. As viewers, we understand the conventions of a film and are able to piece together meanings from visual cues, dialogue and other aspects—including costumes.

Now, it's this last part that gets a little tricky. The messages that are encoded within the film are not necessarily the same messages the audience will take away from it. One reading of *The Devil Wears Prada* can be that work or career goals shouldn't overshadow more "important" things like friendship and romance. This would likely be what Hall would call a "dominant reading" of the film—one which most people in a given context would agree with.[24] For example, in *The Devil Wears Prada*, when Andy upsets her friends and boyfriend by dedicating so much time to work, most people would see that she had the wrong priorities. However, another reading of the film might be that Nate is a terrible boyfriend who doesn't understand Andy as an ambitious woman. Generally, this can be understood as a "negotiated reading" since it clearly uses the same code but reads it in a different way.[25] While this might have been a revolutionary reading of the film when it was released in 2006, by the later 2010s writers for sites like *Cosmo* and *Man Repeller* were pushing such readings of the film into the mainstream.[26] Such a reading acknowledges the dominant code, but plays within its interpretation. Finally, it is possible to put an entirely different framework on the film in what can be considered as "oppositional reading."[27] In *The Devil Wears Prada*, an oppositional reading might be that capitalism, as an economic system, is harmful to all who participate in it, and fashion, in particular, gives people a deluded sense of the world. For such a reading, we could draw off of Miranda's insistence that everyone wants to be like her, as well as the emotional distress career aspirations cause Andy, Miranda and everyone around them. *The Devil Wears Prada* remains something of a cult classic among those interested in fashion—both popularly and academically—because of its portrayal of the industry and its use of clothing. Patricia Field, notable for her work on *Sex in the City,* was the costume designer for the film. Moreover, Andy's transformation from fashion victim to success story marks a transformation of sorts that can be seen visually. Film scholar Tamar Jeffers McDonald argued that costuming is frequently used to convey transformations on screen as can also be seen in movies like *Grease* (1978) and, yes, *The Devil Wears Prada*.[28]

Seven Names to Know in Film and Television Fashion

Orry-Kelly (1897–1964)—Australian-born costume designer who would work on nearly 300 films, including classic films like *Casablanca, 42nd Street* and *Auntie Mame.* Orry-Kelly would win three Oscars for his costuming of *An American in Paris, Les Girls* and *Some Like It Hot.*[1]

Edith Head (1897–1981)—Began costume designing in 1923 and eventually worked her way up to be chief designer at Paramount from 1936 through 1967 before working at Universal until her death. Head was given more than 1,000 screen credits and was nominated for 35 Oscars, winning eight.[2]

Adrian (1903–1959)—Chief costume designer for MGM during the golden years of Hollywood, Adrian would work on films including *The Wizard of Oz* and dress stars like Greta Garbo, Joan Crawford, Jean Harlow and Katharine Hepburn. After leaving the movie industry, he would design for specialty stores and would notably buck the trend against Dior's New Look in the late 1940s.[3]

Joan Rivers (1933–2014)—Boundary pushing standup comedian and late-night host, Joan Rivers would redefine the award show red carpet with her fashion commentary for E! and later the TV Guide Channel. Eventually she would head the show *Fashion Police* from 2010 until her death.[4]

Elsa Klensch (born 1933)—Longtime journalist who worked at publications like *Women's Wear Daily, Harper's Bazaar* and *Vogue,* Klensch would go on to pioneer fashion television with her CNN series, *Style with Elsa Klensch.* The show would run from the launch of CNN in 1980 until 2001.[5]

Patricia Field (born 1942)—Designer and owner of a New York City punk fashion store, Field would begin designing for film and television in the late 1980s, and go on to costume the *Sex and the City* series (thanks to Sarah Jessica Parker), as well as the TV show *Ugly Betty,* and the film *The Devil Wears Prada.*[6]

Ruth E. Carter (born 1960)—Film designer known for centering Black identity and experience, Carter became the first African-American to win an Oscar for Costume Design for the film *Black Panther.* Carter got her start on Spike Lee's *School Daze* in 1987 and has costumed dozens of films including *Amistad, Malcolm X* and *Selma.*[7]

Representation Issues

This brings us to a second influential theory from Hall—that of representation. Everything we understand about the world—people, objects, styles of dress— is represented in some way. And these representations begin to be meaningful to us. Hall explains it like this:

> At the heart of the meaning process in culture, then, are two related "systems of representation." The first enables us to give meaning to the world by constructing a set of correspondences or a chain of equivalences between things—people, objects, events, abstract ideas, etc.—and our system of concepts, our conceptual maps. The second depends on constructing a set of correspondences between our conceptual map and a set of signs, arranged or organized into various languages which stand for or represent those concepts. The relationship between "things," concepts and signs lies at the heart of the production of meaning in language. The process which links these three elements together is what we call "representation."[29]

Essentially, what Hall is saying is that we first learn and understand the world and then give meanings to things or concepts we come into contact with. For example, we understand what clothing is as a concept and develop a sense of how this clothing interacts with concepts like gender and occupation. As such, if we understand what scrubs are—the lightweight shapeless clothing worn by medical professionals—and we encounter someone who is wearing them, we might connect that she is a doctor or a nurse. We may make this assumption of someone we encountered on the street or someone we see in a film or television show. Taken to the next level, we may also make assumptions about the person in scrubs—maybe they are intelligent or caring or whatever else we assume medical professionals to be.

Hall's work draws on other social theorists, like Ferdinand de Saussure, Michel Foucault, and Roland Barthes, to argue that representation works in all forms of communication starting with language and then can be seen in more complex ways.[30] For example, we can take the term "white hat." Colloquially, the term refers to something of a savior who comes in to save the day. "White" is loaded with connotation but generally represents what is good and the hero of the story. On-screen, this has come to be shown by people wearing a . . . white hat. For example, the US television show *Scandal* (2012–2018) starred actress Kerry Washington as Olivia Pope, a Washington "fixer" who made political problems go away. The character was frequently shown wearing white—including a white hat—and frequently referred to herself and her colleagues as being "white hats." The term became synonymous with the series as press headlines peppered in references such as "Olivia Reclaiming the White Hat" and "Olivia Pope Hangs Up Her White Hat for Good" as the series wound down.[31]

The final part of Hall's argument is that linguistic and visual representations always have an element of power to them. For example, language and visual codes are not neutral representations, but bestow a form of power through what they represent or *how* they represent particular subjects.[32] This can be seen problematically throughout film history as films, from 1915's *Birth of a Nation* to 1961's *Breakfast at Tiffany's,* have used racist portrayals and stereotypes. Issues of representation have not gone away, even as more recent films like *Moonlight* (2016) and *Crazy Rich Asians* (2018) have been less derogatory and more inclusive. At the same time, representation matters not just in race, but in other aspects like ethnicity, sexuality and body type. Moreover, these issues are not just in television and films, but take place in all media forms, including print media and advertising.

There have been many discussions about the way we make sense of a media text—some which take into account the author's intention and some that do not. Both Barthes and Foucault wrote on the figurative "death of the author"[33] in relation to how we understand media texts. For his part, Foucault argued that what we understand as an "author" is a historic construction to ground a text.[34] In both of these views, however, what the author or creator intended to communicate doesn't matter or at least isn't given priority over what an audience *takes* from the text in question. While centering the author's intention might have made sense in an era when authors had sole control over a text, in the contemporary complex world of media creation, it is rare that a single person has complete control over a product. As such, even if we could achieve perfect communication where the author's intended message is accurately shared, who should be considered the author? A film's director? Editor? Screenwriter? The producer who financed the film?

"Reading" Texts and Costumes

Therefore, if we can't prioritize the author's intention within a given film or television program, we need some other way to understand it. Before we get too far down this rabbit hole, it should be noted that there are a plethora of research methods that can be applied to film and television, from written diaries (as conducted during Herbert Blumer's early Payne Fund Studies) to reader-responses, interviews and focus groups. However, to look at the text itself—which is largely what we'd do if we were concerned with the costuming— there are a few theories of visual analysis that can come in handy.

Semiotics and Myths

Barthes is influential in many aspects of visual culture, but his book *Mythologies*, which developed the idea of a "myth", might be the most influential. Here, visual representations work on two levels. On a surface level, the images on the screen represent the real-life versions of what's on-screen.[35] So, for example, the film *La La Land* (2016) signifies Emma Stone and Ryan Gosling as it is their images that appear on the screen. That's the first layer of signification: the image of Emma Stone represents *Emma Stone*. However, once we get over that hurdle, we can understand the second (and third and maybe even fourth) levels of signification. Within the film, Stone's image is not intended to represent her, but rather her character, Mia. In this case, the meaning of the initial sign (Emma Stone) is emptied and replaced by the meaning of the character (Mia). From there on, each scene can be understood at various levels of a "myth": What does it mean when Mia wears a yellow dress? What does it mean when she interacts with Sebastian (Gosling's character)? At each layer, the previous meaning is replaced with a new one to represent a different level of the signification chain.

The "Gaze"

When examining films and television, the term the "gaze" deals with who is able to do the "looking" or who has the power to create visual products. Perhaps this is most closely associated with film theorist Laura Mulvey and her article "Visual Pleasure and Narrative Cinema," where she developed the idea of the male gaze. Based within psychoanalysis, Mulvey argues cinema displays a "division of labor" where men are active and do the work of looking, while women are passive and are (generally) looked at. In this way, the role of films and other visual mediums is that it creates roles for viewers: either you're the looker or the looked at.[36]

As others like John Berger and bell hooks have acknowledged, that power plays into who is allowed to do the looking;[37] women, people of color, the young and the less wealthy are reprimanded or taught not to gaze, while those in a position of power are allowed. hooks takes an intersectional approach to note that black women have a unique gaze in relation to films—one that both racial and feminist discussions of the gaze omit. Understanding the text from these various perspectives offers different insights and what the audience is gaining from their consumption.

Both semiotics and the various understandings of the gaze can be applied to costumes. Generally, costumes have been analyzed in relation to their use within the narrative. However, Stella Bruzzi made the case that film costumes are more than narrative props. In doing so, she shows that costumes within films can be understood through their links to other fields beyond the parameters of the visual medium. Specifically, Bruzzi noted that clothing doesn't only gain significance in relation to the characters and that the goal of costumes is not *always* for its wearer to appeal to the opposite sex.[38] Further, Bruzzi showed a permeable boundary between on-screen depictions and historical situations and influences, just as others have noted costume's influence on retail and consumption.

Fashion and Celebrity Culture

The idea that what happens on screen doesn't stay *on screen* is also at the heart of celebrity culture. As Pamela Church Gibson has noted, the intersection of celebrity and fashion works to sustain and promote consumerism in ways not altogether different than the cinema shops in the early department stores.[39] Stars of film and television have long been used as spokespeople for specific brands;[40] however, today they have largely become brands in and of themselves. Basketball player Michael Jordan might be seen as an early precursor to some of today's celebrities: through his collaboration with Nike, Jordans (the various incarnations of basketball sneakers) became a household name while Jordan himself would go on to star in the semi-animated film *Space Jam* (1996).

The 1990s not only saw the rise of Jordans, but also the rise of celebrity-endorsed clothing lines by model Kathy Ireland and TV personality Kathie Lee Gifford—the latter would cause a stir when it was revealed that the line was produced in sweatshops. While not all celebrities have transitioned successfully to fashion, some have. Singer-turned-reality-show star and actress Jessica Simpson would successfully transition into mass market clothing and accessories, while Mary Kate and Ashley Olsen would find success with their more luxurious line, The Row. Rihanna's Savage x Fenty lingerie line has gained attention for its inclusive models (including two who were pregnant during its Fall 2018 show).[41]

At the same time as celebrities were getting into the fashion game, designers were increasingly becoming celebrities in their own rights. Church Gibson traced this back to Chanel who has become mythologized within the fashion world despite some questionable actions during the Second World War.[42] A host of other designers have also become household names from Vivienne Westwood to Karl Lagerfeld. In the past decade or so, documentaries have helped this process including *Valentino: The Last Emperor* (2009), *Dior and I* (2014) which featured Raf Simmons, and *Jeremy Scott: The People's Designer* (2015). Moreover, designers have also become a presence on reality television: Michael Kors and Zac Posen were judges on the US version of *Project Runway*, and Isaac Mizrahi and Georgina Chapman were judges on the All-Star edition. At the same time, the show's most prominent winner, Christian Siriano, has gained popularity through his designs—including his gender-bending 2019 Oscar dress for actor Billy Porter[43]—*and* for becoming the design mentor for the later seasons of the show that made him famous.

Fashion News, Criticism and "Reality" Television

The primary thrust of this chapter has been on the use of clothing within fictional products; however, like celebrity culture spilling into other arenas, the coverage of fashion has been a mainstay of news coverage for decades now. Prior to the 1980s, however, fashion coverage on television was limited to fashion specials, makeovers and morning show pieces. Deidra Arrington noted that changed with the development of *Style with Elsa Klench* (1980–2001), which aired on CNN. The show became the highest rated on the 24-hour news network and would set the stage for fashion coverage in the future. Moreover, Klench's show helped introduce haute couture and luxury fashion to the masses who had previously relied on department stores for the latest looks.[48]

Insight: Pushing the Boundaries on the Red Carpet

What creates a good red carpet look has formed the basis of immense coverage in magazines and on television. From Joan Rivers' coverage of the Oscars to André Leon Talley's commentary at the Met Gala, celebrities are expected to show up and dress the part. Often, this involves designer gowns and eye-catching accessories: musicians like Cher, Björk, and Lady Gaga have all turned heads with various looks, while actors like Sharon Stone and Billy Porter have broken the rules of glamor in other ways. Consider some of these fashion highlights.

Actress Elizabeth Hurley gained attention when she wore a black Versace dress to the London premiere of *Four Weddings and a Funeral* in 1994. The black dress had a thigh-high slit, a low-cut top, and a midriff cutout that was seemingly held together with safety pins. Hurley, who was in attendance with then-boyfriend Hugh Grant, caused a sensation and was propelled onto the A-List. While the dress would go down in red carpet history, years later, Grant and Hurley would acknowledge that the dress was chosen at last minute because other designers had snubbed the then little-known Hurley.[44]

Actress Sharon Stone wore an outfit from her closet to the Academy Awards in 1996: A long black skirt paired with a black turtleneck from the Gap. The shirt reportedly cost $22 and caught the brand by surprise. "If we would have known she was going to wear it," Richard Crissman, Gap's vice president of public relations, told a reporter at the time, "it certainly would have been in stores today."[45] Stone was credited with bringing red carpet looks at "bargain basement" prices.

Actress-turned-musician Jennifer Lopez wore a green Versace dress to the 2000 Grammy Awards. The dress was made of jungle print, had sheer sleeves and skirt and a plunging neckline that was cut to Lopez's waist. The dress caused a sensation on the early internet with people using search engine Google to see what the star had worn. Later, Google would acknowledge that it was the resulting interest in the dress that would spur the development of Google Images.[46]

Icelandic singer-songwriter Björk turned heads at the 2001 Academy Awards when she wore a dress designed to look like a swan draped around her neck. The dress was designed by Macedonian designer Marjan Pejoski, who reportedly did not know the singer wore the dress until the following morning. Despite being widely criticized as a "worst dressed" look, the dress would help build Björk's artistic bona fides and remained a pop culture reference for years.[47]

top © Kevin Mazur via Getty Images; middle © Steve Granitz via Getty Images; bottom © Mirek Towski via Getty Images.

MTV's *House of Style* (1989–1997), hosted by Cindy Crawford, would help "democratize" fashion for young people and strengthened the connection between fashion and music. And, Joan Rivers would become famous for her red carpet critiques starting in the mid-1990s up until her death. While Rivers was instrumental in making the red carpet an award show staple, she would later go on to star on *Fashion Police* (2010–2017), which would continue for three years after Rivers' death. The show, which starred Rivers along with Giuliana Rancic, George Kotsiopoulos and Kelly Osborne, featured a variety of segments on celebrity fashions and criticisms thereof.[49]

As fashion journalism and critiques were being taken more seriously, a second avenue helped push fashion into more homes: reality television. In the early 2000s, reality-based and competition shows would further expand the prominence of fashion, clothing and style on television. Perhaps the first show in this vein was *What Not to Wear*, featuring Trinny Woodall and Susannah Constantine, which debuted in the UK on BBC 2 (2001–2007) and eventually spawned global versions including on the US network TLC, which starred Stacy London and Clinton Kelly (2003–2013). Another show in the same vein, *Say Yes to the Dress*, began airing in the US in 2007 and also since expanded to networks around the globe. Both of these shows deal with clothing and appearance; in the case of *What Not To Wear*, the hosts teach the less stylish how to better present themselves to achieve personal or professional goals. Comparatively, *Say Yes to the Dress*, follows a group of sales associates who help brides to buy their wedding dress. Perhaps the most prominent examples of these shows was *Extreme Makeover* (2002–2007), which aired on the US broadcast network ABC, and included not only styling, but also weight loss and even plastic surgery advice; and *Queer Eye for the Straight Guy* (2003–2007), later just *Queer Eye*, where five gay experts would transform a hapless "straight guy." *Queer Eye* would win an Emmy in 2004 and be closely linked to the rising prominence of the "metrosexual"—and get a Netflix revival in 2018.[50]

Such shows stand in contrast to what many generally think of as "reality TV"—which is more of a *reality competition* show. These shows generally pit various contestants against each other for a prize. The most obvious examples are *Big Brother*, which began in the Netherlands, and *Expedition Robinson* (as it's known in Sweden) or *Survivor* as it's known throughout most of the world. In 2003, the Tyra Banks-created *America's Next Top Model* would debut in the US, where Banks and a panel of judges would help a group of women (and later men) work toward being a "top" model. Most winners received a cash prize and a photo shoot for a US magazine. Like other shows, *ANTM* would spawn international versions around the world.

Figure 6.3 *One Day You're In ... Hosts of* Project Runway, *Tim Gunn, left, and Heidi Klum speak at a runway show in 2017.* © *Dimitrios Kambouris via Getty Images.*

However, *Project Runway,* which debuted in 2004 on US cable channel Bravo, is the reality competition show that had fashion at its forefront. The show, originally hosted by Heidi Klum and Tim Gunn (Figure 6.3), features twelve or more designers competing in weekly competitions around various concepts including using non-traditional materials, designs for celebrities or particular brands. The final challenge generally included designers debuting a show at New York Fashion Week. The winner would win money to support their own fashion line along with other prizes including magazine spreads and a car. *Project Runway* would become something of a cultural phenomenon garnering an Emmy nomination in its first season (and 58 nominations overall), and making Gunn a household name (Heidi Klum was already an internationally known model). The hosts would win their own Emmy in 2013.[51] While *Project Runway* would spur intentional editions, none were as successful as the US version, which is still on air. The show would also create multiple spinoffs including *Project Runway All Stars* (2012–2019) and *Project Runway: Junior* (2015–2016).

There would be other reality competition shows which had varying levels of success and taste. The US show *The Swan* (2004) might have been the most questionable of the genre; it was a makeover competition show where "homely" contestants were given a host of medical and cosmetic procedures to make them more attractive with one being dubbed a "winner" via a pageant competition. The "swan" would win a modeling contract and other prizes. Meanwhile, the US show *Fashion Star* (2012–2013) featured model Elle McPherson, designer John Varvatos, and celebrities Jessica Simpson and Nicole Richie, and would have designers compete to have their work purchased by buyers from Macy's, Saks Fifth Avenue and H&M (in the first season) or Express (in the second). *Fashion Star* aimed to be a more commercially friendly (and mass market) than *Project Runway* as designs would be "picked up" and were literally on sale in stores the following day.[52]

Reality-based shows, as well as fashion news and criticism, still present representational issues within the mass media. Tania Lewis noted that these shows have helped transform our idea of the self and that the "experts" within lifestyle shows act as cultural intermediaries who translate "elite" or "high class" tastes.[53] Katherine Sender added that these shows promote a self-reflexiveness among audiences, regarding consumption and self-regulation.[54] Moreover, even as the contestants and subjects of these shows are intended to represent "ordinary" people, shows are generally edited or manipulated to seem more extraordinary or archtypical.[55] Regardless, there is a clear trajectory whereby fashion, clothing and personal appearance have been receiving more coverage and airtime since the 1980s. Although, the number of these shows has tapered dramatically in the 2010s, they seem to have foreshadowed the rise of streetstyle, beauty blogs and social media influencers.

Digital Fashion Films and Documentaries

While there has been considerable crossover between film, television and the commercial considerations of fashion, one clear way visual media has promoted fashion has been the *fashion film*. When discussing a fashion film, it's generally seen more as a commercial or a piece of promotional material rather than a film about fashion. Meaning, films like *Funny Face* and *The Devil Wears Prada* would not be considered a "fashion film" since they are not promotional in nature, even if they do deal with a fictional account of the fashion world. A fashion film is more commercially driven, often with the goal of promoting products, designers or brands.[56]

Fashion films can be traced back to the beginnings of cinema: Marketa Uhlirova suggested early corset commercials were made in the final years of the 1800s and, by the 1910s, the likes of Paul Poiret had begun using film as a substitute for live fashion shows.[57] These types of films would turn toward documentary styles (which continue through today) and would be used for artistic and business purposes rather than promotion to the larger public. However, by the later 1990s and early 2000s, designers were beginning to experiment with the use of film during fashion shows as the rise of digital culture created more opportunities for convergence of media. Fashion films remained muted in the early days of the internet due to technological limitations like low bandwidth, which made them hard to watch online. However, the first decade of the 2000s would see their increased use as digital platforms made their distribution easier and those within the industry saw the potential for increased, cheap distribution.

At the same time, the presence of fashion documentaries, which are not straight advertisements but are certainly promotional in nature, have become more commonplace in the past decade. Beyond the designer-focused documentaries mentioned earlier, others have centered on various aspects of fashion media. *The September Issue* (2009), follows Anna Wintour and the staff of US *Vogue, Bill Cunningham: New York* (2010) documents the life of the well-known streetstyle photographer, and *The Eye Has to Travel* (2012) interrogates Diana Vreeland's life and legacy. These documentaries can be seen to straddle the line between objective storytelling and public relations messaging, for example, *The September Issue* followed the literary and cinematic success of *The Devil Wears Prada*, which was a not-so-subtle criticism of Wintour. Moreover, *Dior and I* followed Raf Simmons' first collection for the famed fashion house, in the wake of John Galliano's firing due to anti-Semitic comments.[58]

Cultivation Theory

Finally, any chapter discussing the effects of television would be remiss without a discussion of Cultivation Theory. Originally outlined by George Gerbner, Cultivation Theory was developed in relation to media effects (i.e. in the vein of the "magic bullet" theory discussed in Chapter 5) and paid particular attention to increasing television viewership. This theory essentially held that those who were *heavy television viewers* were more likely to have a skewed perception of the world, and generally understood it to be more violent. The premise is that no single media event would ultimately change a viewer's perception, but the repetition of these events had a cumulative effect. Gerbner's work was especially focused on televised violence and, as such, he ultimately argued that those who watch a lot of television are likely to see the world as a more violent place. Dubbed the "Mean World Syndrome," heavy television viewers were more likely to overstate their chances of being a victim of violent crime and believe violent crime is rising, and, as such, be more likely to socially isolate themselves.

Gerbner's work was focused on a macrolevel and was interested in widespread meanings and the long-term acculturating effect of television viewership. While some have attempted to empirically test the theory—including Gerbner himself—statistical measurements showed little support for it. However, attempting to study such a process through content and statistical analysis seems increasingly difficult given the contemporary media landscape. Instead, it has been argued that a more precise scope in cultivation research—along genre lines, for example—might be more productive. As such, researchers have been putting more specific examples into practice, including examining the views of masculinity among those who consume different media genres (e.g. sports, reality television, and sitcoms) and the views of consumption among teens who watch a lot of reality television.[59]

Regardless of the statistical evidence in support or opposition to Cultivation Theory, the idea that repeated exposure to the same messages will shape one's worldview is at the heart of other research as well. Frequently, this premise is used within research into advertising with studies like Erving Goffman's *Gender Advertisements* and Jean Kilbourne's video series *Killing Us Softly* looking at the repetition of gendered messages within the media. Moreover, while Cultivation Theory has not been applied to clothing in an consistent way—generally, clothing is viewed as an indicator of larger issues like sexuality—repeated media messages are really the way we understand what is *in* fashion at a given time. This is less about the distortion of the world and more about how we understand what is happening around us.

Further Reading

While there are not a lot of works on medium ecology or medium theory that address clothing or costuming, several works are rather canonical within media studies. Neil Postman's *Amusing Ourselves to Death* (Random House, 2005) is perhaps the most widely known. Postman's work draws off of ideas in *Understanding Media: The Extensions of Man* by Marshall McLuhan (MIT Press, 1994), which also involves a brief essay on clothing as a medium. The other key book from a communication studies standpoint is *Communication as Culture: Essays on Media and Society* by James W. Carey (Routledge, 2009), which crosses US media studies with perspectives from cultural studies and media ecology.

There are a few foundational books specifically looking at costuming within fashion and television. The volume *Fabrications: Costume and the Female Body* by Jane Gaines and Charlotte Herzog (Routledge, 1990) is one of the earliest books on the topic, but Stella Bruzzi's *Undressing Cinema: Clothing and Identity in the Movies* (Routledge, 1997) is credited with arguing for the study of film costume in its own right. Likewise, Adrienne Munich's simply titled volume, *Fashion in Film* (Indiana University Press, 2011), is an update and further develops the study in this area. The book *Fashion on Television: Identity and Celebrity Culture* (Bloomsbury, 2014) by Helen Warner, does a great job of bringing costume studies to television series, which has been underdeveloped. Pamela Church Gibson's book *Fashion and Celebrity Culture* (Berg, 2011), the volume she edited with Stella Bruzzi, *Fashion Cultures Revisited: Theories, Explorations and Analysis* (Routledge, 2013) and the journal she heads, *Film, Fashion and Consumption* all do a nice job of connecting visual screen cultures to the wider cultural processes.

Finally, while the the work of Stuart Hall is highly influential, the volume *Representation: Cultural Representations and Signifying Practices* edited by Hall, Jessica Evans and Sean Nixon (Sage, 2013) is a useful collection of Hall's work and many related articles and chapters. Meanwhile, Laura Mulvey's article "Visual Pleasure and Narrative Cinema" (1975), John Berger's *Ways of Seeing* (Penguin, 1990) and Roland Barthes' *Mythologies* (Hill and Wang, 1957) are all useful methods for understanding and interrogating visual screen cultures.

1   Postman, Neil (2005). *Amusing Ourselves to Death*. New York: Random House.

2   McLuhan, Marshall (1994). *Understanding Media: The Extensions of Man*. Cambridge, MA: The MIT Press.

3   Carey, James W. (2009). *Communication as Culture: Essays on Media and Society*. New York: Routledge.

4   Gaines, Jane and Charlotte Herzog, eds. (1990). *Fabrications: Costume and the Female Body*. New York: Routledge.

5   Bruzzi, Stella (1997). *Undressing Cinema: Clothing and Identity in the Movies.* New York: Routledge.

6   Munich, Adrienne, ed. (2011). *Fashion in Film.* Bloomington, IN: Indiana University Press.

7   Warner, Helen (2014). *Fashion on Television: Identity and Celebrity Culture.* New York: Bloomsbury.

8   Church Gibson, Pamela (2011). *Fashion and Celebrity Culture.* New York: Berg.

9   Bruzzi, Stella and Pamela Church Gibson (2013). *Fashion Cultures Revisited: Theories, Explorations and Analysis.* New York: Routledge.

10   Hall, Stuart, Jessica Evans and Sean Nixon, eds. (2012). *Representations: Cultural Representations and Signifying Practices.* Thousand Oaks, CA: Sage.

11   Mulvey, Laura (1975). "Visual Pleasure and Narrative Cinema." *Screen,* 16(3): 6–18. doi: 10.1093/screen/16.3.6.

12   Berger, John (1990). *Ways of Seeing.* New York: Penguin.

13   Barthes, Roland (1957). *Mythologies.* New York: Hill and Wang.

Figure 7.1 *Meet the Abercrombie Models. Shoppers pose with Abercrombie & Fitch's famous male models when the chain's Munich flagship store opened in 2012. © Hannes Magerstaedt via Getty Images.*

7

Ads, Brands, and Retail Considerations

Picture it: Summer 1999. The summer has been called the "last, innocent, giddy summer."[1] The dot-com bubble was still in full force as Napster was introduced to the world and Beanie Babies were all the rage. *The Blair Witch Project* was a surprise hit at the box offices and future pop princesses Britney Spears and Christina Aguilera were still shedding their *Mickey Mouse Club* image. And, in the midst of it all, pop trio LFO introduce the world to "Summer Girls," which would become the song of the summer and the group's defining hit. Peaking at number 3 on the Billboard Hot 100 chart,[2] the song became synonymous with teen clothing brand Abercrombie & Fitch, thanks to a reference in the song's refrain.

The brand was on something of an upswing after being saved from the dustbin of history by the Limited Brands, and was being led by CEO Mike Jeffries. Abercrombie & Fitch was in the process of becoming an iconic teen lifestyle brand, selling jeans, T-shirts and flip-flops in stores hidden by white shutters and low light that emanated dance music and the brand's signature cologne. It was an idyllic teen dream with its risqué magazine-catalogue hybrid that featured photography by Bruce Weber, and the dream was brought to life by the "cool kids" working in Abercrombie & Fitch stores, including shirtless male models, with whom customers would take photographs.[3]

Given the brand's position, it might be assumed that it paid for the placement in LFO's song, however, both the brand and the band denied a relationship.[4] Perhaps it was just a happy coincidence for the brand or a foreshadowing of what was to come with Abercrombie's growing cultural image. At the time, Abercrombie was already becoming shorthand for "cool" in high schools across the US,[5] yet the connotations of exclusivity and sex appeal would outlive its financial usefulness and become a cultural punchline. By 2014, the film *Neighbors*, in which new parents (played by Seth Rogan and Rose Byrne) engage in a protracted fight with a group of fraternity brothers (led by Zac Efron and Dave Franco) ended with Efron getting a job as a shirtless Abercrombie & Fitch greeter.[6] That same year CEO Jeffries would depart the company after years of losses and lawsuits.[7]

Fashion brands frequently act as conduits for cultural meaning both through interpersonal communication and across the popular culture landscape. For example, in the book of *The Devil Wears Prada*—which is already a loaded reference to Prada!—Miranda Priestly is known for wearing Hermès scarfs. Elsewhere, in popular music, 5 Seconds of Summer reference American Apparel in the song "She's So Perfect" while Cardi B's "Bodak Yellow" references the red soles of Christian Louboutin's shoes.[8] Ultimately, in today's world, brands have become a complex and contested form of media,[9] some of which we even use to adorn our bodies. This, however, was not always the case. Throughout the 1800s and early 1900s brands were understood to be a marker of quality rather than culturally significant repertoires of meaning.

A Brief History of Fashion Brands

As an overall process, branding is generally traced back to the British Empire in the late 1800s, even though the term "brand" did not enter the lexicon until the 1920s. Still, trademarked names, precursors to the modern brand, began to adorn products such as soap in the 1870s, with names like Sunlight, in the UK, from 1876 and Ivory, in the US, from 1879. From roughly the same time, producers of food products began putting their names on offerings, including Folger coffee in 1872 and Kraft cheese in 1903.[10]

A bit earlier, a designer by the name of Charles Frederick Worth was making a name for himself as a clothing designer in Paris. Worth is considered the first couturier of modern times. He moved from England to Paris in 1846 and worked at the apparel business Gagelin-Opigez et Cie, where his designs were awarded a medal for dressmaking. Eventually, Worth and his label "Worth et Bobergh" became a favored designer of Empress Eugénie, wife of Napoleon III, and he designed much of her wardrobe. He gained an impressive list of royal clients during the 1860s and while his initial label would be shuttered during the Franco-Prussian War, he would go on to found the House of Worth thereafter. Worth, and his children, who eventually joined the fashion house and succeeded him, were worried about design piracy, leading them to help develop the Chambre Syndicale de la Haute Couture Parisienne in 1868 and to create the fashion label, which was stamped in gold to identify the garment as an original coming from the house.[11]

The piracy of fashion brands remained an issue as designer Paul Poiret found out when he debuted a line of dresses in the US. Initially, the designs were given a special label to be identified as a "authorized reproduction" but the piracy persisted. Designer Madeleine Vionnet, who was known for her ability to work with fabric, took labels to the extreme and would include her fingerprint on garment labels to prove their authenticity.[12]

Still, by the early 1900s, designers were truly coming to understand the power of their names and product lines. Poiret began a line of perfume, Rosine, in 1911, which would predate Coco Chanel's eponymously named Chanel No. 5, by a decade. It was the perfume and other cosmetics that would make Chanel a financial success. After the perfume became popular Chanel would enter into an agreement with Pierre Wertheimer giving him and his family, owners of the biggest cosmetics company in France, 70% of the profits. While there was some legal wrangling before and during the Second World War (where Chanel tried to seize the cosmetic company from the Wertheimers who fled to the US), Chanel's boutique continued to sell the perfume. After the war, she was accused of treason and exiled to Switzerland, however, in 1954, the Wertheimers bought her fashion house for the rest of her life and allowed her to design again.[13]

Chanel's licensing of her name for the perfume would set the stage for licensing to take on a greater importance. Christian Dior, who you might remember from Chapter 4, saw his Maison Dior business take off after his famed "New Look." As a way to meet demand while expanding the business, Dior first opened an American branch in 1948 and then separated the American and French operations. Finally, Maison Dior opened specialized branches and expanded licensing agreements with various manufacturers. There were subsidiaries to produce perfume, shoes and menswear in France, while the US focused on ready-to-wear and accessories. After Dior died in 1957, his assistant, Yves Saint Laurent, would take over as chief designer until he left the company in 1960. In 1961, design operations between Dior-New York and Maison Dior (in Paris) were fully separated with each setting out their own designs and selling them locally. The company would continue to expand its licensing business, but the model set up by Dior kept the house afloat after the designer's death and remains the preeminent model of a fashion business.[14]

Outside of licensing, the development of the mass media also had massive implications for branding—including fashion brands. Contemporary brands, which are seen as highly complex and meaningful, needed forms of mass media to communicate their messages. Branding today is understood as a set of connotations applied to goods and services through various communication channels—such as names, logos, design and advertising.[15] In their "Practical Model of Fashion Brand Management," Stephen M. Wigley, Karinna Nobbs and Ewa Larsen have noted that tangible brand communication (i.e. the things we can experience through our senses) is built into intangible elements of the brand (i.e. things we cannot experience through our senses) (Figure 7.2).

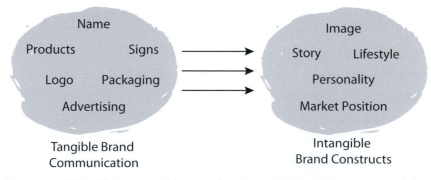

Figure 7.2 *Tangible to Intangible. Brand communications that we can see help us create an immaterial understanding of the brand.*

Tangible brand elements include (1) names and logos, (2) packaging; (3) products; (4) the store experience; and (5) marketing communications.[16] These various elements then get assembled into ideas like images, personalities, stories, lifestyle, heritage and even market position, most of which will elicit some type of consumer response. Others have added that once brands are created, they take on something of a life of their own, helping to shape understandings, expectations and even financial considerations.[17]

Brands as a Social Construct

Before we can get into more specifics of how branding works, it's important to take a step back and consider what a brand actually is. While brands are generally understood as a sign attached to goods and services, the term has been expanded in a multitude of ways to the point that marketing professor Philip Kotler says, "Everything is a brand."[18] In fact, defining what is and isn't a brand has been something of a "Holy Grail" for marketing researchers and theorists.[19] However, perhaps the easiest way to understand a brand is that it's a *social construct* that we accept as true or factual.

You might have heard the term "social construct" used somewhat offhandedly that many things in our world and concepts as diverse as race, gender, geographical designations like cities, states, and nations, classes, and even grades are social constructs. The idea of social construction (the process that works to make social constructs) is credited to Peter L. Berger and Thomas Luckmann who wrote the book *The Social Construction of Reality*. In it, they argue that everyday life is created through the process of social construction— everything we do is learned and then re-enacted by us helping to sustain it, including language and how we use tools and objects.[20] This is somewhat subjective as we each learn and understand the world around us in our own way. However, once we come to know it, we all primarily agree on the "objectiveness" of the world.

Think about it: What makes a clothing store, a *store*? We might recognize a clothing store as an open space with stacks of folded clothing, mannequins displaying the latest styles and a cash register where you pay for the products.

Abercrombie & Fitch played with that idea through their low light and loud music, and without the clothing, the space could double as a dance club. Likewise, Amazon's "Go" stores are doing away with cash registers and cashiers, using cameras and QR codes to charge customers for the products they want to "buy."[21] So, in the future, stores with cashiers may be the exception, not the rule. In fact, the idea of money and "paying" for products are all an element of social construction as well, as there are other ways to share goods, such as bartering or charity. Despite social constructs being learned and essentially accepted by everyone, that doesn't mean they aren't powerful. Once they are established they are generally slow to change.

For branding, we need to both have an understanding of what a "brand" is and what a specific brand means.[22] This is largely what we'll be discussing for the next several pages as the tangible brand communications help build the immaterial or *socially constructed* parts of a brand. In order for brands to be meaningful to *us* we have to have a working knowledge of what the brand is, what it represented and the way others view that brand. For example, a student once shared that she was wearing a pair of Lululemon leggings out in rural Virginia one day. Lululemon products, as you might know, are identified by a circle with a stylized "A" or what might be misconstrued as a female head. In any case, a woman approached the student and told her she had a "sticker" on the leggings; of course, the woman was talking about the logo. For someone aware of Lululemon, the symbol indicates perhaps the price of leggings as well as the brand's messaging and culture power. However, for someone who didn't recognize the logo and a brand, the sign just looked like a "sticker" or something that didn't belong on them. In this case, while Lululemon is socially constructed, it had little power to someone who didn't recognize the symbol.

Tangible Brand Communications

To understand contemporary branding, it's best to start at the heart of the matter—the product. As Liz Moor points out, brands were largely developed from product design that allowed products to be distinguished from one another,[23] and making something distinctive remains an important part of branding. Think about it: if every car looked and acted in the same manner, it wouldn't matter whether you had a Toyota or a Jaguar, since there would be no difference. Likewise, it would make sense that clothing was on the front lines of branding since it was handmade and designs made visible differences between garments. In comparison, creating differences in appliances or other products would take significantly more technological development.

In any case, at the heart of the branding is the product that is being sold. For clothing, this largely includes material properties, such as design, fit, feel and even color. Designer Jeanne Lanvin was known for using a signature blue hue in her designs.[24] And, closely related to the design is the logo, or symbol, which ultimately represents the brand. Everyone is likely familiar with the Nike swoosh, and nearly all brands have a logo. It's easy to recognize garments produced by Lacoste, Polo Ralph Lauren and Hollister by their respective alligators, horses and seagulls. The prominence of logos on clothing waxes and wanes, much like fashion trends themselves. In the 1990s, Tommy Hilfiger was known for white T-shirts adorned with his large flag logo, and later clothing brands from Gap to Abercrombie & Fitch proudly displayed their logos on all types of wear. While this was a successful strategy for a while, eventually the tide turned against the conspicuous logos and mass market fashion brands began to turn away from the practice.[25] Brands like Lululemon and Uniqlo still use logos, but do so in a less visible way, while fashion brands like Fendi have gone to the other end of the spectrum and repeat their logos seemingly endlessly.

Of course, clothing, as a product, is not only about the way it looks, but also about how it feels, how it fits and how it lasts. The famed slogan, "The touch, the feel of Cotton," struck right at the heart of this dynamic by implying the haptic qualities made it "the fabric of our lives." The stretch softness of a T-shirt and the stretch of yoga pants can play into the tangible qualities of certain products and, by extension, the brand. Clothing from places like Primark and H&M may feel rougher than garments sold by more upscale stores. In the same vein, fit can be used as a means of branding. The store 5-7-9—once a staple of US malls—only stocked clothing in those three sizes, while more recently the Brandy Melville chain has taken to selling its clothing in "one size."[26] Likewise, during its heyday, Abercrombie & Fitch didn't stock women's clothing in XL or XXL in an effort to limit who could buy its clothing.[27] Finally, how long a garment lasts is also integral to the branding process—if we ever had a shirt shrink in the wash, pill or develop a hole shortly after purchase, we might have surmised that the brand isn't very high quality.

Seven Names to Know in Fashion Design and Business

Charles Frederick Worth (1825–1895)—Englishman turned early Parisian designer, Worth is usually credited with establishing haute couture. While there were other prized designers before him, Worth's couture house and promotion of himself as an artist has created a lasting legacy in the fashion field.[1]

Gabrielle "Coco" Chanel (1883–1971)—French designer and shrewd businesswoman, Chanel opened her first shop in 1913 where she sold stylish yet utilitarian daywear and romantic eveningwear. She would come to be associated with the little black dress, her wool tweed and jersey suits and, of course, the licensing of her name to the popular perfume, Chanel No. 5.[2]

Christian Dior (1905–1957)—French designer who established the House of Dior in 1946. Dior would become synonymous with the "New Look" of the late 1940s. He would create a global fashion business by establishing subsidiaries and licensing agreements in the US and elsewhere outside of Europe.[3]

Stanley Marcus (1905–2002)—American retailer who took over the Dallas-based department store, Neiman Marcus, which was founded by his father, aunt and uncle. Marcus turned the store into a global force with an emphasis on fashion and luxury. Marcus created the Neiman Marcus Awards for fashion which honored the likes of Chanel, Dior, Yves Saint Laurent and Valentino.[4]

Amancio Ortega (born 1936)—Notably press shy, Spanish businessman Ortega is the man behind fast fashion retailer Zara and majority owner of its parent company, Inditex, the world's largest clothing retailer. Ortega opened the first Zara store in 1975 and has overseen the store's growth around the globe.[5]

Bernard Arnault (born 1949)—French businessman and president of LVMH, Arnault controls more than 75 luxury brands including Dior, Louis Vuitton,

Fendi, Hennessy, Dom Pérignon, and Sephora. Thanks to Arnault, LVMH is the largest luxury conglomerate in the world and the second most valuable company in Europe. And, thanks to LVMH, Arnault is the fourth richest man in the world.[6]

Tadashi Yanai (born 1949)—Founder and president of Fast Retailing, Yanai oversees the fourth-largest apparel business in the world. After taking over his father's clothing store chain in 1984 and founding a new store that would become Uniqlo, he saw Fast Retailing grow to encompass brands like Helmut Lang, Theory and J Brand.[7]

Beyond the product, "packaging" also helps to communicate a brand image. While clothing and accessories aren't packaged in the way some other products are, shoe boxes are generally designed and include the brand's logo, and if we've ordered something online, it might have come with distinctive packaging. Superdry, for example, mails orders in bags with its signature orange and logo in white. The other way we can think about the "packaging" of clothing is the bags stores use. Think about the bags you got the last time you bought something; the bags you were given were likely distinguished in one way or another. Bags from Japanese clothing store Uniqlo are usually solid white with its logo in red but, at times, it has used bags adorned with various Japan-inspired imagery. Meanwhile, Bloomingdale's "brown bags" have become an icon in their own right.[28]

Moving on from the physical qualities of products and packaging, one of the most prominent ways people understand a brand is through their experience with it. And, by "experiential branding"[29] we're not only talking about the experience with the product, but rather the experiences we have when we're shopping. For example, Abercrombie & Fitch stores were well-known for promoting a club-like atmosphere. Meanwhile, Nike stores were known for their emphasis on sports and still allow people to shoot hoops in some of its stores. Largely, these types of branding exercises are more frequently used in flagship locations, which are seen as the pinnacle of firms' branding efforts. While physical experiential retailing remains a driving force, the internet has changed the way consumers interact with brands, which has been a particular problem for luxury brands who relied on a feeling of exclusivity during their transactions.[30]

The element of tangible communication that helps shape the brand can broadly be described as "marketing communications" and could include things like print advertisements in newspapers and magazines, billboards, television commercials, flyers or other promotional materials distributed in stores like branded publications or catalogs, social media messages and advertisements, and even press releases. Each of these work to build a brand in specific ways. For example, one famous element of Abercrombie & Fitch was its self-produced magazine-catalog hybrid (often referred to as a magalog), which included order forms, pictures of the clothing, the fashion photography of Bruce Weber and articles covering topics like travel advice, drinks recipes and celebrity profiles. In comparison, brands like Target and Gap used television advertisements and catchy pop music to help brand themselves as "cool." Elsewhere, public relations professionals for brands Oscar de la Renta and DKNY developed social media personas—Oscar PR Girl and DKNY PR Girl—to help humanize their brands.[31] Regardless of the medium, brands use each of these channels to distinguish themselves from each other, enforce the messages from other elements (such as an in-store experience) and build intangible brand elements that bring value to a brand in several different ways.

Intangible Brand Communication

Intangible brand communication is more frequently discussed by brand managers, researchers and industry insiders than your everyday consumer, but it is powerful nonetheless. These constructions are largely unseen, but make brands more desirable and valuable—both in what we pay for products *and* what companies will pay each other for trademarks and licensing. It's not quite useful to go into each one individually, so let's take them in two different groupings: the first will be the cultural constructions of a brand, and the second will be the financial constructions of a brand.

The intangible, cultural constructions of a brand are the aspects that give it meaning and how we understand that meaning. These can largely be understood in overlapping ways, which is why it's difficult to discuss one as completely different than the other. But, here are a few rough definitions:

- *Brand image*: Consumer perceptions of a brand that give symbolic value.[32]

- *Brand personality*: Consumer perceptions that personify a brand (i.e. assume it to have human characteristics).[33]

- *Brand myth*: Symbolic meaning provided to and by brands that purport to help consumers fix contractions present in contemporary society.[34]

- *Brand story*: A narrative structure in which a brand can fit into. This may include elements like characters, conflict and plots.[35]

- *Brand lifestyle*: Beliefs, meanings and aspirations given to specific brands and, in turn, transposed onto the brands' consumers.[36]

- *Brand heritage*: Largely the qualities a brand draws from its past, whether from older offerings or lasting success.[37]

Lumping these various understandings together under one umbrella may seem a bit confusing since they do, in fact, imply or refer to different aspects of a brand. However, they would all fit within a postmodern view of branding whereby the intangible and immaterial aspects of brands provide additional meaning and value.[38] This value may be financial, but may also provide affective or symbolic meaning for consumers. Realistically, we might understand that purchasing a North Face jacket won't turn us into an outdoors person nor that a new pair of Quicksilver board shorts will make us a beach bum, but that doesn't mean those messages are any less powerful or persuasive.

Brand Images and Personality

Perhaps the oldest and most widely known of these intangible meaning structures is that of brand image. This idea has its roots in research of the 1950s first by Burliegh B. Gardner and Sidney J. Levy. In their joint article, they wrote, "The *image of a product* associated with the brand may be clear-cut or relatively vague; it may be varied or simple; it may be intense or innocuous," and noted that "These sets of ideas, feelings and attitudes that consumers have about brands are crucial to them in picking and sticking to ones that seem most appropriate."[39] Levy would later go onto expand upon this idea suggesting, essentially, that people aren't rational in their purchasing and that we buy products for "what they mean."[40] Among factors that play into these images, Levy included gender, sex, age, class and taste (which can also imply class).

In comparison, Jennifer Aaker defines a brand personality as "the set of human characteristics associated with the brand."[41] This plays into the anthropomorphizing (i.e. the assigning of human attributes to nonhuman things) of brands, including the fact that people form relationships with them and the understanding that they act with intention. Researchers have examined traits like sincerity, excitement, competence, sophistication, ruggedness, warmth and capability.[42] Not all researchers accept this personification, however, as Mark Avis, Sarah Forbes and Shelagh Ferguson have demonstrated that, when asked, consumers are willing to assign personality traits to decidedly non-interactive entities—in their case, rocks.[43]

Somewhat more productively, these discussions—whether brand image or brand personality—have been used toward attempting to line up consumers' understanding of themselves with the brands they purchase and use.[44] The assumption being, of course, that if consumers see themselves within the brand, they are more likely to buy it. This is a similar assumption used by some anthropologists, like Grant McCracken (who you might remember from Chapter 4); however, anthropologists are generally more interested in where and what the meaning is, rather than testing whether or not it lines up with consumers' sense of self. In the first instance, researchers rely on surveys and statistical analysis of responses, whereas the second more often relies on descriptive accounts and/or personal experience.[45]

Myths, Storytelling and Fashion

Building on the ideas of brand image, myths and storytelling take the branding process to the next level. Myths aim to answer some sort of social contradiction for consumers while storytelling draws on cultural meanings to grow brands. Douglas B. Holt suggests that the best way for a brand to achieve success and become an "icon" is through mythmaking. For brand managers, this involves finding a specific social contradiction that needs to be resolved and telling a story—through tangible communication—that answers it for a set of consumers. For example, Holt uses the example of working-class men who found the social order changing around them in the 1980s, as outsourcing and women within business helped change the expectations of men and definitions of masculinity. In response, brands from Budweiser to Harley-Davidson to Mountain Dew offered myths that helped reconcile these tensions. For example, Harley-Davidson built an "outlaw myth" around its motorcycles, while Mountain Dew changed several times over the years from a hillbilly myth to a redneck myth to the Slacker myth. In these cases, the myth helped solve the cultural contradiction. If jobs are less plentiful and blue-collar men are being forced out of work, then being an "outlaw" gives them a different identity. Likewise, if jobs aren't available or are hard to come by, why not slack off and have fun? In these cases, images presented by the brand change to meet the mood of consumers, but also provide a more in-depth meaning than the aforementioned brand image.[46]

In a similar vein, storytelling is one of the most productive ways to imbue mass-produced clothing with a meaning.[47] Within a brand storytelling model, the goal is to provide a full narrative of the clothing: including characters (Who's wearing it?), setting (Where are characters wearing it?) and plot (What are they doing while wearing it?). This is clearly easier for some brands than for others. A clothing brand like Billabong, which emphasizes swimsuits and board shorts will have an easier time creating a story since their clothing is specifically made for beach activities. A brand that offers less specific clothing—say Levi's or True Religion—might have more work to do in relation to storytelling since jeans rarely have a specific meaning (as discussed in Chapter 2).

Storytelling in this manner is usually done in an integrated marketing sense, whereby the story is communicated within various channels, but with the same end goal in mind. However, various brands have utilized some modes of communication more than others. Abercrombie & Fitch was dominant in its in-store shopping experience. A brand like Calvin Klein has long been known for its print and billboard advertising from early Marky Mark advertisements to more recent photoshoots featuring Justin Bieber and Shawn Mendes.

One place where storytelling has been important has been within runway shows. Documentaries like *Dior and I* (2014) and *Jeremy Scott: The People's Designer* (2015) have explored how collections thematically come together for the runway. Yet, this process is a somewhat recent phenomena—early "runway" shows were only done for buyers, magazine editors or elite clients. Those early shows were more about the clothing than the shows. However, as designers grew in importance and popularity across the social landscape, so too did runway shows. Designer Alexander McQueen was well known for the storytelling within his collection and on the runway. His memorable runways shows included his Highland Rape collection, which told the story of eighteenth-century Scotland through its use of plaid, torn garments and fake blood.[48] In these cases, while the storytelling is done via a runway show, it also trickles down into the clothing and non-couture designs of the fashion house.

Lifestyles and Branding

One of the newest—and perhaps least finite—concepts when it comes to branding is the idea of a lifestyle or lifestyle brand; however, that has not stopped it from being used for a variety of brands from Ralph Lauren to Apple to McDonald's. If you're surprised to hear that McDonald's wanted (perhaps still *wants*) to be a lifestyle brand—you're not alone.[49] The idea that a purveyor of fast food, which has been branded as low quality and unhealthy (Hat tip: Morgan Spurlock and *Supersize Me*) could want to *promote its lifestyle* seems a bit counter-intuitive.

Part of the reason why McDonald's and Starbucks[50] have been dubbed lifestyle brands is that the term is often misused—as is the concept of lifestyle itself. Theorists have suggested that lifestyles are both a part of "modern" society and also a postmodern construction.[51] David Chaney explains, "Lifestyles are patterns of action that differentiate people" and that they are modern in that they are structured by social order.[52] Comparatively, lifestyles have also been seen as part of the flexible "consumer culture", the aestheticization of living and blurring the structure and conditions of what is generally understood as "modernity."[53] Usually, these lifestyles are communicated to us through tastemakers and other cultural intermediaries (as we discussed in Chapter 5).

Some brands will be dubbed a lifestyle brand when they sell more than one product: For example, Calvin Klein attempted to turn ck one, the name of its popular fragrance line, into a "lifestyle brand" by selling jeans, underwear and swimwear.[54] Theoretically speaking, someone could live in ck one using both its clothing and its fragrance, just like someone *could* both eat at McDonald's and wear its clothing. However, Stefania Saviolo and Antonio Marazza explain that a lifestyle brand is more than a brand that competes in different product categories. Instead, they suggest that lifestyle brands are a form of "symbol intensive brands" (i.e. brands with a strong identifiable meaning, myth or story) that offer social benefits to people, such as signaling their membership in a particular social group.[55] These brands signal other ideas about the wearer's way of life and/or consumption patterns, but all of a person's consumption does not have to be wrapped up in that particular brand. Consider German shoemaker Birkenstock for a moment. Birkenstock is well-known for comfort, even if the brand's shoe lines go in and out of fashion. However, Birkenstock is associated with a wealth of cultural connotations in relation to environmentalism and eco-consciousness. As a brand, the shoes emphasize their quality and use the outdoors to provide a general sense of wellness. While Birkenstock sells *some* accessories—like belts and skincare products—the brand's power comes from the connections of how a wearer *lives* not because it offers multiple products.

Insight: What Does Your Brand Stand For?

As discussed elsewhere in the chapter, brands are seen as adding symbolic meanings to products. Our understanding of the brand has advanced considerably from simply being a marker of quality to where brands stand for any number of qualities and commitments.[56] However, today, brands and the firms that create them are increasingly taking—or being *forced to take*—social positions on important issues. This may come in the form of eco-consciousness and environmentalism or in support of social justice, is often dubbed as being "socially conscious" and may or may not be a cynical ploy to increase sales. Consider the following brands:

TOMS Shoes was founded in 2006 with the premise that for every pair of shoes purchased, one will be donated to a child in need. TOMS signature

shoes were rather simple and plain looking, but came with the promise
of doing good. Today, the brand states that it has given away more than
60 million pairs of shoes, while expanding its philanthropy to eyewear, clean
water and maternal care.[57]

Nike made waves in 2018 when they kept supporting former football player
Colin Kaepernick and, in so doing, strongly supporting the Black Lives
Matter movement. As the quarterback for the San Francisco 49ers,
Kaepernick became a lightning rod for criticism when he refused to stand
for the national anthem: first by sitting, then later kneeling to protest police
brutality of Black people. Kaepernick donated cash to causes and started a
movement among athletes, but public opinion remained divided, even more
so as politicians weighed in. Despite Kaepernick not being on any team,
Nike still made him the face of a Just Do It ad campaign with the phrases:
"Believe in something. Even if it means sacrificing everything." While some
protested the move, others applauded Nike's decision, including actress
Jenifer Lewis who wore a Nike outfit to the Emmys in support of
Kaepernick.[58]

Figure 7.3 *"Controversial" Kaepernick. Nike stuck by Colin Kaepernick
even after he was released from the NFL because of his protest against
police brutality. © Donaldson Collection via Getty Images.*

Internet startup Everlane has promoted a "radical transparency" to its
clothing. This included working with suppliers to push for more sustainable

practices and making sure its clothes are not produced in sweatshops. While Everlane wasn't the first to use ethical factories—American Apparel had promoted this concept before—the transparency of its supply chain helped the brand extend its social consciousness in more directions. Everlane also allows customers to "choose" what they pay, where customers are presented with a base price, but can choose to give more to help with overheads and product development.[59]

What is clear is that consumers are expecting brands to take a stand on social and environmental issues and largely back their claims. Cosmetics companies like Lush and The Body Shop promote their animal-friendly and environmentally friendly products, respectively, while others like lingerie store Aerie push body positivity.[60]

Financial and Market Creations

Beyond the various cultural elements of brands, there is also a financialization that comes from tangible communication. Don Slater explains that it is impossible to separate economics from culture and, largely, the two are interdependent. Markets—themselves social constructs—are "malleable and fluid" while advertisers and brand managers help to define products, competitors and target audiences. As such, all of the tangible communications put out by a brand are not competing within a market but helping to define what the specific "market" is.[61] For example, the Hot Topic brand was closely associated with emo and goth subcultures through much of the 1990s and 2000s. In this way, it would have been competing with other retailers targeting those of "alternative" subcultures. While there are few "goth" retailers, Pac Sun and Zumiez, who both sell clothing in the skate and surf veins, would likely have been competitors. However, Hot Topic moved its offering toward hardcore fans of a variety of media, redefining itself and the market.[62]

Likewise, brands frequently develop their images in relation to one another in a process of associations and differentiation.[63] Some firms will own multiple brands that target different market segments. Carmaker General Motors is largely seen as pioneering this approach when it positioned its brands within a "Ladder of Success" hierarchy on social class.[64] Chevrolet was seen as the lowest tier—the "every person car," if you will—while Pontiac, Oldsmobile, Buick and Cadillac were all positioned as more expensive (and desirable). The idea was that as a Chevrolet driver grew up and earned more money, they would graduate into other General Motors vehicles, thus providing new goods for consumers, but also keeping them a General Motors customer for life. While General Motors discontinued the Pontiac and Oldsmobile brands during the 2008 financial crisis, this type of differentiation remains important (if simplified) in many car companies. Three obvious examples are the Ford/ Lincoln, Honda/Acura and Toyota/Lexus setups where lower and company namesake brands (e.g. Ford, Honda and Toyota) are intended for the mass market while the others are intended for a luxury market.

You're likely already thinking of some, but this happens with clothing companies too. Consider the brands owned by Gap Inc: Old Navy is positioned as cheaper and somewhat funkier than mid-tier Gap and business casual Banana Republic. Likewise, Abercrombie & Fitch more clearly defined its brands in terms of ages: Abercrombie was for children, Hollister for fourteen-to-eighteen-year-olds, Abercrombie & Fitch for high school and college demographic, and the short-lived Ruehl No. 925 was aimed at twenty-to-thirty-year-olds.[65] Brands have also used this differentiation to explore new markets; Abercrombie & Fitch and American Eagle moved into lingerie with the Gilly Hicks and Aerie brands, respectively, while Gap moved into athleisure wear with its Athleta brand.

Moreover, the valuation of a brand largely takes its tangible aspects— including those which are generally interpreted qualitatively—and makes quantitative calculations about them. In this way, it is the evaluation tools which help create a brand's value. It is also this perceived value that encourages brands to be bought, sold and reinvented throughout their lifetime.[66] However, this is not always a success. For example, early catalog retailer and later department store behemoth Montgomery Ward went bankrupt in 2001 closing all of its stores. However, the brand was revived in 2004 when a marketing firm purchased the intellectual property (i.e. the brand name and related trademarks) and relaunched the brand as an online retailer. In comparison, a similar fate befell Abercrombie & Fitch in its original incarnation as a sporting goods retailer back in the 1970s. However, it was later revived by Oshman's, taken over by The Limited and turned into the teen retailer we're familiar with today.[67]

The Use (and Abuse) of History

One area that contemporary brands continue to mine for meaning is the past: both actual and fictional. In its widest sense, a brand's heritage includes the history, structure and memory of the company behind it and continues to influence the organization and, through it, the public perception of the brand. Brand heritage can include moments when a brand took unprecedented action, such as when Johnson & Johnson pulled Tylenol from shelves over tainted pills, and ritualized actions, like the Walmart cheer which has been with the company since 1975. Fashion brands can also benefit from this history: Levi's uses its long history as a seller of blue jeans and the fact that it was first to patent copper rivets as support for the sturdiness and desirability of their current jeans.[68]

There are several different uses of history within a brand's heritage according to Brandford T. Hudson and John M.T. Balmer, they write that a brand's heritage can be formed in one of four ways. The first is structural heritage, where a brand is linked to a "pedigree" and moment of inception.[69] This can include dates of a brand's beginning or references to its founder, for example, Abercrombie & Fitch frequently referenced its founding in 1892 and the name itself references its founders, David T. Abercrombie and Ezra Fitch. The second is an implied heritage, which invokes the brand's longevity in support of superiority and can be displayed through brand museums, like The World of Coca-Cola Museum or the Guinness Storehouse Museum. The last two types of brand heritage take a bit of a liberty with the historical record. With reconstructed heritage, the past is somewhat reimagined and retold. For example, the contemporary Abercrombie & Fitch has little to do with the past, but that didn't stop the brand's tangible communications from invoking and repositioning Fitch in more teen-friendly ways. Lastly, mythical heritage invents the past and can be partly or wholly fictional.[70] This is what Abercrombie & Fitch attempted to do with their ill-fated Ruehl No. 925 brand, which told the fictional story of German, immigrant leathermakers, who opened a store in Manhattan in the mid-1800s. As *The New York Times* noted, the story was fictional right down to the address of the "original store."[71]

Some researchers have noted that by repurposing the past in this sense, a new type of temporality is being created as the heritage is using some of the source material, if you will, within different contexts and to new ends. The various uses of history can help sustain images, myths and stories, as well as supporting brand valuations; the fact that these "heritages" have the potential to be re-imagined, if not downright fictional, illustrates criticisms that advertising and the mass media have warped our understanding of reality.[72]

Advertising and branding have long been criticized as one of the most prominent aspects of capitalism and consumer culture, as well as being highly problematic in its own right.[73] Moreover, Sarah Banet-Weiser has explored how brands have moved into realms generally thought to be outside of commercial culture, such as politics, religion and art.[74] And while much of this criticism is undoubtedly true and should be addressed, advertising and branding remain powerful communicative forces, especially when it comes to clothing. These brands have become part of popular culture, appearing in films and television shows, but, by paying attention, we can use these messages to support companies and brands that align with our own values and use branded clothing and accessories to communicate with others.[75]

Further Reading

Much of the work done on advertising and branding has approached it from a business perspective and with practical advice. However, several business-oriented pieces are quite insightful with regard to aspects of communication. Articles like "The Product and the Brand" by Burliegh B. Gardner and Sidney J. Levy and "Symbols for Sale" solo-authored by Levy, date from the 1950s but provide good foundational work for understanding contemporary brands. Meanwhile, works like *Gender Advertisements* (Harper & Row, 1979) and *Advertising as Communication* (Routledge, 1982) were early to interrogate ads as a unique medium of communication.

Some more recent works in the vein of meaning-making for business purposes include *Culture and Consumption II* (Indiana University Press, 2005) by Grant McCracken, as well as Douglas Holt's article, "Why Do Brands Cause Trouble?" and book, *How Brands Become Icons* (Harvard Business Review Press, 2004). Around the same time, brands were getting a lot of critical attention. *No Logo* (Picador, 1999) by journalist Naomi Klein is probably the most critical and broadly influential, taking aim at advertising and branding as a tool of control and deception. More academically oriented critical works include *Brands: The Logos of the Global Economy* (Routledge, 2004) by Celia Lury, *Brands: Meaning and Value in Media Culture* (Routledge, 2006) by Adam Arvidsson, and *The Rise of Brands* (Berg, 2007) by Liz Moor. Both Lury and Arvidsson look at brands as a media object, while Moor focuses a bit more on history and aesthetics. Somewhat related to this vein of research would be several articles from an Actor-Network Theory view, including Lury's "Brand as Assemblage" and especially Joanne Entwistle and Don Slater's "Models as Brands" and "Reassembling the Cultural", both of which interrogate brands as a more complex network of practices as seen through the modeling industry.

The specific intersection of fashion and branding is somewhat less interrogated than it could be, but Joseph H. Hancock's *Brand/Story* (Bloomsbury, 2016) provides one of the most accessible reads on the topic and the article "Making the Marque" by Stephen M. Wigley, Karinna Nobbs and Ewa Larsen provides a rich, practical understanding of these processes. Moreover, the journal *Fashion Practice*, edited by Sandy Black and Marilyn DeLong, produced a variety of valuable articles about this intersection over the past decade including looking at the branding of urban menswear and designer collaborations.

1   Gardner, Burleigh B. and Sidney J. Levy (1955). "The Product and the Brand." *Harvard Business Review,* 33(2): 33–39.

2   Levy, Sidney J. (1959). "Symbols for Sale." *Harvard Business Review,* 37(4): 117–24.

3   Goffman, Erving (1979). *Gender Advertisements.* New York: Harper & Row.

4   Dyer, Gillian (1982). *Advertising as Communication.* New York: Routledge.

5   McCracken, Grant (2005). *Culture and Consumption II: Markets, Meaning and Brand Management.* Bloomington, IN: Indiana University Press.

6   Holt, Douglas B. (2002). "Why Do Brands Cause Trouble? A Dialectical Theory of Consumer Culture." *Journal of Consumer Research,* 29(1): 70–90.

7   Holt, Douglas B. (2004). *How Brands Become Icons: The Principles of Cultural Branding.* Boston: Harvard Business Review Press.

8   Klein, Naomi (1999). *No Logo.* New York: Picador.

9   Lury, Celia (2004). *Brands: The Logos of the Global Economy.* New York: Routledge.

10   Arvidsson, Adam (2006). *Brands: Meaning and Value in Media Culture.* New York: Routledge.

11   Moor, Liz (2007). *The Rise of Brands.* New York: Berg.

12   Lury, Celia (2009). "Brands as Assemblage: Assembling Culture." *Journal of Cultural Economy,* 2(1–2): 67–82.

13   Entwistle, Joanne and Don Slater (2012). "Models as Brands: Critical Thinking about Bodies and Images," in Joanne Entwistle and Elizabeth Wissinger (eds), *Fashion Models: Image, Text and Industry.* New York: Bloomsbury.

14   Entwistle, Joanne and Don Slater (2014). "Reassembling the Cultural: Models, Brands and the Meaning of 'Culture' After ANT." *Journal of Cultural Economy,* 7(2): 161–77.

15   Hancock, Joseph Henry II. (2016). *Brand/Story: Cases and Explorations in Fashion Branding.* New York: Bloomsbury.

16   Wigley, Stephen M., Karinna Nobbs and Ewa Larsen (2013). "Making the Marque: Tangible Branding in Fashion Product and Retail Design." *Fashion Practice,* 5(2): 245–64.

Figure 8.1 *Not so Clueless. Cher's (Alicia Silverstone's) computer in the film* Clueless *helped her pick out the perfect outfit. © CBS Photo Archive via Getty Images.*

8

Digital Communication, Social Media, and Mediatization

The now-classic Amy Heckling film *Clueless* is remembered for introducing the world to snappy catchphrases like "Whatever!" and "As if!" and memorable actors Brittany Murphy and Stacey Dash. However, one scene in the film that seemed rather fanciful has come to be a bit more predictive.

For those of you not in the know, *Clueless* was a 1990s retelling of Jane Austen's *Emma*. In it Cher, played by Alicia Silverstone, is trying to make her way through high school with her friend Dionne (Dash). Cher lives a relatively charmed life taking care of her high-powered lawyer father since her mother's passing. Like most high schoolers, Cher is concerned about getting her driver's license—even though she's a terrible driver—and interested in dating college men who she deems more mature than the "boys" in high school. Cher and Dionne decide to transform newcomer Tai (Murphy) and hijinks ensue as Tai's popularity eclipses Cher's leading to a turf war. Without giving too much away, there's a happy ending that borders on incest, but is rather sweet if you don't think about it too hard.

However, early in the film when Cher is getting ready to go to school, she enters her large, walk-in closet and she sits in front of her desktop computer, which helps her choose her clothing for the day. After scrolling through her options of tops and bottoms, she settles on a outfit only to be told "Mis-Match!"

when she hits the "Dress Me" button. Eventually, the computer suggests Cher settle on the yellow plaid outfit, with a pair of white Mary Janes with a slight kitten heel and thigh-high stockings—which the computer displays on a photo of her. Thankfully, the computer got it right since the outfit is now a 1990s movie icon.

However, more to the point, this scene was intended to be seen as overly extravagant to down-right fantasy, but today it seems like it might be coming to pass. Now, the Echo Look from Amazon allows users to take photos in different outfits and its algorithm will tell you which outfit "looks" better based on "fit, color, styling and current trends."[1] And, it's not just digital cameras: Uniqlo's San Francisco store includes a mirror that allows customers to change the color of the clothing they are trying on and captures a 360-degree image of them, while a mirror at Neiman Marcus allows you to take photos wearing different sunglasses and compare them side-by-side. Amazon has a patent for a mirror that allows you to try on virtual clothing, a step toward solving fit issues in online clothing retail.[2] It's easy to see how something that was far-fetched in the 1990s has now come to pass.

However, digitalization and technology didn't have to be so dramatic to greatly influence the fashion industry. Developments in communication technology from laptops and smartphones to blogging and social media have greatly shifted both personal communication and the media. This chapter will explore the ways technology has changed communication and the fashion system, revisiting some of the themes discussed in previous chapters. After exploring the history of the web, this chapter will look at how the digital communications reshaped ourselves and how we communicate with each other, before exploring its effect on the media industries and how it altered the landscape of advertising, branding, and retailing. Taken together, it's possible to see how technological developments have had a lasting impact on fashion communication.

Some History and Theory of the Web

The internet was first developed in the 1960s and 1970s for military purposes: the idea was to have an interconnected communication system that was dispersed and could continue to function in the event of a catastrophic attack.[3] Broadcasting, which at the time was the predominant way people could communicate with a group over long distances, was dependent upon physical towers to communicate, so if something happened to that tower, communication would be severely restricted. For example, during the attack on the World Trade Center on September 11, 2001, broadcast antennas were destroyed when the North Tower collapsed leaving local stations without a way to get their signals out. While both cable and the internet were already in wide usage at the time, the impediment of New York's broadcasting abilities spoke toward the original fears.

The internet was originally developed by a consortium of universities, including the University of California, Los Angeles (UCLA), Stanford University, the University of California, Santa Barbara and the University of Utah, along with the Advanced Research Projects Agency within the US Department of Defense. What came from those was a packet-switching network, meaning that when information was sent through this network, it would be broken down into small "packets" of information which were sent via the quickest path. The receiving computer would then reassemble the information. While the early internet would be used by the government and universities during the 1960s and 1970s, it would take until 1989 for commercial networks to get onto the internet, led by CompuServe and America Online (now called AOL).[4]

The early internet was somewhat different than what we're accustomed to now, in that it was largely text-based and largely consisted of email and listservs. Even early computer operating systems were text-based and it would take until Windows 95 for the graphic interface to be widely adopted. (There had been earlier versions of Windows and Apple had a graphic-based operating system for Macintosh computers, but all were bit players.) Eventually, the European Organization for Nuclear Research, known as CERN, would help to develop the "World Wide Web," which would standardize web addresses and coding language. This would allow the development of web browsers and led to the "internet" we're accustomed to using today.[5]

In the 1990s there was significant interest and growth in the internet as search engines like Yahoo, Excite and Lycos, email providers like Hotmail, and interest-driven space like the women's site iVillage dominated. Website building and blogging also grew in prominence: sites like Geocities, Tripod and Angelfire allowed users to build their own websites, while Live Journal and Xanga were dedicated blogging platforms. While many internet firms were successful and decided to go public (i.e. sell stock), many went bankrupt in what would be known as the "dot-com bubble" in the early years of the 2000s. Some firms consolidated after the bubble burst, while other firms like Google, Yahoo, eBay and Amazon would end up as the dominant internet sites.

However, in the 2000s there would be another revolution: social media. The simple social network site, Friendster, launched in 2002, and both LinkedIn and MySpace launched in 2003. This opened the door to the sites that still dominate the social media landscape like Facebook (originally launched for college students in 2004 and opened to everyone in 2006), YouTube (2005) and Twitter (2006).[6] There would be other hiccups along the way such as the check-

Seven Names to Know in Digital Fashion

Julia Wainwright (born 1957)—American tech entrepreneur, Wainwright founded the online luxury consignment site, The RealReal, which autheniticates and helps resell luxury goods. Wainwright had previously worked with the startup Pets.com, which went bankrupt, before founding The RealReal in 2011.[1]

Scott Schuman (born 1968)—After quitting his fashion career, Schuman became one of the earliest streetstyle photographers and started the blog, The Sartorialist, in 2005. Since then, he's expanded to Instagram and released a number of books, including one documenting fashion in India.[2]

Imran Amed (born 1975)—Canadian-British consultant-turned-entrepreneur, Amed is the CEO and editor-in-chief of the website The Business of Fashion, which he started in 2007. The site's profile was raised when it received $2.5 million in seed funding in 2013. It currently publishes fashion news and various industry reports, including the BOF 500 ranking the most influential people in fashion.[3]

Jennifer Hyman (born 1980)—American businesswoman, Hyman founded the tech startup Rent the Runway with partner Jennifer Fleiss.[4] The site allows customers to rent clothing individually or as part of a subscription service which has led to a host of more established retailers doing the same.

Arielle Charnas (born 1987)—Blogger-turned-influencer-turned-designer, Charnas is known for her brand Something Navy. Charnas first collaborated on a product line with US department store Nordstrom in 2017, where it reportedly sold $4 million one day, and later announced plans to develop her own, independent lifestyle brand.[5]

Tavi Gevinson (born 1996)—Young blogger who first created the blog Style Rookie in 2008 at age eleven. She would become a known commodity from her attendance at fashion shows and the creation of the online magazine, *Rookie*, which she founded when she was fifteen. *Rookie* closed in 2018.[6]

Kylie Jenner (born 1997)—Reality star-turned-businesswoman, Jenner first rose to prominence on the show *Keeping Up with the Kardashians*, which documented her famous family, including sister, Kim, and parents, Kris and Kaitlyn. Jenner used the show as a launch pad to become a successful social media influencer, and later created her own brand of makeup, Kylie Cosmetics.[7]

in-based Foursquare (now Swarm), the short-video-based Vine, and the anonymous geo-locator YikYak—all of which grew quickly in popularity only to fade shortly thereafter. Photo-based platforms including Pinterest (2009) Instagram (2010) and Snapchat (2011) would take off a bit later and are still in wide use as of this writing, as is TikTok (2016), the short video-based platform.

It's worth taking a brief pause here to explain the difference between social network sites and social media. Many of the sites we consider "social media" started out as social network sites that allowed users to create profiles and connect and communicate with their network.[7] However, as smartphone technology grew and these sites expanded and developed as publishing platforms, they helped build what we now call social media. Today, social media is generally understood to include social networking sites and other forms of internet-based media, which allow users to connect with others, produce content (in whatever form), communicate with others and customize their profiles.[8] We'll come back to some of these points in the following pages.

In many ways, the internet and digital communications are unlike any of the media that has come before it due to its flexibility and interactive nature. For example, Mark Poster noted that the internet is largely underdetermined, meaning that it can be used in a variety of ways. The fact that the "world wide web" became the dominant way for us to use the internet wasn't predetermined nor is it the only way for us to use it.[9] While many people might not have the technical knowledge to run their own servers, it remains a possibility. For example, the peer-to-peer file sharing network such as BitTorrent (currently) and Napster (formerly) do not use the world wide web; neither do smartphone applications. Both the openness in communication and the new capabilities provided by social media would have a profound impact on the ways in which we communicate.

Given the internet's vast underdetermination, its development—along with subsequent development of smartphones, thus making the "internet" portable, and the "apps" for phones and tablets—has had wide-reaching implications for a variety of industries. At the same time, "the internet" has become something of a catch-all term for all of the technological, communicative and media changes that have taken place over the past three decades or so. As such, while the rest of this chapter will use the internet to refer to increased usage of computers, smartphones and related technology, keep in mind that, unlike previous forms of media, the internet cannot be neatly summed up as one thing since it enables us to do *a lot* of things!

Updating Ourselves

In the early chapters of this book, we discussed how we come to know ourselves and how we use our appearance to communicate about ourselves. As such, it should come as no surprise that the internet had profound implications for the way we communicate. For example, theorists like Jenny Sundén and Tom Boellstorff have explored the internet as a sort of "virtual world" to see how we understand ourselves in that space. Sundén noted that, especially in the early days of the internet, users had to "type" themselves into existence,[10] otherwise they would not be known in that space. While that was certainly true for chat rooms and text-based applications, it remains true for things like social media—without creating a profile you don't officially exist in that network. Boellstorff took this a step further as he examined the avatar-based chat program Second Life and argued that what happens on the internet isn't all that different from what happens in the "real" world and, as such, used the terms "virtual world" for what happens on the internet and the "actual world" to denote what happens in the physical world. Still, Boellstorff noted that within Second Life people have the ability to portray themselves in whatever way they want,[11] something that still has implications for social media, where we continually put our best foot forward.

Russell W. Belk, who earlier theorized that material possessions help create our "extended selves", added that our social media profiles and the things we associate with also become part of our identity. Rather than consuming items privately or getting rid of them once they have been consumed, Belk pointed out that we frequently leave a digital trail online.[12] Some of this we might have done willingly: our social media profiles are likely littered with pictures from nights out with friends, special events with family and any number of other things. These photos are a digital memory of the places we've been, the things we've done and the clothing we wore. At the same time, digital algorithms help to keep a memory of the products we've looked at and purchased, which can help offer up ads to us later. While this isn't the same public performance as we post on social media (even though there have been some failed attempts at publicizing our purchases), it still has the ability to inform and shape our future consumption.

Likewise, our social profiles have enabled us to see ourselves in new ways. One method in particular that has gotten a lot of attention is the process of "branding" yourself. Researchers including Alison Hearn, Jefferson Pooley and Alice Marwick have all written about this phenomenon in various ways. Hearn suggests that the idea of branding ourselves took place within various realms—e.g. both reality television *and* social media—and indicates a blurring of capitalistic practices and the construction of the self. The use of social media platforms to promote or "brand" ourselves creates somewhat unique demands on our time that other people are monetizing. The implications of this raise important questions with regard to labor, production and consumption, which we'll come back to later in this chapter.[13]

Rather than seeing the internet as a wide open space for creating and expressing oneself (as Sundén and Boellstorff suggest) or as a primarily money-making venture (as Hearn and Marwick suggest), Jefferson Pooley lands somewhere in between. He notes that social media pushes people toward a "calculated authenticity" whereby people are doing, saying and acting in a manner to get others to like them. However, Pooley points out that this idea has long roots, citing Dale Carnegie's *How to Win Friends and Influence People,* which was published in 1936, as the epitome of this idea, but he also ties it to Erving Goffman's idea of performance[14] (which we talked about in Chapter 2). Played out on social media, Pooley argues that these platforms have forced a dichotomy between being authentically expressive and performing or branding ourselves. You may or may not spend a lot of time thinking about what you post to social media and what it makes you look like, but if you've ever done something "for the 'gram'" you've taken part in this strategic representation of yourself.

Updating the Media

Beyond the changes to how to present ourselves, the internet and social media has revolutionized the way we understand the "media." Prior to the development of the internet—and as we've more or less discussed in the previous chapters— each type of media was good for one thing. Books were good for saving and sharing information. Newspapers and magazines were able to print in a more timely way, and magazines were able to use new photography and design techniques. Films were for long visual storytelling; radio for audio productions, and television had the timeliness of radio and the visual of film. However, the internet allows us to do all those things, and more. This is an example of what we call media convergence, where text, photographs, video and audio all live side-by-side.

Jay Botler and Richard Grusin called this process "remediation" and argued that the internet is "mediating" older forms of media. In this telling, each new medium attempts to make things seem more real, while minimizing the fact that it is a medium. The internet put text, video and audio together in new ways; the basis of this—written language, photos and videos—are still ultimately the same and the "new media" (e.g. the internet) was simply *re*mediating the old media forms. Botler and Grusin used Marshall McLuhan's line, "The 'content' of any medium is always another medium. The content of writing is speech, just as the written word is the content of print, and print is the content of the telegraph." In short, this process didn't start with the internet and has been happening throughout history since art began to recreate the real world.[15]

Agnès Rocamora centered her attention on fashion blogs and explored both their hypertextual nature and their remediation. Hypertext—the ability to link within one text to another—is one of the ways the internet is different than older media. Where a printed text could simply reference another article, the hypertext helps to make the story interactive, allowing us to click and visit another page. (Anyone who has used the internet has likely done this, whether or not you've called it a hyperlink.[16]) Rocamora goes on to note that fashion blogging involved significant amounts of remediation of the fashion press. Bloggers frequently discussed fashion magazines or, barring that, used similar styles of photography and representation in their work. At the same time the publishing industry began to use the content produced in blogs, remediating that content in print.[17]

Beyond the remediation, the computers and internet created two other major implications for the media: convergence culture and the fall of the gatekeepers. Convergence culture was coined by Henry Jenkins and refers to how we make sense of the world through various different means. Jenkins suggests that the internet is not going to replace older forms of media—just like television didn't kill radio, film or newspapers—but that media, and consumers, would adapt and use the internet in various ways.[18] Convergence culture allows consumers to produce and rework popular culture and better interact with those producing it. Further, the rise of the internet, blogs and social media was seen as a leveling of the media playing field, allowing everyone to participate in production. Shorthandedly, this has been chalked up to a "fall of the gatekeepers"—or a way to circumvent the cultural authority figures we discussed in Chapter 5. Some of the rosiest predictions suggested that bloggers would take the place of journalists and the mass media since it was so easy to self-publish.[19] While some of the news predictions have come true—just look at social media during a "breaking news" event— much of this also undermined the ability of media professionals to keep out the crazies and has opened the floodgates to conspiracy theories and misinformation.[20]

Brooke Erin Duffy closely examined the way women's magazines responded to these changes and noted that rather than remaining print-media specific, these organizations were harnessing the convergence culture to become brands. For those who worked for the magazine, the internet has forced them to develop a broader skillset beyond writing, editing or design. Now, magazine editors not only edit for a print edition, but might work on a digital edition, run social media feeds, blogs and apps. Likewise, as magazines transition to the web, their readership has changed as well. As we noted back in Chapter 5, magazines were largely predicated on developing a narrow, target audience, such as girls between the ages of 14 and 18 (*Seventeen, Teen Vogue, CosmoGirl*) or high-class travelers (*Condé Nast Traveler*) to any number of demographic, psychographic, geographic or interest-based groups. However, many online audiences are younger than their print counterparts and there is little overlap between print subscribers and online readers. Moreover, there is also the potential for online content to be picked up by search engines, requiring editors to consider search engine optimization (SEO), and providing the opportunity for anonymous audiences to find the work. Finally, Duffy noted that magazines have attempted to harness the power of their audience including creating blogger networks to which people could contribute content on magazine sites.[21]

So You Want to be an Influencer?

While there are some blogs still around, much of the attention in recent years has moved onto *influencers*. You've likely heard the term tossed around, but maybe haven't figured out *exactly* what an influencer is. As journalist Taylor Lorenz points out, "influencer is a platform-agnostic term. It describes anyone who leverages social media to create a following and exerts influence over that following in order to make money."[22] While people like Kim Kardashian West, Kylie Jenner and Bella Hadid might come to mind when you think of an "influencer," the term would also include people like Arielle Charnas of Something Navy, and beauty blogger-turned-face-of-CoverGirl James Charles. Really, as Duffy points out, the media narrative has long been that "anyone" can become an influencer.[23] Too bad that's more fiction than fact.

Influencers stand at a unique intersection of personal identity and business considerations. As mentioned previously, social media has forced people into a type of contrived authenticity that can be "branded" in a certain way, while also appearing relatable. What gets lost in this process is that an influencer's content (whatever it might be) is time- and labor-intensive. While the exact process would depend on which platform people are involved in, for a budding influencer on Instagram the process might take the form of scouting locations, setting up photoshoots and lighting, taking the photos, editing the photos, writing captions, scheduling the post and then following up to interact with followers once the content is posted. And, despite myths to the contrary, this *isn't* just like posting to your everyday account. To be an influencer, you need to post content regularly and always be calibrating your posts for viewer interest.[24]

Various researchers have attempted to theorize labor in this sense, often with various terms and implications. To clarify, when people talk about "labor" they are usually referring to it in the Marxist sense where those without other resources sell their time in exchange for money. Traditionally, this has meant workers would produce a product that would be sold for more than its value in order to pay for the raw materials, the worker's wages and still have excess capital (i.e. money) for owners and/or upper management.[25] Until relatively recently, the production aspect—including its labor—was seen as one side of the equation and the people who purchased and used the goods that were made were seen as the "consumers" or those engaging in consumption. However, the internet and convergence culture has helped turn many people into both producers *and* consumers. This process is often referred to as the portmanteau (i.e. the combining of two words) prosumption and those who engage in it as prosumers.[26] Think about it: when we use social media, most of us are engaging in prosumption since we're likely posting text or photos while consuming that of our friends, families and anyone else we follow.

Outside of prosumption, there have also been various discussions of labor within this space. Since this labor is only producing communication, rather than a material good like a T-shirt or pair of shoes, it has been called immaterial labor.[27] Consider the following forms of immaterial labor:

- Entrepreneurial labor is where workers accept high-status jobs with low pay and potential personal financial risk for the possibility of future rewards. Working in fields like modeling and digital media usually comes with the understanding that the worker is an independent contractor working on their own, investing in their own careers, and not officially part of a larger organization.[28]

- Aspirational labor is where people produce content in the hope of getting paid in the future. Duffy found that those who engage in this type of labor—including bloggers and potential influencers—highlight authenticity, affective relationships and brand devotion.[29]

- Glamour labor is the work people do in all manners to make themselves seem "cool." This may be dieting, exercising or dressing in a certain way in the physical world, and posting statuses, photos and snaps to enhance your online persona.[30]

Regardless of how exactly we describe it, these various understandings of labor all suggest that we are working in an *unpaid capacity* with the hope of getting paid in the future. Some of this isn't new[31] and may seem commonsense to students who are already *laboring* in classes with the hopes of making money in the future. However, the key difference here is that while we participate within social media our work *is* being monetized. The firms behind Facebook, Twitter and TikTok are making money by selling ads against the content users create *for free*; this is how these companies have become billion-dollar firms.

The draw of becoming an influencer, of course, is that you get to do something you enjoy—and might even be doing anyway!—and get paid for it. Lorenz has pointed out that the number and types of influencers are ever changing and advertisers are spending millions of dollars to work with influencers to promote their products. While this has not escaped the attention of researchers, critics and even the government, some suspect there are deceptive marketing practices where influencers are being paid to support a product or brand, and keeping the payment a secret.[32] Beyond that, while some influencers *are* making money, the vast majority of social media users are not—even if they want to be! Those engaging in aspirational or entrepreneurial labor may never see a financial return on their time commitment or even their monetary investments. And, as Duffy has pointed out, many of the people banking on this strategy won't have a fallback in the traditional career fields as everything is moving in a precarious and unstable direction.[33]

Finally, an inherent question of fairness is rippling across the employment world. Creative industries from modeling to acting to journalism and public relations are making assessments of people's social media when they apply for jobs. Therefore, many are expected to put in time and energy to develop their personal brand even before they are hired. This is, essentially, unpaid labor people are being expected to do before they are even to be *considered* for a job. Despite it not being obvious, someone is making money from this work—just not really the creators.

Changes in Retail and Shopping

Where the internet and digital media has altered our personal communication and vastly affected the media landscape, it has had a pronounced effect on fashion advertising, branding and retailing. Some of this is directly related to the internet's communicative changes: brands need to be monitoring social media for customers' complaints and are often waiting for their "viral moment." Other changes have been somewhat indirect, including new retailers

Insight: Photo Manipulation in Advertising and Social Media

The fashion and beauty industries have long been criticized for promoting unrealistic standards for people to live up to, as has been touched upon in previous chapters. And, while the art of photo editing has long roots, digital manipulation of photos has become easier to do—initially through computer programs like Adobe Photoshop and more recently with apps like Facetune and even now standard Instagram filters. This has the potential to change the way we understand the world, but also undermines how exactly we learn about the world. One such "hoax" has been a shark—originally shot for *National Geographic*—which has "appeared" in places such as highways during hurricanes.[34] Still, much of the photo manipulation we see isn't fake in that way, just a gussied up version of reality.

However, US drugstore CVS took aim at digitally edited photos when it started a "Beauty Mark initiative" and a commitment to identifying visually altered advertising photos. Originally announced in 2018 with a target start date of 2020, the store partnered with beauty brands like Olay, L'Oreal and Maybelline to shoot and promote "realistic" images for in store and online.[35] As *Fast Company* noted, this was a step in a trend toward body positivity embraced by fashion brands like Aerie and spearheaded by Dove, and already legally required in countries like France.[36]

While editing our personal photos for social media may seem like second nature, some are suggesting that the process can cause body image problems. Dubbed "Snapchat dysmorphia," some doctors have suggested it is the cause of a rise in plastic surgery procedures. Some new filters aren't intended to make you look "better," but instead give you other means of self-expression. Some filters allow for metallic, glossy and even cyborg looks while other allow users to play with age and even gender—the last of which has been floated as therapeutic for trans people.[37]

coming onto the scene, largely made possible by the ease of the internet. In early 2019, one former startup, Amazon, became the world's most valuable company.[38] But, before we can get into the specific logistics, let's look at the big picture. The internet has made it possible to find, buy and even sell products around the world, in ways that were scarcely even imaginable a few decades ago.

Sociologist Sharon Zukin suggests that the ease of internet shopping has created a few paradoxes. The first is that the internet makes us shop more, despite its promises of making shopping easier and less time-consuming. While some facets of shopping (think: grocery shopping) have become easier as sites like Fresh Direct make it possible to purchase groceries, we spend more time on "shopping" for other products, like comparing models of televisions, reading reviews of cars or gadgets, or just browsing clothing sites. And, while Zukin wrote this before the rise of social media, think how easy it is for us to get pulled into "shopping" through advertisements on social media platforms and even through influencer posts. The second paradox is that the internet doesn't help marketing.[39] This has been an ongoing concern and has led some researchers to suggest the internet has allowed customers to cut through advertisements and see the "value" at hand.[40] And, perhaps unsurprisingly, people haven't been eager to embrace brands and advertising, rebuffing those that ventured into the social media realm and leading to an ongoing discussion of how brand managers can engage online. There are also other factors at play including algorithms, which can influence the advertisements and social media messages we see.[41]

As mentioned above, fashion retailers are starting to better utilize technology to help people try on and shop for their clothing. Uniqlo, the Japan-based clothier, has used technology in various ways. In addition to its mirrors, Uniqlo stores include an online shopping portal (Figure 8.2) that allows customers to order products from its website that might not be currently available in the store. And, in an attempt to be accessible in places where stores aren't always possible, such as airports, Uniqlo has begun selling select clothing through vending machines. In truth, these are just the latest steps stores are taking to make shopping and purchasing easier for customers. More commonly, stores like Walmart, Macy's and J.C. Penney allow customers to purchase online and pick up the products in store, and many retailers allow purchases online with free shipping, with both free and in-store returns.

Beyond moving many brick-and-mortar retailers toward click-and-mortar retailing, the internet has also given rise to various internet-only (or, perhaps it's better to say *originally* internet-only) retailers. These often target niche markets or offer a niche product—like the shorts companies Chubbies and Birddogs. Both originally sold variations of men's athletic shorts aimed at post-collegiate, but not yet "adult" (read: boring) men. Journalist Sam Grobart named those brands along with the likes of Criquet and Untuckit "brotailers" as they were targeting young men frequently dubbed as "bros."[42] While the internet provided a space for these brands to gain traction and a following, many have leapt into the physical realm. For, example Untuckit launched in 2011 with the idea of selling men's shirts that are shorter and thus aren't expected to be tucked into pants. The brand, founded by two Columbia University alums, was online only until 2015 when it opened a New York City store, following by stores in Chicago, Los Angeles and San Francisco in 2016. And, suit makers

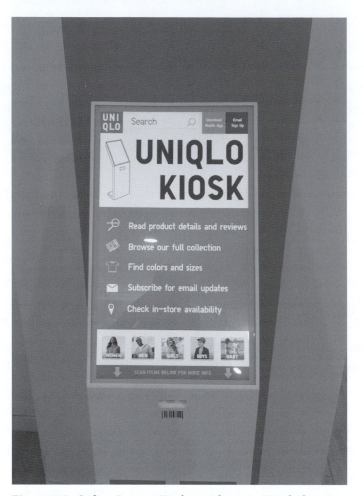

Figure 8.2 *Online Instore. Kiosks inside some Uniqlo locations allow customers to find items online while physically in the store.*

Bonobos and Indochino, eyeglass retailer Warby Parker, shoe retailer Allbirds, and more all-purpose clothiers like Outdoor Voices and Marine Layer have also made the leap into physical retail.[43]

The internet has also helped revolutionize the very idea of *buying* at all. Consider Rent the Runway. Founded in 2009, the service focused on renting one-time formalwear for women who would want new outfits for different events. One of its founders, Jennifer Hyman, said her inspiration for Rent the Runway came from seeing her sister overspend on formal dresses and, when questioned about it, her sister said since she was photographed in a dress and the picture was on Facebook she couldn't be seen wearing it again.[44] In short, Rent the Runway customers can select a garment—or garments—to rent for an amount of time, returning it when they are finished and receiving something new. The number of garments and the length of time customers can keep them depends on which level a customer buys into. The idea took off and spurred copycat offers from mass market brands as diverse as Vince, Ann Taylor, Express and Urban Outfitters, as well as inspiring the rental of furniture, home décor and small appliances.[45] While the renting of furniture wasn't new, per se (Rent-A-Center long predates this movement), Rent the Runway moved upmarket what had been seen as a déclassé practice, reserved for people with poor credit. These services were made possible by widespread internet and digital technologies, which allowed people to easily find and order items.

Another way the internet has helped change the face of retail has been with the growth of luxury consignment sites like The RealReal. While second-hand and consignment shops have been around for quite some time—they can be dated to Renaissance times,[46] if not before!—there has been a uptick in these stores in recent years. Sites like eBay spurred the buying and selling of all sorts of goods, and chains like Buffalo Exchange and Plato's Closet have been reselling clothing of all stripes. In these spaces, The RealReal has been a relative newcomer, not only reselling luxury goods, but also attempting to verify their authenticity. While the firm has been met with skepticism by some, and at least one lawsuit from Chanel, The RealReal's founder, Julia Wainwright, has suggested the site both introduces younger people to the world of luxury and helps to support the luxury market as a whole.[47]

One final way the internet has changed retail has been through a firm's ability to offer customizable products. While shoe brands like Adidas, Under Armour and Vans all provide customizations, Nike's offering dates back to 1999. Over time, even luxury brands like Burberry and Louis Vuitton have experimented with the idea; however, the process is costly for retailers and can take several weeks for delivery relegating the process to a niche market of people who care—and are willing to wait.[48]

Mediatization, Algorithms and Apps

Beyond the specific ways in which the internet has changed communication there remains some broad changes digital communication has brought that are shaping everyday life in various ways. Perhaps the most notable has been increased mediatization, or how media permeates and alters our world.[49] Rocamora had applied this concept to clothing and designers to argue that it has altered fashion shows and retail. Like some of the aforementioned digital changes within retailing, Rocamora suggests that retail establishments are becoming more like websites, using displays and digital screens to recreate product offerings and choices one would expect online. Likewise, Rocamora has suggested this has also played out with brands beginning to produce their own niche, media content. For example, the luxury online retailer Net-a-Porter launched their own weekly magazine, *The Edit*, which replicated a traditional glossy magazine online and made it "shoppable" or able to buy products featured with a few clicks.[50] On the flip side, magazines like *Vogue* and *GQ* have also created looks that can be purchased from various shopping websites.

At the same time algorithms—the computer code that works to show users content they might want or like—have also shaped how we shop. Websites and applications as diverse as Facebook, Google and Netflix, and even advertisements you might not notice, use information about us to target content. Within social media we have some control over the algorithm: we select which accounts to follow and how often we engage with them, and can tell the algorithms to show us information less often or not at all. However, beyond that we don't have much of a say. Instagram (and Facebook and Twitter) show content based on what the algorithm thinks you'll like and interact with—whether or not it's accurate.

Tarleton Gillespie notes that algorithms have six dimensions through which they can shape culture. They are:

- Patterns of inclusion—what content is included within a set of information.

- Cycles of participation—what the algorithms intend to get users to do.

- Evaluation of relevance—how algorithms determine if information is relevant to users.

- Promise of objectivity—an implied assumption that the algorithm is impartial.

- Entanglement with practice—how algorithms respond to user actions.

- Production of calculated publics—how users understand themselves and those around them as displayed through the algorithm.[51]

On the whole, these elements are pretty self-explanatory and they could easily be mapped on to fashion: whether that is fashion media or shopping for clothes. Algorithms in social media and search engines determine what articles we might see from *Vogue* or other producers. At the same time, shopping algorithms—say from Gap or Amazon—determine what items to show you based on your purchasing or browsing habits.

More critically, though, algorithms should not be understood to be an objective application. They are constantly evaluating users based on the information provided to them and—at the end of the day—algorithms are biased in whatever way programmers create them. Think about it this way: in Chapter 5 we discussed how tastemakers help shape which stories are written and *how* they are written. Here, the coders who create algorithms determine whether you're provided with the information *at all*. This can lead to some delicate territory if coders aren't careful with what they are producing.[52] Likewise, this underscores the need for diversity among coders—a topic that has frequently been overlooked by the tech industry.

As the previous pages have showed, the internet and digitalization has transformed the way we communicate in untold ways. However, one of the latest developments has been the use of smartphone applications—"apps" for short. If you have a smartphone, you likely use apps all the time, but may not give them much thought. Developed by any number of developers and with some pre-loaded on our phones, apps seem natural to the smartphone environment. Still, they do present special considerations given the ease with which they can be attained and used (in comparison to more traditional software) and how they are created by third-party firms and distributed through "stores" moderated by the likes of Apple and Google.[53]

Again, apps have affected fashion in different ways—many of which have yet to be interrogated by researchers. However, media production companies have developed their own apps in order to entice users, even as more utilitarian apps, like Apple News, have begun offering magazine content to subscribers. At the same time, stores across the fashion spectrum have developed their own apps, which makes shopping easier. Finally, apps have given rise to a new set of casual gaming that has united fashion, gaming and celebrity culture. For example, in *Covet Fashion*, users create outfits using brand-name garments; these looks are then pitched against outfits created by other players. And, in *Kim Kardashian: Hollywood*, where users help turn themselves into A-list celebrities through jobs and appearances, players are able to "buy" clothing and accessories for their characters.

Further Reading

As this chapter attempted to illustrate, the rise of the internet and digital media has resulted in so many changes that it is nearly impossible to cover all of them in one book. However, several books and articles are useful on various aspects of these changes. *Point of Purchase: How Shopping Changed American Culture* by Sharon Zukin (Routledge, 2005) is a good sociological foundation for shopping as the internet was beginning and Chapter 9 of the book specifically deals with the internet. Similarly, Elizabeth Wissinger's *This Year's Model: Fashion, Media and the Making of Glamour* (NYU Press, 2015) does a great job of linking contemporary culture, including digital media usage, to the rise of the 1990s supermodel.

Russell W. Belk's article, "Extended Self in a Digital World" is useful for thinking about how we understand and create ourselves in the digital realm. Moreover, the book *Status Update: Celebrity, Publicity and Branding in the Social Media Age* by Alice E. Marwick (Yale University Press, 2013) contains a good interrogation of the self-branding phenomenon, as do Alison Hearn's article, "'Meat, Mask, Burden': Probing the Contours of the Branded 'Self'" and chapter, "Brand Me 'Activist.'" Brent Luvaas' *Streetstyle* (Bloomsbury, 2017) offers a slightly different perspective by taking an auto-ethnographic lens to becoming a streetstyle blogger and, along the way, he interrogates some of the issues that come with this terrain. Two books by Brooke Erin Duffy are also insightful at the intersection: *(not) Getting Paid to Do What You Love* (Yale University Press, 2017) specifically looks at the motivation and laboring of influencers, while *Remake, Remodel: Women's Magazines in the Digital Age* (University of Illinois Press, 2013) provides a nice overview of how magazines have been reimagined for the digital realm. Agnès Rocamora has provided perhaps the most substantial theorizing of digital fashion media. Her articles "Hypertextuality and Remediation in the Fashion Media: The Case of Fashion Blogs" and "Mediatization and Digital Media in the Field of Fashion" interrogate how media changes have altered the fashion press and fashion retailing, as does her chapter, "Mediation and Digital Retail," in *The End of Fashion: Clothing and Dress in the Age of Globalization*, which expands on the aforementioned articles.

Additionally digital media-oriented books such as *The Daily You* by Joseph Turow (Yale University Press, 2011), and *The Social Power of Algorithms* (Routledge, 2018) and *Popular Culture and Media: The Politics of Circulation* both by David Beer (Palgrave Macmillan, 2013) help explain some of the outcomes of algorithmic culture as does Nicholas Carah's various articles, including "Algorithmic Brands: A Decade of Brand Experiments with Mobile and Social Media." Finally, the edited collection, *Appified: Culture in the Age of Apps* by Jeremy Morris and Sarah Murray (University of Michigan Press, 2018) begins the discussion of "app culture." While these books don't address fashion directly, they will undoubtedly influence how we think about digital fashion media moving forward.

1 Zukin, Sharon (2005). *Point of Purchase: How Shopping Changes American Culture.* New York: Routledge.

2 Wissinger, Elizabeth (2015). *This Year's Model: Fashion, Media and the Making of Glamour.* New York: New York University Press.

3 Belk, Russell (2013). "Extended Self in a Digital World." *Journal of Consumer Research,* 40(3): 477–500.

4 Marwick, Alice (2013). *Status Update: Celebrity, Publicity, and Branding in the Social Media Age.* New Haven, CT: Yale University Press.

5 Hearn, Alison (2008). "'Meat, Mask, Burden': Probing the Contours of the Branded 'Self.'" *Journal of Consumer Culture,* 8(2): 197–217.

6 Hearn, Alison (2012). "Brand Me 'Activist,'" in *Commodity Activism: Cultural Resistance in Neoliberal Times.* New York: New York University Press.

7 Luvaas, Brent (2016). *Street Style: An Ethnography of Fashion Blogging.* New York: Bloomsbury.

8 Duffy, Brooke Erin (2017). *(not) Getting Paid to Do What You Love: Gender, Social Media and Aspirational Work.* New Haven, CT: Yale University Press.

9 Duffy, Brooke Erin (2013). *Remake, Remodel: Women's Magazines in the Digital Age.* Champaign, IL: University of Illinois Press.

10 Rocamora, Agnès (2012). "Hypertextuality and Remediation in the Fashion Media: The Case of Fashion Blogs." *Journalism Practice,* 6(1): 92–106.

11 Rocamora, Agnès (2017). "Mediatization and Digital Media in the Field of Fashion." *Fashion Theory,* 21(5): 505–22.

12 Rocamora, Agnès (2019). "Mediation and Digital Retail," in A. Geczy and V. Karaminas (eds), *The End of Fashion: Clothing and Dress in the Age of Globalization.* New York: Bloomsbury.

13 Turow, Joseph (2011). *The Daily You: How the New Advertising Industry is Defining Your Identity and Your Worth.* New Haven, CT: Yale University Press.

14 Beer, David (2018). *The Social Power of Algorithms.* New York: Routledge.

15 Beer, David (2013). *Popular Culture and New Media.* New York: Palgrave Macmillan.

16 Carah, Nicholas (2017). "Algorithmic Brands: A Decade of Brand Experiments with Mobile and Social Media." *New Media & Society,* 19(3): 384–400.

17 Morris, Jeremy Wade and Sarah Murray (2018). *Appified: Culture in the Age of Apps.* Ann Arbor, MI: University of Michigan Press.

Figure 9.1 *Record Breaking Sweater. Nirvana frontman Kurt Cobain takes a break from performing during* MTV's Unplugged *in 1993. © Frank Micelotta Archive.*

9

Fashion, Clothing and/as Art

Throughout the 1990s, *MTV Unplugged* was one of the music channel's mainstays. Artists from Eric Clapton and Bob Dylan to Mariah Carey and Shakira appeared on the show playing acoustic versions of their hits. In November 1993, the grunge band Nirvana played an unplugged show where they mostly performed lesser-known songs and covers. During the performance, lead singer Kurt Cobain played an acoustic guitar while sitting on a stool in front of a simple mic. The set up was typical for the *Unplugged* shows. Cobain's clothing spoke to his signature grunge look: he wore a pair of jeans, with a white graphic T-shirt, under an unbuttoned, striped button down and an olive green acrylic and mohair cardigan.

The show would go on to be one of Cobain's final television appearances; he would die by suicide almost five months after the *Unplugged* taping on April 5, 1994.

Months later, the *Unplugged* performance would be released as a stand-alone album in November 1994, and it would peak at #1 on the Billboard 200.[1] Cobain's untimely death would turn him into something of a rock music legend, joining the ranks of Janis Joplin, Jimi Hendrix and Elvis Presley—who all died during the height of their popularity. While Cobain's wife, Courtney Love, and bandmate Dave Grohl, would go on to find success with the bands Hole and Foo Fighters, it is Cobain who is remembered as the grunge pioneer.

More than two decades later, Cobain's possessions fetch large sums in auctions. A custom-made Fender guitar, which had been on display at the

Rock and Roll Hall of Fame, sold for $340,000. And, Cobain's olive green sweater—*unwashed* since the 1993 performance—initially sold for $137,500 during a November 2015 auction. Then, in May 2019, a different sweater Cobain wore in his final photoshoot with Nirvana sold for $75,000 dollars. And, five months later, the sweater worn during the *Unplugged* appearance would sell for $334,000, making it the most expensive sweater ever sold at auction. The president of the auction house called the sweater, "the holy grail of any article of clothing that he ever wore" and is emblematic of how "rock & roll memorabilia has become an investment." In fact, the owner who bought the sweater in 2015 had every intention of carefully preserving the garment and re-selling it.[2]

While a stained and unwashed sweater we've saved from 1993 might not be worth nearly the same amount, there is a form of cultural prestige associated with Cobain and his once-worn sweater. The sweater now signifies Cobain's musical talents and influence, and could easily be exhibited in rock museums. However, there's a collective reification of both the power and value of the sweater—one that would not hold for our individual items. In the previous chapters, we've explored how clothing can be a means of communication and the ways in which we communicate *about* clothing, largely how the media helps create the fashion system. This chapter will take a slight turn from the others and will look specifically at the intersection of art and clothing. While there have been volumes written about fashion and art, their relationship remains somewhat complex since neither term has clear boundaries. And, while we'll get into that in the coming pages, this chapter is also about something different: cultural prestige.

Designating something as "art" changes the way we understand it and communicate about it. Calling something art or *an art* confers a status on it and its related actions, thereby giving it greater cultural prominence and prestige. This status is generally given to works by cultural institutions including museums, critics and award organizations.[3] Generally (although certainly not exclusively nor uncontroversially) films that win "Best Picture" by the Academy of Motion Picture Arts and Sciences, and the "Best Song" and "Best Album" award by The Recording Academy are seen as more prestigious products of the year. Over the course of history, the fashion industry has presented a variety of awards, previously, the Neiman Marcus Fashion Award and the Coty American Fashion Critics' Award were presented for decades, while both The Fashion Awards, overseen by the British Fashion Council, and the Council of Fashion Designers of America's Fashion Awards are still presented annually.

This chapter picks up on some of the themes of how we understand *fashion* from Chapter 4 and our understanding of tastemaking from Chapter 5 to look at how these ideas intersect with cultural institutions. Clothing, especially the pieces that are regarded as *fashion*, have inhabited a strained space within the art world straddling craft and more celebrated works of art. Clothing and garments are physical pieces of culture that had found their way into museums prior to more fashionable garments, but fashion exhibits are increasingly common in institutions of serious art. The Metropolitan Museum of Art in New York has gained prominence for its annual fashion gala and exhibit, and it is not uncommon for more regional venues to feature fashion exhibits; for example, museums in the Dallas-Fort Worth area (not widely known a fashion center) featured two major fashion exhibits in 2019 alone.

At the same time, art is frequently used as a form of inspiration for both couture and mass market designs. While seeing a relationship between high-end clothing and art is common,[4] today brands like Uniqlo and Vans have partnered with museums to use famed artwork within their designs. This has the dual benefit of raising the profile of these brands, but also circulating representations of the artwork more widely. It's a joint branding exercise that offers prestige on both sides of the relationship.

To understand the linkage of clothing, art and cultural prestige, this chapter first explores what art *is* and how we come to understand that. From there we can turn toward the various ways fashionable clothing design and production can be understood in different ways and how fashionable clothing has become a museum object. Afterward, we'll tackle how visual displays within museums and department stores align, before briefly turning our attention to music's influence on fashion. Finally, we'll end with a discussion of promotional culture and how art and clothing both operate under its logic to different ends.

What is Art?

Whether or not you've given it much thought, you undoubtedly have interacted with or at the very least experienced art in some way. Frequently, art is considered to be a visual medium like a drawing, a painting or a sculpture. Think about the types of activities you might have engaged in when taking a high school "art" class. Maybe you discussed color theory, practiced sketching or learned about famous works. This is different than what you might learn in "music" class, which is also an art, but not a visual art. In this way, we usually see art in two ways: first as a process and second as a specific work. For example, painting, drawing and sculpting are all actions which can lead to artworks in the form of paintings, drawings and sculptures. Now, certainly not all of these products are understood as a "work of art," which is generally something held in high regard. Consider works like Leonardo Da Vinici's Mona Lisa or Claude Monet's Water Lilies; both are held in high esteem and, as such, are considered works of art. In this way art is a "honorific title" given to some projects and not others.[5]

Visual art—and what constitutes art in this sense—is often linked to aesthetics and taste. Immanuel Kant suggested that art is something objective speaking not only to our individual taste, but also to a larger understanding of beauty. He believed that these determinations could be made in a detached or objective sense and understood universally. This is the basis for the role of critics and criticism as unbiased or objective observers. Kant believed that aesthetic judgements could only be made through visual and aural means since they are the only senses that are applicable at a distance; we must be much closer to items to touch, taste and smell them.[6]

In comparison, John Dewey believed that we could determine art through the "experience" of it. Rather than seeing art as something that is rarified and placed in museums or other establishments, Dewey notes that art was once seen as more integral to everyday life. In moving art from the realm of the everyday and toward more exclusive sittings, these works lose their power of expression. Instead of a work of art being enjoyed for what it communicates, it becomes subject to external conditions which influence our understanding of it. Art, in Dewey's telling, should not be sectioned off from the public and everyday aspects of life, but art should help to create experiences for the general population.[7] In this light, art isn't working toward an objective aesthetic to be admired, but rather is something each person can experience. As such, something like Michelangelo's statue of David and Andy Warhol's prints can be considered art, but so can Banksy's various contemporary art installations and the performance art by Marina Abramović.

Sociologist Howard Becker adds another layer to this discussion when he notes that many or most works of art are made as part of an "art world" that brings it to fruition. In this way, art isn't just an idea that can be created by a singular artist, but rather is a complex process that helps materialize that idea.[8] Think about it: a painter may have the idea for a portrait they'd like to paint, but they will generally purchase the paint, brushes and canvas (rather than making these elements themselves). In more intangible art forms, like film, television and music, a host of people support the pieces. Not only those who work specifically on the film, show or album, but also the people who manufacture and distribute it as well. And, in the contemporary world where work is distributed digitally, those who code websites and run online stores would also be part of this process.

Meanwhile, critical theorist Walter Benjamin argued that mass production specifically worked against the creation of art. In this understanding, art is dependent upon the experience of it: seeing the original Mona Lisa is an impactful experience because of its originality. However, once we start making reproductions or prints of the Mona Lisa, it no longer has the same artistic value because it is commonplace and viewed outside of its intended setting. For Benjamin, it was the reproduction that undermined the significance of the work.[9]

Despite these various discussions, it is important to refer back to something we touched upon back in Chapters 4 and 5. Taste is both subjective and largely socially constructed. This means that what was understood to be good is determined by those in power, usually those with significant economic, social and cultural capital. These ideas are created and shared to the general population through a process of cultural intermediation that involves a variety of jobs such as news reporters, critics and advertising executives, among others. As such, Kant's ideas of an "objective" beauty crash against social realities where aesthetic judgements run up against any number of obstacles, including racism, sexism and classism.[10]

Clothing, Art Worlds and Artification

The intersection of clothing, fashion and art has remained a fraught discussion, which has its roots in the internal divisions of those working within fashion studies. Some, like Anne Hollander, hold that clothing is a form of art in a Kantian sense, and because the image of how we dress is of paramount importance, the way fashion literally feels is a lesser concern. Others have generally seen production of clothing as more of a skill or useful craft than an art. And, in many ways, this debate goes back to the earliest couturiers. Designers like Charles Frederick Worth and Paul Poiret used art within their salons to elevate design and clothing making to a skilled craft. Poiret went so far as to disavow the commercial aspects of fashion as clothing and insisted that his designs were something more.[11] In comparison, Coco Chanel believed she was creating a commodity for sale, not a higher art form.

Beyond art worlds requiring various roles and jobs to create art, they also establish conventions used to produce the art. Becker uses the example of the music stanza as a convention,[12] but we could easily see it through the famed VHS/Betamax debate or even digital file formats. These conventions and processes can generally be determined through strict delineations put in place by a guild, other groups *or* by the workings of the market economy. The latter process has been at work regarding home videos—first with the VHS/Betamax battle back in the 1970s and more recently with Blu-ray and HD DVDs in the 2000s. While market structures largely dictate conventions today, we can see the examples of guilds or other formal structures in two places: professional organizations and schools. Organizations like the Academy of Motion Picture Arts and Sciences or the Council of Fashion Designers of America help to set the standards of industries by declaring genres and award categories.

Additionally, the educational system helps to create classifications and bestow prestige. Angela McRobbie called art schools "legitimizing agencies"[13] because of the power these institutions have on various forms of art. Within the UK art schools, fashion was generally understood in the same vein as dressmaking—a feminized craft that was tied to industry and of a lower class than the fine arts taught within schools. In order for fashion to be taken seriously within the academy, it had to separate itself from the more practical dressmaking and begin to separate the various elements that go into the fashion system: design, production and manufacturing. This divide would ultimately take root within schools as different courses of study would tackle the differing aspects of the fashion system. McRobbie classifies the resulting approach to fashion as professional, managerial and conceptual.

- Professional fashion is geared toward upscale production—including but not limited to haute couture—that aims to be edgy and high end.
- Managerial fashion is that which is geared toward creativity within the business world and jobs beyond design, including marketing, publicity, styling and forecasting.
- Conceptual fashion is that which is intended to be creative without concern for the business side of the industry.[14]

Conceptual fashion has been the most useful in raising the status of fashion as an art form both inside and outside the academy. In fact, some have argued that creativity within such fashion designs—not truly intended to be "practical or utilitarian"—ultimately proves that fashion *is* an artform.[15] Moreover, some of these designs have been intended to critique the fashion system of social structures as a whole. Francesca Granta's work on experimental fashion argues that designers and artists like Rei Kawakubo, Leigh Bowery and even Lady Gaga have used clothing to critique normative discourses and bodily presentations. Examples like Kawakubo's padded dresses and Leigh Bowery's drag performances question the materiality and artifice of our personal appearance.[16] When used in this way, clothing and appearance aims to be a more meaningful expression than the "consumable" way we generally think of clothing.

Some fashion designers may not be looking to earn the status of artist, but rather use their designs to "access a form for symbolic capital that improves their status as fashion designers," as Diana Crane writes.[17] In some of these cases, the looks aren't meant to move fashion at all, but rather display creativity and skills. Raising the symbolic capital of the designer can be useful for career prospects of individuals or to make a fashion house or brand more notable. This can also help sales of related, but more mass market ready-to-wear lines and other products including licensing for perfume and accessories.

Seven Names to Know in Museum Curation

Diana Vreeland (1903–1989)—After being dismissed from *Vogue* in 1971, Vreeland's friends would help her land a position as a consultant for the Costume Institute at the Metropolitan Museum of Art in New York. Despite a lack of formal education, she helped to establish fashion as a formidable part of museum work—even if some of her interpretations were not historically accurate.[1]

Richard Martin (1946–1999)—American curator and scholar who led the Met's Costume Institute from 1993 until his death. Martin took a more scholarly approach to fashion and wrote more than 100 scholarly papers and multiple books on fashion.[2]

Harold Koda (born 1950)—American curator best known for heading the Met's Costume Institiute from 2000 to 2016. Koda worked with Vreeland, Martin and Bolton at various times, and curated exhibits such as *Giorgio Armani* at the Guggenheim in 2000 and *Charles James: Beyond Fashion* in 2014 for the Met.[3]

Valerie Steele (born 1955)—American researcher and curator, Steele has been the director of the Museum at FIT in New York since 1997. Steele has curated more than 25 exhibits during her tenure and has written more than two dozen books. Steele is also the founder and editor-in-chief of the first scholarly journal of fashion studies, *Fashion Theory: The Journal of Dress, Body and Culture.*[4]

Andrew Bolton (born 1966)—Wendy Yu Curator at the Met's Costume Institute who became curator-in-chief after Koda. Bolton has curated some of the most successful fashion exhibits including 2011's *Alexander McQueen: Savage Beauty* and *Heavenly Bodies: Fashion and the Catholic Imagination* in 2017, which would become the most attended exhibit in the museum's history. Bolton previously worked for the Victoria & Albert Museum.[5]

Nathalie Bondil (born 1967)   Former executive director and head curator at the Montreal Museum of Fine Arts from 2007 until 2020, Bondil has designed exhibitions on music, cinema and fashion. Bondil's sudden firing caused a stir among the art world.[6]

Oriole Cullen (born 1977)—Irish curator, Cullen is currently the Victoria & Albert Museum's curator of fashion and textiles. Cullen previously worked at the Museum of London and has curated exhibits like *The London Look: Fashion from Street to Catwalk* and *Christian Dior: Designer of Dreams*.[7]

Crane suggests that fashion designers can challenge the accepted norms in five different ways. The first is the use of unconventional materials for clothing. A notable example of this, remains Coco Chanel who was able to skirt French laws on couture houses by using jersey instead of more acceptable materials for clothing. The second means is through transgression, which essentially is violating underlying conventions. This is what the experimental fashion, discussed by Granta, does. The third, subversion, satirizes clothing and its place within contemporary society. Jeremy Scott's use of fast food symbols within his 2014 Moschino Ready-to-Wear line would be a prominent example of this. Surrealism, connecting clothing and fashion with other material items is the fourth means to challenge norms. Elsa Schiaparelli is perhaps best known for her surrealist styles, such as her high-heeled shoe hat which was inspired by the painter Salvador Dali.[18] Finally, pastiche, a postmodern form of production whereby styles from different periods are brought together, is the fifth way to challenge conventions. The flamboyant styles of Madonna and Cyndi Lauper in the 1980s are sometimes chalked up to pastiche, but could also be said of Lagerfeld's updating and reworking of Chanel's classic designs.

The process of recognizing something that was not previously considered to be art, well, an *art*, is called "artification." Crane notes that the process of artification has wide implications for the artist and cultural institutions associated with the new art. These implications include changes of who engages in the practice, changes in the pieces of art, the creation of organizations to promote said art, and the status of the art within governmental and heritage organizations.[19] Specifically, as a creative undertaking begins to be seen as art, it becomes embedded within cultural institutions (such as museums and schools), which require the "artists" or those participating within the art form to possess more cultural and social capital, frequently developed by increased formal education. Tailoring and dressmaking, from its early days, was not held in high regard and the trade was often passed from one expert to another. Early designers were often apprentices who then went on to run their own houses. However, today, a host of formal institutions train wannabe designers, including the Fashion Institute of Technology in New York and Central Saint Martin's College of Art and Design in London. This is a formalization of education practices that previously were completed under the tutelage of established experts in the field.

Clothing, Fashion and the Museum

Beyond schools and universities, museums are another important cultural establishment that can work toward artification. Museums have acknowledged clothing and dress as important cultural artifacts dating back to the late 1700s, however, the first *fashion* exhibits generally were displayed within the 1900s. Exhibiting "fashion" or fashionable clothing, rather than national costumes or historic artifacts, would grow in popularity throughout the intervening century.[20] While this would come with some detractors, fashion exhibits became more extravagant and popular over time. Marie Riegels Melchior suggests this change indicated a transformed view of museology, or the practice of organizing museums. Early museums had a "dress museology" whereby individual garments were to be collected for the social and cultural significance. Such a perspective was interested in the conventional aspects of the textiles, and understanding clothing within the context of a given cultural and historic moment was prioritized.[21]

The museology perspective would shift dramatically in the 1970s, first with the Victoria & Albert Museum's *Fashion, an Anthology by Cecil Beaton* which was curated by the famed photographer himself, and later with exhibitions at The Metropolitan Museum of Art in New York, which former *Vogue* editor Diana Vreeland would consult on.[22] Vreeland proved to be a lightning rod for criticism during her time at the Met and her impact remains somewhat contested today. Vreeland, as discussed in Chapter 5, worked with *Harper's Bazaar* and as the editor-in-chief at *Vogue* before becoming a special consultant to The Met's Costume Institute. Vreeland was not a trained curator and was more interested in the spectacle of fashion than the reality of the garments or the exhibits; she has been quoted as saying, "I don't want to be educated . . . I want to be drowned in beauty!"[23]

There were two major criticisms of Vreeland's exhibits. First, they were not intended to be historically accurate. At some points, Vreeland styled historic Chinese clothing with a 1980s aesthetic and had Hollywood costumes copied when she couldn't locate original items. The second criticism was the museum's turn toward consumerism. In particular, Vreeland staged an exhibit of the work of Yves Saint Laurent—the first notable museum exhibit of a living designer; critics suggested the show was little more than a full scale advertisement for the YSL brand.[24]

Despite the criticism, Vreeland is seen as a pivotal figure in regard to how clothing is displayed within a museum. Her exhibits worked to shake the stodginess of clothing exhibits and excited the public. While curators since have paid more attention to accuracy, some even concede that, despite her indifference to history, Vreeland captured the feeling of the fashion at a given time.[25] Following in Vreeland's footsteps, curators Richard Martin, Harold Koda and, most recently, Andrew Bolton, have continued to create spectacular fashion exhibits at the Met. Still, questions remain over the interpretation and representation of fashion within a museum.[26]

Fashion exhibits, along with their spectacle and allure, have helped to move museums toward what Melchior described as a "fashion museology". In this sense, museums need to seem contemporary rather than a cultural repository of artifacts and information. Staging or attracting dynamic fashion exhibits is one way to do that. While the Met has long been considered the "gold standard," fashion exhibits have helped propel the museum into the popular imagination. Within the past decade, the Met Gala, in support of the Costume Institute, has become a star-studded, red carpet event and was featured in the documentary *The First Monday in May* (2016) directed by Andrew Rossi. *Vogue* editor Anna Wintour has been chairwoman of the gala since 1995 and has been instrumental in raising money for the Costume Institute. (Wintour's support has been so successful that in 2014 the Met renamed the Costume Institute the Anna Wintour Costume Center.) The Met Gala, now annually held on the first Monday of May, ushers in a fashion exhibit for the museum. Several of these exhibits have gone on to become some of the most attended exhibits in the Met's history, including 2018's *Heavenly Bodies*, which was the most visited exhibit ever. Others, like *Alexander McQueen: Savage Beauty* and *China: Through the Looking Glass*, also remain among the most viewed exhibits at the museum.[27]

Insight: Uniqlo's Nights at the Museums

Museums are a repository of cultural history and memory, but they ultimately take a lot to maintain. It takes a serious amount of financial investment to purchase and keep a collection, let alone maintain the building and appropriate staff. While some museums—such as the Smithsonian museums in the US, the Victoria & Albert and the British Museum—are government-run and sponsored, others, such as the Metropolitan Museum of Art are not. These museums generally rely on a mix of private donations from wealthy benefactors and entrance fees to keep them going. In New York, both the Met and the Museum of Modern Art now cost $25 USD to enter, which caused some hand-wringing at the time. Of course, museums attempt to balance their accessibility with their costs, not wanting to prohibit people from experiencing collections.

Enter corporate sponsorships.

Uniqlo, the Japanese clothier, has entered into agreements with both New York's Museum of Modern Art and the Tate Modern in London. Since 2013, Uniqlo has sponsored Free Fridays at the MoMA, taking over the partnership from department store Target. And, in 2016, the store began sponsoring monthly late-night programs at the Tate, dubbed "Tate Lates." Both endeavors have been successful: 1.6 million people visited the MoMA for Free Fridays between 2013 and 2017, while more than 350,000 visitors attended the Tate Lates.[28]

This collaboration was not just good press for Uniqlo: the MoMA also licensed some of the artwork for use in Uniqlo's SPRZ NY lineup. SPRZ NY (aka "Surprise New York") started with much fanfare in 2014 as Uniqlo dedicated an entire floor of its Fifth Avenue flagship store to the clothing and product line which featured the work of artists, including Andy Warhol, Keith Haring, Jenny Holzer and Man Ray. These designs were sold within Uniqlo locations *and* within the MoMA's gift shop. While the brand claimed to be spreading art around the world, the close association with the museum and the artworks provided the retailer with a cultural cache.

Despite fashion's increasing place within the museum, it is still frequently considered a lesser art because of its close ties to commerce. Speaking to a journalist, Koda suggested that contemporary art frequently manipulated commerce in what he suggested was "Warhol on steroids."[29] The presentation of clothing, especially *fashionable clothing*, within the museum simply makes the connection between what is considered "high art" and commerce explicit and bestows cultural legitimacy on fashion along the way.

Museums and Curation as Cultural Intermediation

Museums are generally large, complex organizations working together to preserve and display artifacts within their collections. A form of cultural intermediation can be seen in both the collection *and* the curation within museums. First, the collection and preservation of works of art is a resource-heavy endeavor—especially when it comes to fashion. As such, the selection of which items to purchase is, in and of itself, a form of cultural mediation. While there are other ways museum collections receive items (such as gifts from benefactors) finding a piece important enough to hold is making a value judgement about it. These decisions are made by curators while conservators make sure the physical objects are maintained within the collection and are able to be displayed. While curators are largely the public facing and better-known figures, exhibitions of clothing and other material goods would not be possible without conservation staff. Conservators have also become more important with fashion researchers' renewed interest in objects or the "material turn" of research.[30]

On the other hand, curators act as cultural intermediaries when they create exhibits for the public. As mentioned in the last section, these exhibits have become more elaborate, but also allow curators to tell a story in their own right. This can be done in a variety of ways, including the selection of mannequins and the settings of the exhibit, including the spaces, props and other artwork included.[31] For example, *Alexander McQueen: Savage Beauty*, which was put on by The Met in 2011 and the V&A in 2015 included a variety of rooms that played up different themes. The rooms had different styles of mannequins and some were adorned with facemasks in an attempt to recreate the atmosphere of

McQueen's runway shows.[32] Moreover, the traveling exhibit *Dior: From Paris to the World* included several rooms that were recreated to give visitors a 360-degree viewing experience (Figure 9.2).

Clothing, unlike other works of art, is unique in that it has both visual and tactical dimensions. While yes, you might be able to run your hand over a painting or feel the marble of a sculpture, clothing is generally intended to be felt as it sits on our skin. As Julia Petrov writes, "Fashion within the museum environment in particular takes on a heightened visuality at the expense of hapticity, due to the norms and rules surrounding the need for the preservation of objects, the physical arrangement of objects in the space, and the physical and visual relation of visitors to objects on display."[33] Moreover, clothing is generally a three-dimensional object that can be viewed from all sides; leaving clothing on a hanger or flat against a wall doesn't display all of its attributes. As such, many fashion exhibitions are more of an installation whereby the works of art (i.e. the clothing) take up physical space within the museum. Petrov notes that there is no one way to display clothing and fashion within a museum and the preferred means of curation have changed over time.[34] In addition to the extensive blockbuster shows that have been dominating museums, institutions are now turning to digital and online means to catalog and share specific pieces and exhibitions.

Figure 9.2 *Dior in Dallas. Famed styles from the House of Dior can be seen on display at the Dallas Museum of Art during the exhibit* Dior: From Paris to the World.

However, as curators and museums act as cultural intermediators deciding what is culturally significant and important to keep, they are not the only institutions who help to construct a cultural memory. In particular, corporate archives also help to save the past, so to speak, by keeping copies of their designs.[35] At times, these have been used in various museum exhibits, perhaps most notably when corporations have helped sponsor the exhibits. Nonetheless, these are important repertoires of memory and work to signify the importance of garments, designs and those who brought them to fruition.

Influence of Art and Museums

While critics have taken issue with the blurred line fashion and clothing create between culture and commerce, the overlap and influence of these spheres is undeniable. Beyond the direct influences and collaborations we'll get into in the coming pages, fashion scholars have also acknowledged this interplay by linking museum-applicable terms like curating and installation to commercial practices. Additionally, museums—being influenced by the consumer revolution and marketing considerations—have formed more explicit relations with commercial entities.[36]

It would, however, be an oversight to suggest art has only recently been used for commercial ends. As mentioned previously, early designers like Worth and Poiret included art in their salons in an attempt to highlight the craft in their designs. While the linkage of fashion and art here might be somewhat explicit, it also speaks toward other issues within consumption, namely cultural capital. Cultural capital, as you might remember from Chapter 5, is the working knowledge or taste judgements made by the dominant groups within society. Those who are understood to have "good taste" might be viewed as being better by others and being able to engage in, appreciate or share this taste can be a means to earn financial capital. However, these taste assessments imply that some items—including particular forms of art or fashion—are better than others. As such, linking fashion to more heralded art forms was a way to raise its cultural prestige.

In many ways, store displays drew off of display tactics used elsewhere, namely through the Great Exhibition halls that were once prominent in major cities.[37] Today, merchandising displays both within stores and in store windows draw on techniques used to display works of art, especially within luxury stores. Display windows for department stores like Macy's and Bergdorf Goodman become particularly prominent during the holiday season and their unveiling is often featured in the popular press. Moreover, Selfridges in London has used its display windows to share mannequins from Japanese artist Yayoi Kusama. And, to underscore the blurred lines of art and retail display, Annamari Vänskä and Hazel Clark note that part of the Selfridges' window display later became an installation at the Helsinki Art Museum.[38] Moreover, much in the same way that Poiret used art to support his fashion house, brands continue to use art to support their luxury and high-class associations. While writers were critical of Vreeland's promotion of Yves Saint Laurent, brands including Chanel, Dior and Louis Vuitton have sponsored museum exhibits in an attempt to imbue their brands with the connotations of art.[39]

Similarly, when brands use art within products or associate themselves with specific artists, they are curating and acting in the role of a cultural intermediary, which helps to promote and circulate particular artists and artwork.[40] For example, when the shoe company Vans partnered with the Van Gogh Museum and printed the artists' works on its shoes, it worked to give cultural relevance to the artwork as well as becoming a selling point for Vans products. Moreover, using known artworks like Van Gogh's self-portrait and Starry Night helps to maintain the profile of those works.

One example of a brand carefully curating its association with an artist can be found in the use of Robert Mapplethorpe's work by Uniqlo. Mapplethorpe was well-known for photographing sadomasochist and bondage scenes in the late 1960s and 1970s. However, when Uniqlo reproduced his artwork on a line of T-shirts, the works were sanitized and primarily used Mapplethorpe's still life images of flowers showing little or no representation of the bondage images. While even the Robert Mapplethorpe Foundation describes those sadomasochistic images as "shocking," sanitizing the photographer's work in the name of commercial interest provides a real sense of erasure or, at the very least, a recasting of a prominent artist.

Fashion and Music

While the previous pages have primarily focused on visual artwork, clothing interacts with one other prominent form of art: music. While the connection between clothing and music is not as readily available, apparent or visible as that of other art forms there are several points of connection where the two collide. In fact, next to the songs themselves, clothing and appearance is perhaps one of the defining features of music—both for the artists and for the fans. The Beatles are remembered for the Mod-style suits they first debuted on The Ed Sullivan Show while Salsa legend Celia Cruz was known for her dazzling costumes.

Frequently, fans of a particular musical artist or a particular genre are lumped together based on their clothing and personal appearance. For example, members of the punk community are frequently associated with leather, spikes, safety pins and Dr. Martens boots, while early fans of hip-hop and rap music were known for wearing looser fitting (i.e. baggy) pants and athletic brands like Adidas. (Run-DMC even recorded as a song called, "My Adidas.") When clothing—sometimes known as "merch"—is purchased and worn in support of a specific band or artist, it can lead to the development of subcultural capital, as we discussed in Chapter 3. Spending money to purchase clothing with an artist's name or logo is a direct way to support the artist, but it also identifies the person as a fan or even a member of a particular community.[41] More broadly, clothing plays into how we understand and relate to musical artists—even if we're not buying their merch.

Janice Miller suggests that clothing and image play an intricate role in the perceived authenticity of musicians—namely through associations with a "bohemian lifestyle," but also any type of artistic production.[42] Specifically, Jochen Strähle and Anna-Christina Kriegel outline various intersections between fashion and music. These include (1) the overlap in tastes in both fashion and music; (2) popular music's influence on fashion trends; and (3) music's use in fashion branding and experiential retail.[43] While it is somewhat difficult to link fashion and music trends, consider how dancing or even playing music might be affected by our clothing. Some dances, like the Charleston, which was popular in the 1920s, would be easier to do in the flapper dresses of the time. Likewise, imagine doing some more contemporary dances—say the Electric Slide or even twerking—in something like Dior's New Look or nineteenth-century hoop skirts. At best, it would be uncomfortable; at worst it would be impossible.

Musicians are often linked to their styles of dress even within a particular subcultural style. Alphonso McClendon has documented how the stages of jazz music, ragtime to blues to swing, each brought a distinctive style of dress via the popular musicians with each turn. In a more contemporary setting, clothing can also be seen as supporting mainstream and niche artists. Boybands have used their style of dress to seem both masculine and sensitive, while musicians like David Bowie and drag artists like RuPaul play with expressions of sex and sexuality.[44]

Finally, music has become an important part of fashion branding, whether it's music that accompanies runway shows or the background music in retail locations (sometimes referred to as the brand name Muzak). During its peak influence of the late 1990s and early 2000s, Abercrombie & Fitch was known for the loud music that emanated from its stores, which replicated a dance club environment. This became integral to the company's branding, so much so that A&F Radio could be streamed through the store's website.[45] Elsewhere, brands like Apple and Target have effectively tied stylish commodities to pop music through their advertising.[46]

One final and important crossover between music and fashion comes in the form of music videos. Music videos came of age during the rise of MTV in the 1980s, but they added a visual means to music that wasn't always present previously, especially if you couldn't see live performances. (After all, there's a reason MTV's first video was The Buggles' "Video Killed the Radio Star.")[47] Music videos frequently include a type of intertextuality between the song lyrics, the visuals on screen and imagery elsewhere in popular culture. Sometimes this is more obvious: 5 Seconds of Summer's reference to "American Apparel underwear" in "She's So Perfect" creates a clear link between the music and the brand. Elsewhere, Miller has noted that the video for Gwen Stefani's "Rich Girl" has similar aesthetics to advertising campaigns of John Galliano and Vivienne Westwood. This created a multi-leveled intertextual relationship between Stefani's music, the brands of Galliano and Westwood, *and* the singer's own clothing line L.A.M.B.[10] All said, the links between fashion and music are complex and multiple, and can involve live performances, celebrity culture and visual imagery.

Fashion, Art and Promotional Culture

One aspect that underlies fashion and visual art (and fashion and music) is that of circulation and promotional culture. As initially outlined by Andrew Wernick, promotional culture deals with the circulation of ideas and objects within society. In the case of something physical—say a painting or vase to use Wernick's example—either the item or a replication needs to be physically moved in order for it to be seen or experienced.[49] However, through its circulation, the objects can gain attention and praise. As noted earlier in this chapter, what we understand as "art" is created at the nexus of a variety of actors and actions from critics, journalists, historians and patrons.

Promotional culture largely understands circulation to be the key factor in an object's value. With that, we can understand the relationship between clothing and art in three potential ways. First, when clothing is *in* art, it becomes a signifier in and of itself. This is something that was discussed in Chapter 6 with clothing within films and television, but it also occurs within paintings and other visual arts. Moreover, clothing within these pieces of art help to provide an historical record of ways of dressing and what garments and trends were "in style."[50] Secondly, in some cases, the fact that a garment or a designer's work is important enough to be included in a piece of art provides an element of cultural significance and prestige. Consider the famed Richard Avedon piece "Dovima with Elephants." The fact that the model was wearing a Dior dress in the photos raises the profile of the dress and the House of Dior.

The third intersection comes from clothing that uses artwork within its design. Take, for example, the aforementioned collaboration between the Van Gogh Museum and Vans. The fact that Vans collaborated with the Van Gogh

Museum (or similarly, as discussed in the Insight, Uniqlo collaborating with the Museum of Modern Art) gives the artist and the artwork more cultural significance. In this case, it's through direct circulation: the advertisements for the products *and* the products themselves as they are purchased and publicly consumed help ensure the artwork remains culturally significant for future generations.

Further Reading

Given the complex intersection of clothing and art, it can be explored from a number of different directions. Anne Hollander's *Seeing Through Clothes* (University of California Press, 1993) and *Couture Culture: A Study in Modern Art and Fashion* by Nancy J. Troy (MIT Press, 2003) are both from art history and somewhat foundational within fashion studies. At the same time, Howard Becker's *Art Worlds* (University of California Press, 1982) approaches art from a sociological perspective, although the book doesn't address fashion and discusses more traditional fine arts. The volume *Fashion and Art* edited by Adam Geczy and Vicki Karaminas (Bloomsbury, 2012) helps to pull different disciplinary perspectives together, including art history, sociology and museology.

Looking particularly at museums, curation and clothing and fashion, Valerie Steele's 1998 article "A Museum of Fashion is More Than A Clothes-Bag" and her 2008 article "Museum Quality: The Rise of the Fashion Exhibition" both from *Fashion Theory* are incredibly insightful. Moreover, there are several illuminating recent books. *Fashion and Museums: Theory and Practice*, edited by Marie Riegels Melchior and Birgitta Svensson (Bloomsbury, 2014), *Curating Fashion: Critical Practice in the Museum and Beyond,* edited by Annamari Vänskä and Hazel Clark (Bloomsbury, 2017) and *Fashion, History and Museums: Inventing the Display of Dress* by Julia Petrov (Bloomsbury, 2019) all provide great insight into the role of fashion and clothing in museum exhibitions and curations writ large. Vänskä and Clark's volume along with Geczy and Karaminas' book *Fashion Installation: Body, Space and Performance* (Bloomsbury, 2019) do a nice job of explaining curation and display outside of the museum setting.

Meanwhile, likely due to the immaterial nature of music, the relationship between fashion and museum has been less interrogated. However, Janice Miller's *Fashion and Music* (Bloomsbury, 2011) and the recent volume *Fashion & Music* edited by Jochen Strähle (Springer, 2008) are extensive works on the topics. Finally, while taking a wider view, *Experiencing Music Video: Aesthetics and Cultural Context* by Carol Vernallis (Columbia University Press, 2004) and *Music/Video: Histories, Aesthetics, Media* edited by Gina Arnold, Daniel Cookney, Kirsty Fairclough and Michael Goddard (Bloomsbury, 2019) both include discussions of clothing and appearance within music videos.

1   Hollander, Anne (1993). *Seeing Through Clothes*. Berkeley, CA: University of California Press.

2   Troy, Nancy J. (2003). *Couture Culture: A Study in Modern Art and Fashion*. Cambridge, MA: MIT Press.

3   Geczy, Adam and Vicki Karaminas, eds. (2014). *Fashion and Art*. New York: Bloomsbury.

4   Steele, Valerie (1998). "A Museum of Fashion is More Than a Clothes-Bag." *Fashion Theory*, 2(4): 327–335.

5   Steele, Valerie (2008). "Museum Quality: The Rise of the Fashion Exhibition." *Fashion Theory,* 12(1): 7–30.

6   Melchior, Marie Riegels and Birgitta Svensson, eds. (2014). *Fashion and Museums: Theory and Practice.* New York: Bloomsbury.

7   Vänskä, Annamari and Hazel Clark, eds. (2017). *Curating Fashion: Critical Practice in the Museum and Beyond.* New York: Bloomsbury.

8   Petrov, Julia (2019). *Fashion, History and Museums: Inventing the Display of Dress.* New York: Bloomsbury.

9   Geczy, Adam and Vicki Karaminas (2019). *Fashion Installation: Body, Space and Performance.* New York: Bloomsbury.

10 Miller, Janice (2011). *Fashion and Music.* New York: Bloomsbury.

11 Strähle, Jochen, ed. (2018). *Fashion & Music.* Singapore: Springer.

12 Vernallis, Carol (2004). *Experiencing Music Video: Aesthetics and Culture.* New York: Columbia University Press.

13 Arnold, Gina, Daniel Cookney, Kirsty Fairclough and Michael Goddard, eds. (2018). *Music/Video: Histories, Aesthetics, Media.* New York: Bloomsbury.

Notes

Preface

1 Wilson, 2004: 379.
2 Couldry and Hepp, 2016.
3 Entwistle, 2015: xiii.
4 Kalbaska, Sádaba and Cantoni, 2018.

Chapter 1

1 Littlejohn, 1996: 6.
2 Beebe, Beebe and Ivy, 2016: 5.
3 Edwards, Edwards, Wahl and Myers, 2016: 7; Beebe, Beebe and Ivy, 2016: 5.
4 Littlejohn, 1996: 18–19.
5 See McCracken, 1986, or Hamilton, 1997, for formulations on this division.
6 Trenholm, 2014: 278.
7 Duffy, 2013: 115–118.
8 Gillmor, 2004: 136–157.
9 Duffy, 2013; Luvaas, 2016: 215–252;
10 Lasswell, 1948 qtd in McQuail and Windahl, 1993: 13.
11 Ibid.: 14.
12 Ritchie, 1986; McQuail and Windahl, 1993: 16–17.
13 McQuail and Windahl, 1993: 16–17.
14 Hanson, 2017: 7–12.
15 Beebe, Beebe and Ivy, 2016: 9–10.
16 McQuail and Windahl, 1993: 17–18.
17 Beebe, Beebe and Ivy, 2016: 10–11.
18 McQuail and Windahl, 1993: 19–20.
19 Beebe, Beebe and Ivy, 2016: 11–12.
20 Beebe, Beebe and Ivy, 2016: 7; Edwards, Edwards, Wahl and Myers, 2016: 7; McQuail and Windahl, 1993: 20–21.
21 Griffin, 2009: 279.
22 Ibid.: 280–284.

23 Foss and Griffin, 1995: 3.

24 Ibid.: 5.

25 Foss, "Framing" 2004; Foss, "Theory", 2004; Edwards, 2009; Miles and Nilsson, 2018.

26 Del Gandio, 2008: 14–18.

27 Beebe, Beebe and Ivy, 2016: 56.

28 Ibid.: 83.

29 Belk, 1988; Solomon, 1983; Stone, 1962 1995.

30 Campbell, 2007.

31 Eicher and Roach–Higgins, 1993; Eicher, 2010; Kawamura, 2005: 3; Barnard, 2006: 10–11.

32 Barnard, 2002: 11.

33 Roach and Eicher, 2007: 109.

34 Kaiser, 1997: 4.

35 Goffman, 1959.

36 Stone, 1962 1995; Kaiser, 1997: 5.

37 Stone, 1962 1995.

38 Kawamura, 2005: 3–4.

39 Kawmaura, 2005: 5.

40 Veblen, 1899 2009: 198–222; Simmel, 1904 1957; Blumer, 1969; McCracken, 1986; Lipovetsky, 1994.

41 Polhemus, 2011: 31.

42 Kawamura, 2005: 1.

43 Eicher, 2011.

44 Ibid.

45 Polhemus, 2011: 41–43.

46 Hollander, 1994: 18.

47 Cahoone, 2003: 8–9.

48 Charles, 2009: 390–391; Baudrillard, 2003: 426; Jameson 1991: iv; Lyotard, 2003: 260.

49 Tseëlon, 2016: 218–223.

50 Beebe, Beebe and Ivy, 2016: 43–46; Edwards, Edwards, Wahl and Myers, 2016: 26–38.

51 Barnard, 2002: 72–100; Barthes, 1990.

52 De Saussure, 1983: 15–17.

53 Barthes, 1990: 60–64.

54 Lurie, 1981; Barnard, 2006.

55 Davis, 1992: 7.

56 Campbell, 2007.

57 Beebe, Beebe and Ivy, 2016: 7.

58 Barnard, 2007: 176–177.

59 Miller, 2010: 31–38.

60 Kaiser, 1997: 58–63.

61 Barnard, 2002: 73–100; Davis, 1992: 8.

62 Zukin, 2005: 35–62.

Chapter 2

1 Bacon, 2018.
2 Hegarty, 2018; Bush, 2018; Carter, 2018; Clinton, 2018; Obama, 2018.
3 Ebbs, 2018; McCammon, 2018.
4 Heil, 2018.
5 Trump, 2018.
6 Bourne, 2018; Cillizza, 2018.
7 Givhan, 2018.
8 Friedman, 2018, "Melania Trump, Agent of Coat Chaos".
9 BBC, 2018.
10 *20/20*, 2018.
11 "The Power of Style", 2017.
12 Farhi, 2011.
13 Weaver, 2018.
14 Crane, 2000: 15.
15 Beebe, Beebe, and Ivy, 2016: 35.
16 Miller, 2016: 50.
17 Sullivan, 1997; Wolgast, 2009.
18 Goffman, 1959, especially see page 15.
19 Davis, 1992: 15–18.
20 Entwistle, 2015: 6–9.
21 Craik, 2005: 7; Mauss, 1973.
22 @ChurchCarlton, 2018; Bologna, 2018; Gieseler, 2017.
23 Paoletti, 2012: xvii, 89–93, 95.
24 Pearson and Davilla, 2001: 7.
25 Spinner, Cameron and Calogero, 2018; Reich, Black and Foliaki, 2018; Fulcher and Hayes, 2018; Klass, 2018; Zimmerman, 2017.
26 Stone, 1995: 21, 23.
27 Barnard, 2010: 29.
28 Kaiser, 2012: 12–27.
29 Nike, 2018.
30 Douglas and Isherwood, 1979: 56–58; Dunn, 2008: 8–11.
31 Greenhouse, 2010; Klein, 2010: 328–329.
32 Cooley, 1902: 164–169.
33 Blumer, 1969: 2; Kaiser, Nagasawa and Hutton, 1991: 168–169; Stone, 1995: 19.
34 Beebe, Beebe and Ivy, 2016: 201.
35 Folger Shakespeare Library.
36 Goffman, 1959: 106–140.
37 Cupach and Metts, 2006.
38 Wilson, 2003: 123–125; Crane, 2000: 22–23.
39 Blumer, 1969: 50.
40 Mackinney–Valentine, 2017: 31–41.
41 Goffman, 1959: 4.

42 Kaiser, Nagasawa and Hutton, 1991.

43 Solomon and Theiss, 2013: 5.

44 Edwards, Edwards, Wahl and Myers, 2016: 152.

45 Beebe, Beebe and Ivy, 2016: 156.

46 Kaiser, 1997: 61–63.

47 Beebe, Beebe and Ivy, 2016: 180.

48 Knobloch and Solomon, 2002.

49 Corrigan, 2008: 113–117; Lascity, 2018; McCracken, 1988: 84–85.

50 Legal Information Institute; Shackelford, 2014: 374.

51 ACLU, "Tinker v. Des Moines"; United States Courts, n.d.; Shackelford, 2014: 376.

52 Oppenheimer, 2017; Hudson and Ghani, 2017; ACLU, "All Dressed Up".

53 Lurie, 1981; Barthes, 1990; Campbell, 2009; Davis, 1992: 12–15.

54 Beebe, Beebe and Ivy, 2016: 57.

55 McQuail and Windahl, 1993: 17.

56 Campbell, 2009.

57 Beebe, Beebe and Ivy, 2016: 58; Edwards, Edwards, Wahl and Myers, 2016: 57–58.

58 See Goffman, 1959: 4, for this use in verbal and nonverbal communication.

59 Crane, 2000: 99–107.

60 Miller and Woodward, 2012: 7, 89–92.

61 Solomon and Theiss, 2013: 337–339; Beebe, Beebe and Ivy, 2016: 210–211.

62 Johnson, 2010.

63 Craik, 2005: 14.

64 Abnett, 2016; Magsaysay, 2018.

65 Entwistle, 2015: 16–35.

66 Peretz, 1995; McIntyre, 2016; De Casanova, 2015.

67 Franz, 2005.

68 Pettinger, 2004; Peretz, 1995: 25.

69 Consumerist, 2013.

Chapter 3

1 Eicher, 2011; Edwards, 2011: 20–29; Aspers and Godart, 2013.

2 Arch, 2010.

3 Arch, 2010; Craik, 2005: 15.

4 Craik, 2005: 17.

5 Ibid.: 29, 33.

6 Arch, 2010.

7 The Salvation Army, n.d.

8 Craik, 2005: 45–46; Arch, 2010.

9 Craik, 2005: 52, 64.

10 Craik, 2005: 40–42, 57–58, 62–64; McVeigh, 2010; Webster, 2010; Yagou, 2010.

11 Webster, 2010; Craik, 2005: 58.

12 Craik, 2005: 71.

13 Oppenheimer, 2017; Plante, 2017.
14 McVeigh, 2010.
15 Handy, 2002; Lester, 2011.
16 CNT Editors and C. Kwak, 2018; Sheppard, 2014; Williams, 2016; Feitelberg, 2019; Del Valle, 2019.
17 Craik, 2005: 17; Cole and Deihl, 2015: 39–40.
18 Craik, 2005: 17.
19 Beebe, Beebe and Ivy, 2016: 18–19.
20 Ibid.: 201.
21 Anderson, 2006: 5–6, 44–45.
22 Hofstede, 2011: 9–16.
23 Beebe, Beebe and Ivy, 2016: 133; Hebdige, 1979: 3.
24 Keblusek and Giles, 2017.
25 Brewer, 1991: 477–479.
26 Miller, 2010: 38–41; Hollander, 1994: 17.
27 Paoletti, 2012: 33–35.
28 Paoletti, 2012: 36.
29 Cook, 2004: 3, 12–14; See Schor, 2004, for discussion on consumption and childhood.
30 Paoletti, 2012: 37.
31 Corrigan, 2008: 110–113.
32 Massoni, 2010: 130–138.
33 Palladino, 1996: 103–104.
34 Chaet, 2012.
35 Church Gibson, 2000: 81.
36 Chernikoff, 2014; Mackinney-Valentin, 2017: 31–32, 37–39.
37 De Casanova, 2015.
38 Grobart, 2016.
39 Hollander, 1994: 22, 64–65.
40 Hollander, 1994: 77; Paoletti, 2015.
41 Crane, 2000: 102.
42 Moeslein, 2018; O'Malley, 2018; Tschorn, 2018; Henderson, 2018.
43 Paoletti, 2012: 98–99.
44 Levine, 1998: 20–25, 59–65.
45 Sontag, 1966: 275–292, especially 277–279.
46 Friedman, 2018, "Met Costume Institute Embraces 'Camp' for 2019 Blockbuster Show".
47 Friedman, 2016.
48 Italie, 2019.
49 Warner, 2008.
50 Cole and Deihl, 2015: 392; Dockers, n.d.
51 Patterson, 2019.
52 McGregor, 2012; Farooq, 2011; Sellers, 2004.
53 Patterson, 2019; Kadaba, 2019.
54 Carreon, 2019.
55 McGregor and Telford, 2019.
56 Bourdieu, 1984: 114–125.

57 Currid-Halkett, 2017: 49–50.

58 Zukin, 2005: 35–40.

59 Albrecht, 2017.

60 Hume, 2010; 2013; Arthur, 1999: 2.

61 Graybill and Arthur, 1999: 12.

62 Ibid.: 21.

63 Hamilton and Hawley, 1999: 39–40.

64 Graybill and Arthur, 1999: 26.

65 O'Neal, 1999: 126–127.

66 Lewis, 2013; Spellings, 2018.

67 Golshan, 2016.

68 *The Economist,* 2019; Sheftalovich, 2016; Taylor, 2016.

69 Hebdige, 1979.

70 Strings, 2019, especially 122–146.

71 Pham, 2015: 11–12.

72 See Breward and Gilbert, 2006 for examples.

73 Lewis, 2003; O'Neal, 2010.

74 Tulloch, 2011.

75 Hebdige, 1979: 73–80.

76 Bennett, 1999; Bennett, 2011: 495; Maffesoli, 2016.

77 Cheney, 1996: 4.

78 Polhemus, 1994: 130–131.

79 See McCracken, 1988: 118–129 for change in material consumption and class.

80 Thornton, 1996: 11–14.

Chapter 4

1 Buckland, 2008.

2 Cole and Deihl, 2015: 198, 203–204.

3 Ibid.: 208–209.

4 Pujalet-Plaà, 2010.

5 Cole and Deihl, 2015: 211; Pujalet-Plaà, 2010.

6 Walker, 2010.

7 Kawamura, 2005: 4–5.

8 Lipovetsky, 1994: 6–8.

9 Simmel, 1904 1957.

10 Kawamura, 2005: 20–23.

11 McNeil, 2016: 69.

12 See Hunt, 1996 for a discussion and history of sumptuary laws.

13 Blumer, "Fashion" 1969.

14 Ibid.: 288–289.

15 Davis, 1992: 130–131.

16 Polhemus, 1994: 10.

17 Ibid.: 130–134.

18 Polhemus, 1996: 91.

19 Sporles, 1986: 56, 65.

20 Ibid.: 66.

21 Meinhold, 2013: 109–110.

22 De Chernatony, 2009; Ewing, Jevons and Khalil, 2009; Also see Holt, 2002 and Lury, 2004 for discussions for the economic and cultural entanglements of brands.

23 Uniqlo, n.d.

24 Vanderschoot, 2018.

25 Mull, 2019; Pardes, 2018; Syme, 2018; Allbirds, n.d.; Rothy's, n.d.

26 CBS News, 2019.

27 Stone, 1995: 20–23.

28 Kaiser, Nagasawa and Hutton, 1991: 180.

29 McCracken, 1988: 71.

30 Ibid.: 72.

31 Hamilton, 1997: 164; see also Kaiser, Nagasawa and Hutton, 1991.

32 Hamilton, 1997: 167.

33 Aspers and Godart, 2013; Blaszczyk and Wubs, 2018.

34 Lantz, 2016: 6.

35 Blaszczyk and Wubs, 2018: 9, 11–12.

36 Blaszczyk, 2018: 37.

37 Ibid.: 47.

38 Pouillard and Trivette, 2018: 69–70, 77.

39 Pantone, n.d.

40 Quinto, 2015; Falconer, 2018; Bruccullieri, 2019.

41 WGSN, n.d.

42 MacNaughton, 2018.

43 Ibrahim, 2019.

44 Pearl, 2019.

45 Lantz, 2016: 46–47, 51–65.

46 Laver, 1937: 201–208.

47 Geczy and Karaminas, 2016: 86.

48 "The Power of Style."

49 Geczy and Karaminas, 2016: 87–89.

50 Kaiser, 2012: 178–180.

51 Jenss, 2015: 4–9.

52 Kaiser, 2012: 5–6; Jenss, 2015: 23.

53 Agins, 1999: 35–53.

54 Ibid.: 8–16.

55 Geczy and Karaminas, 2018.

Chapter 5

1 Harper's Bazaar Staff, 2014.

2 Biography.com, "Diana Vreeland," 2014.

 3 Biography.com, "Diana Vreeland," 2014; Wilkinson, 2011.

 4 Hare, 2014.

 5 Pettegree, 2014: 58; New York Public Library; Miller and McNeil, 2018: 28–29.

 6 Miller and McNeil, 2018: 70; Ballaster, Beetham, Frazer and Hebron, 1991: 87; Miller, 2013: 17.

 7 Miller and McNeil, 2018: 78.

 8 Ibid.: 88.

 9 Buckley and Clark, 2018: 96; Collins, 2004; Massoni, 2010: 20.

 10 *Elle*, "The Heritage"; Rose, 2000; Rose, 2003; Adlerman, 2015; Massoni, 2010: 20.

 11 Massoni, 2010: 29–38.

 12 Ibid.: 27.

 13 Anderson, 2006: 1–7.

 14 Thornton, 1996: 116–162.

 15 Wright, 1960: 608–9.

 16 Massoni, 2010: 65–68, 72–77, 157–161; Palladino, 1996: 107–108, 112–115.

 17 *The Merchants of Cool*; *Generation Like*.

 18 Memmott, 2013; Pooley and Socolow, 2013; Gumbel, 2009.

 19 Lowery and DeFleur, 1995: 13; Hanson, 2017: 29.

 20 Hanson, 2017: 38.

 21 Weaver, McCombs and Spellman, 1975; McCombs and Shaw, 1993: 61–65.

 22 *The Cut*, "Meet Tavi," 2008; *The Cut*, "Tween Blogger," 2008.

 23 Kwan, 2008; Spiridakis, 2008.

 24 Twohey, 2010; Gevinson, 2011; Trong, 2011; Ortved, 2018.

 25 Van Dyke, 2014; Roy, 2014.

 26 Entman, 1993: 51–52.

 27 Reese, 2001: 9.

 28 Business of Fashion, "Elaine Welteroth"; Headlee, 2012.

 29 Doyle, 2016.

 30 Arnold, 2018.

 31 Kaufman, 2017.

 32 McNeil and Miller, 2014: 46, 48, 57.

 33 Maguire and Matthews, 2014; Bourdieu, 1984; Zukin, 2005; Lynes, 1980.

 34 Lynes, 1980: 5–7.

 35 Zukin, 2005: 169–196.

 36 Powers, 2013.

 37 Twitchell, 1992; Gans, 1999.

 38 Bourdieu, 1984: 13.

 39 Bourdieu, 1984: 319–328.

 40 Thornton, 1996: 11–13.

 41 Kanai, 2016.

 42 Hughes, 2016; Chabbott, 2017; Singer, 2017; Collins, 2018.

 43 *The Eye Has to Travel*.

 44 Czerniawski, 2015: 9–14.

 45 Chia, 2019; Van Meter, 2019; *The New York Times*, 2018.

 46 Anderson, 2004.

47 Box Office Mojo, n.d.

48 Kismaric and Respini, 2008: 34–35.

49 Martineau, 2018: 13, 85; Hall Duncan, 1979: 22–26; Cole and Deihl, 2015: 163.

50 Cheang, 2013: 37–40; *The Eye Has to Travel.*

51 Gamson et al., 1992.

Seven Names to Know in Print Fashion

1 *The New York Times* (1957), "Edna Woolman Chase Dies at 80; Retired Vogue Magazine Editor", *The New York Times,* 21 March. Available at: https://timesmachine.nytimes.com/timesmachine/1957/03/21/86701355.pdf.

2 Tomkins, C. (1994), "The World of Carmel Snow", *The New Yorker,* 7 November, 148–158; Horgan, R. (2015), "Remembering Harper's Bazaar Editor in Chief Carmel Snow", *Adweek,* 16 July. Available at: www.adweek.com/digital/vogue-harpers-bazaar-carmel-snow-conde-nast/

3 Darcella, A. and B. Galopin (2018), "CR Muse: The Discerning Eye of Diana Vreeland", *CR Fashion Book,* 18 September. Available at: www.crfashionbook.com/culture/a23277243/cr-muse-fashion-editor-diana-vreeland/; *The Eye Has to Travel.*

4 *The Business of Fashion* (n.d.), "Anna Wintour", *Business of Fashion.* Available at: www.businessoffashion.com/community/people/anna-wintour.

5 Friedman, V. (2018), "André Leon Talley's Next Act", *The New York Times,* 24 May. Available at: www.nytimes.com/2018/05/24/style/andre-leon-talley-documentary.html.

6 Fernandez, C. (2020), "What Samira Nasr's Appointment Means for Harper's Bazaar and Fashion Magazines", *Business of Fashion,* 9 June. Available at: www.businessoffashion.com/articles/news-analysis/harpers-bazaar-magazine-new-editor-in-chief-samira-nasr.

7 Bullock, M. (2019), "Elaine Welteroth Had to Leave Media to Earn Real Money", *The Cut,* 12 June. Available at: www.thecut.com/2019/06/elaine-welteroth-on-leaving-conde-nast-and-getting-into-tv.html

Chapter 6

1 Encyclopædia Britannica, "HDTV", n.d.

2 Shah, 2016.

3 Ibid.

4 Ibid.

5 Hanson, 2017: 36–38.

6 Griffin, 2009: 312–322.

7 Carey, 2009: 15, 111.

8 Strate, 2004: 7.

9 Hanson, 2017: 190–191.

10 Dirks, n.d.

11 Hanson, 2017: 192–196.

12 Ibid.: 220–222.

13 Peter, 2018.

14 See *The Film is Not Yet Rated* on film ratings in the US.

15 Encyclopædia Britannica, "Newsreel", n.d.

16 Fandango, n.d.

17 Stutesman, 2011: 20–23.

18 Munich, 2011: 5.

19 Gaines and Herzog, 1990: 19; Gaines, 1990: 180–188.

20 Gaines, 1990; Eckert, 1990: 107; Reyer, 2017; Bruzzi, 1997: 7.

21 Feuer, 1995: 141.

22 Warner, 2014: 24, 30; Warner, 2009; Buckley and Clark, 2018: 239–246; Quick, 1999.

23 Hall, 2012: 139.

24 Ibid.: 143.

25 Ibid.: 143.

26 Baxter-Wright, 2017; Ross, 2018.

27 Hall, 2012: 144.

28 Jeffers McDonald, 2010.

29 Hall, 2013: 173–174.

30 Hall, 2013: 174–184.

31 Nededog, 2013; Roberson, 2018.

32 Hall, 2013: 184–190.

33 Barthes, 1977: 142–148.

34 Foucault, 1969.

35 Barthes, 2012: 219–226.

36 Mulvey, 1999: 750–753; Miller, 2016: 54.

37 Berger, 2013; hooks, 2013; Barnard, 2002: 119–125.

38 Bruzzi, 1997: xvi–xvii, 102–103, 165.

39 Church Gibson, 2012: 13–14.

40 McCracken, 2005.

41 Rosenblaum, 2000; Singer, 2019; Fisher, 2018.

42 Church Gibson, 2012: 188–192.

43 Martin, 2019.

44 Golfar, 2019; Clark, 2019.

45 Rubin, 1996.

46 Tashjian, 2019.

47 Cerini, 2019.

48 Luther, 2010; Arrington, 2017.

49 Tietjen, 2017; McFadden, 2014.

50 Kesvani, n.d.

51 Television Academy, n.d.

52 Genzlinger, 2012.

53 Lewis, 2004: 72–73, 150.

54 Sender, 2012: 5–9.

55 Grindstaff, 2013: 409–412.

56 Rees-Roberts, 2018: 5.

57 Uhlirova, 2013: 140–142.

58 Horyn, 2011.

59 Potter, 2014: 1026–1027, 1030–1032; Scharrer and Blackburn, 2018; Opree and Kühne, 2016.

Seven Names to Know in Film and Television Fashion

1   Boyt, S. (2016), "Women I've Undressed by Orry-Kelly, review: 'Old Hollywood Heaven'", *The Telegraph,* 6 February. Available at: www.telegraph.co.uk/books/ what-to-read/women-ive-undressed-by-orry-kelly-review-old-hollywood-heaven/; Yaeger, L. (2016), "Women He's Undressed: A New Film Celebrates Hollywood Costume Designer Orry-Kelly", *Vogue,* 8 August. Available at: www. vogue.com/article/orry-kelly-hollywood-costume-designer-women-hes-undressed-film-marilyn-monroe

2   Sauro, C. (2010), "Edith Head", in V. Steele (ed.) *The Berg Companion to Fashion,* New York: Bloomsbury.

3   Trapnell, J. (2010), "Adrian", in V. Steele (ed.) *The Berg Companion to Fashion,* New York: Bloomsbury.; Polan B. and R. Tredre (2009), *The Great Fashion Designers,* New York: Bloomsbury, 59–61.

4   McFadden, R.D. (2014), "Joan Rivers, a Comic Stiletto Quick to Skewer is Dead at 81", *The New York Times,* 4 September. Available at: www.nytimes.com/2014/09/ 05/arts/television/joan-rivers-dies.html.

5   Finn, R. (2001), "Public Lives: Elsa Klensch, Still in Style, but Out of a Job", *The New York Times,* 13 February. Available at: www.nytimes.com/2001/02/13/ nyregion/public-lives-elsa-klensch-still-in-style-but-out-of-a-job.html.

6   Schulman, M. (2015), "Patricia Field Hangs Up Her Retail Wig", *The New York Times,* 26 December. Available at: www.nytimes.com/2015/12/27/fashion/ patricia-field-hangs-up-her-retail-wig.html.

7   St. Félix, D. (2018), "Ruth E. Carter's Threads of History", *The New Yorker,* 10 September. Available at: www.newyorker.com/magazine/2018/09/10/ruth-e-carters-threads-of-history.

Chapter 7

1 Webster, 2015.

2 Billboard, "LFO" n.d.

3 Denizet-Lewis, 2006; Hancock, "Chelsea on 5th" 2009.

4 Du Lac, 1999.

5 Goldstein, 1999.

6 *Neighbors,* 2014.

7 McGregor, 2014; O'Connor, 2014; Kaplan, 2015.

8 Dempsey, 2007; Gonzales, 2017.

9 Arvidsson, 2005; Lury, 2004: 6–8.

10 Mercer, 2010; Bastos and Levy, 2012: 353–354; Stern, 2006: 217.

11 Polan and Tredre, 2009; Cole and Deihl, 2015: 34–37; English, 2013: 30.

12 Cole and Deihl, 2015: 37–38, 66–67.

13 English, 2013: 30–31; Polan and Tredre, 2009: 47.

14 Cole and Deihl, 2015: 118, 146; Thomas, 2002; Polan and Tredre, 2009: 41.

15 Ibid.: 209; Okawa, 2008; Polan and Tredre, 2009: 84–85.

16 Lury, 2004, 2009; Arvidsson, 2005; Entwistle and Slater, 2012; Moore and Reid, 2008: 429; Danesi, 2013.

17 Wigley, Nobbs and Larsen, 2013.

18 Lury, 2009; Lury and Moor, 2010.

19 Kotler, 2003: 8; Manning, 2010.

20 De Chernatony, 2009.

21 Berger and Luckmann, 1966: 21–23.

22 Johnston, 2018.

23 Nakassis, 2012: 628.

24 Moor, 2007: 26–30.

25 Cole and Deihl, 2015: 145; Polan and Tredre, 2009: 37.

26 Wahba and Skariachan, 2013; Bhasin, 2016; Dishman, 2015.

27 Black, 2018; KTRK, 2017; Rubin, 2014; Ellison, 2017; Lowry et al., 2014.

28 Lutz, 2013; Rees, 2013.

29 Klara, 2015.

30 Pine and Gilmore, 2011.

31 Hancock, 2009; Zukin, 2005: 203–205, 238–244; Kozinets et al., 2002; Doyle et al., 2010; Moor, 2007: 65.

32 Lascity, 2019; Ilyashov, 2015; Smith, McClain and Lascity, 2019.

33 Patterson, 1999: 419.

34 Holt, 2004: 6–7; 56–61.

35 Hancock, 2016: 8.

36 Saviolo and Marazza, 2013: 60.

37 Hudson and Balmer, 2013.

38 Hancock, 2016: 20–21; Holt, 2006.

39 Gardner and Levy, 1955: 35.

40 Levy, 1959: 118.

41 Aaker, 1997: 347.

42 Ibid.: 1997; Fournier, 1998; Fournier and Alvarez, 2012; Kervyn, Fiske and Malone, 2012; Keller, 2012.

43 Avis, Forbes and Ferguson, 2014.

44 Dolich, 1969; Bellenger, Steinberg and Stanton, 1976; Sirgy, 1982; Parker, 2009.

45 McCracken, 1988: 77–79; McCracken, 2005: 175–191.

46 Holt, 2004: 39–61; 155–187.

47 Hancock, 2016: 33–35.

48 Barajas, 2015.

49 Hancock, 2016: 48–49; Cuneo, 2003; Macarthur, 2005; Nudd, 2015.

50 Klein, 2009: 20–21, 118.

51 Cheney, 1996: 4; Featherstone, 2007: 83–84.

52 Cheney, 1996: 4–5.

53 Ibid.: 145–159.

54 Karimzadeh and Naughton, 2010.

55 Saviolo and Marazza, 2013: 37.

56 Bastos and Levy, 2012: 354.

57 TOMS, n.d.

58 Mather, 2019; Draper and Belson, 2018; Yang, 2018.

59 Fast Company, n.d.; Feloni, 2019.

60 Lush, n.d.; The Body Shop, n.d.; Aerie, n.d.

61 Slater, 2002: 63, 68.

62 Mejía, 2019.

63 Lury, 2004: 85–92.

64 Neil, 2009.

65 Kuczynski, 2005.

66 Lury and Moor, 2010: 29–31; Brown, Kozinets and Sherry, 2003; Powers and Pattwell, 2015.

67 Kaufman and Deutsch, 2000; Carpenter, 2007; TIME, 1977; Groves, 1987; *The New York Times*, 1988.

68 Smith and Stedman, 1981; Walmart, n.d.; Hancock, 2016: 119–122.

69 Hudson and Balmer, 2013: 349.

70 Ibid.: 2013: 350–351; Hollenbeck, Peters and Zinkhan, 2008.

71 Kuczynski, 2005.

72 Balmer and Burghausen, 2019; Tseëlon, 2016: 220–223.

73 Goffman, 1979; *Killing Us Softly 4: Advertising's Image of Women;* Klein, 1999: 279–309.

74 Banet-Weiser, 2012: 5–6.

75 Dyer, 1982.

Seven Names to Know in Fashion Design and Business

1 Colman, E.A. (2010), "Worth, Charles Frederick", in V. Steele (ed.), *The Berg Companion to Fashion,* New York: Bloomsbury.

2 De la Haye, A. (2010), "Chanel, Gabrielle (Coco)", in V. Steele (ed.), *The Berg Companion to Fashion,* New York: Bloomsbury.

3 Pujalet-Plaà, E. (2010), "Dior, Christian", in V. Steele (ed.), *The Berg Companion to Fashion,* New York: Bloomsbury; Okawa, T. (2008), "Licensing Practices at Maison Christian Dior", in R. L. Blaszczyk (ed.), *Producing Fashion: Commerce, Culture, and Consumers,* Philadelphia: University of Pennsylvania Press.

4 Prace, E. (2002), "Stanley Marcus, the Retailer From Dallas, is Dead at 96", *The New York Times,* 23 January. Available at: www.nytimes.com/2002/01/23/business/stanley-marcus-the-retailer-from-dallas-is-dead-at-96.html; *Southern Methodist*

University (n.d.), "Stanley Marcus Papers: Overview." Available at: www.smu.edu/libraries/digitalcollections/smp.

5 *Bloomberg* (n.d.), "Amancio Ortega", *Bloomberg.* Available at: www.bloomberg.com/billionaires/profiles/amancio-ortega-gaona/

6 Friendman, V. (2019), "Bernard Arnault Just Bought Tiffany. Who Is He?", *The New York Times,* 25 November. Available at: www.nytimes.com/2019/11/25/fashion/bernard-arnault-tiffany-lvmh.html; *The Business of Fashion* (n.d.), "Bernard Arnault", *The Business of Fashion.* Available at: www.businessoffashion.com/community/people/bernard-arnault.

7 *Business of Fashion* (n.d.), "Tadashi Yanai", *Business of Fashion.* Available at: www.businessoffashion.com/community/people/tadashi-yanai

Chapter 8

1 Amazon, n.d.; See also Goode, 2017; Ong, "Amazon's Echo", 2018.
2 Colliver, 2016; Ong, "Amazon Patents", 2018.
3 Hanson, 2017: 246–248.
4 Ibid.: 2017: 248–250.
5 Ibid.
6 boyd and Ellison, 2007: 212.
7 Ibid.: 211.
8 Hanson, 2017: 256.
9 Poster, 2001: 17–20.
10 Sundén, 2003: 49–55.
11 Boellstorff, 2008: 17–21, 128–138.
12 Belk, 1988; Belk, 2013: 490.
13 Hearn, 2008.
14 Pooley, 2010: 79, 85.
15 Bolter and Grusin, 1999: 45, 11.
16 See De Maeyer, 2013 for a discussion of hyperlinks.
17 Rocamora, 2012: 101–104.
18 Jenkins, 2006: 4–10.
19 Gillmor, 2004.
20 Nichols, 2017.
21 Duffy, 2013: 56–60, 76–84, 106–111.
22 Lorenz, 2019.
23 Duffy, 2015, 2017.
24 Hennessy, 2018: 33.
25 Sullivan, 2016.
26 Ritzer and Jurgenson, 2010; Ritzer, Dean and Jurgenson, 2012.
27 Hearn, 2008: 207.
28 Neff, Wissinger and Zukin, 2005.
29 Duffy, 2016: 446.

30 Wissinger, 2015: 6–7.
31 Neff, Wissinger and Zukin, 2005: 309.
32 Garza, 2019; Sabin, 2019.
33 Thompson, 2019.
34 Keefer, 2018; Ehrenkranz, 2017.
35 CVS, 2018; CVS, 2019.
36 Raphael, 2019; Held, 2017.
37 Davies, 2018; Willingham, 2018; Carman, 2019; Harbison, 2019; McMillan, 2019; Tolentino, 2019.
38 Feiner, 2019.
39 Zukin, 2005: 233–244.
40 Simonson and Rosen, 2014.
41 Fournier and Avery, 2011; Vernuccio, 2014; Schivinski and Dabrowski, 2016; Couldry and Turow, 2014; Turow, 2011; Carah, Brodmerkel and Hernandez, 2014; Carah, 2017; Carah and Angus, 2018.
42 Grobart, 2016.
43 Johnston, 2019; DeAcetis, 2018.
44 *How I Built This*, 2017.
45 Maheshwari, 2019.
46 Palmer and Clark, 2005: 2–3.
47 Jacobs, 2019.
48 Abnett, 2015; Sawyer, 2017; Barker, 2018.
49 Couldry and Hepp, 2013; see also Deacon and Stanyer, 2014; Hepp, Hjarvard and Lundby, 2015.
50 Rocamora, 2017: 509–515; Rocamora, 2018: 101–102.
51 Gillespie, 2014: 168–169.
52 See Seaver, 2017 for a discussion of algorithms.
53 Morris and Murry, 2018: 6.

Seven Names to Know in Digital Fashion

1 Jacobs, A. (2019), "Tycoon of the Pre-Owned", *The New York Times,* 23 January. Available at: www.nytimes.com/2019/01/23/style/the-real-real.html

2 Nordstrom, L. (2019), "Scott Schuman Heads to India for Newest 'Sartorialist' Book", *WWD,* 15 October. Available at: https://wwd.com/eye/lifestyle/scott-schuman-heads-to-india-for-newest-sartorialist-book-1203344261/; *The Business of Fashion* (n.d.), "Scott Schuman", *Business of Fashion.* Available at: https://www.businessoffashion.com/community/people/scott-schuman

3 *The Business of Fashion* (n.d.), "Imran Amed, Founder and CEO of The Business of Fashion", *The Business of Fashion.* Available at: www.businessoffashion.com/about/imran-amed; *You* (2018), "Is Imran Amed the most powerful man in fashion?", *You Magazine,* 4 November. Available at: www.you.co.uk/imran-ahmed/

4   *Business of Fashion* (n.d.), "Jennifer Hyman", *The Business of the Fashion.* Available at: www.businessoffashion.com/community/people/jennifer-hyman

5   Pearl, D. (2019), "Influencer Arielle Charnas is Creating Her Own Brand with the Help of the Investor Who Boosted Michael Kors", *Adweek,* 15 August. Available at: www.adweek.com/retail/the-investor-who-boosted-michael-kors-and-tommy-hilfiger-is-betting-on-influencer-arielle-charnas/; Curotto, M. (2018), "Something Navy's Arielle Charnas is More Successful Than Ever—But at What Price?", *Observer,* 12 December. Available at: https://observer.com/2018/12/something-navy-star-arielle-charnas-launching-nordstrom-holiday-line/

6   Peiser, J. (2018), "Rookie Catalogue a Generation of Girlhood", *The New York Times,* 13 December. Available at: www.nytimes.com/2018/12/13/style/rookie-tavi-gevinson.html; Gevinson, T. (2019), "Who Would I Be Without Instagram?", *The Cut,* 16 September. Available at: www.thecut.com/2019/09/who-would-tavi-gevinson-be-without-instagram.html.

7   Alexander, S. (2019), "Kylie Jenner, Youngest Self-Made Billionaire on Earth", *Bloomberg Businessweek,* 4 December. Available at: www.bloomberg.com/news/articles/2019-12-04/kylie-jenner-the-youngest-and-gen-z-s-first-billionaire-on-earth; Biography.com (2019), "Kylie Jenner", 19 November. Available at: www.biography.com/personality/kylie-jenner.

Chapter 9

1 Billboard, "Nirvana" n.d.
2 Asmelash, 2019; Kreps, "Sweater", 2019; Kreps, "'Unplugged'" 2019.
3 English, 2008.
4 See Bai, 2018 for an example.
5 Becker, 1982: 37.
6 Negrin, 2014: 44; McNeil and Miller, 2014: 61–64.
7 Dewey, 2005: 5–10.
8 Becker, 1982: 34–35.
9 Benjamin, 2012: 38–39.
10 Donnella, 2019.
11 Negrin, 2014: 43; Troy, 2003: 36, 47.
12 Becker, 1982: 40–67.
13 McRobbie, 1998: 8.
14 Ibid.: 38.
15 Clark, 2014: 70; Negrin, 2014: 43.
16 Granata, 2017.
17 Crane, 2014: 104–105.
18 Blanks, 2014; The Metropolitan Museum of Art, "Hat", n.d.
19 Crane, 2014: 105.
20 Melchior, 2014: 1–19; Petrov, 2019: 1–3; Steele, 2008: 9.
21 Ibid.: 2014: 1–19.
22 Ibid.

23 Newhouse, 2006: 190, qtd in Steele, 2008: 11.

24 Steele, 2008: 11–14.

25 *The Eye Has to Travel*; Steele, 2008: 13–14.

26 Steele, 2008: 21–29.

27 Melchior, 2014: 1–19; Steele, 2008: 19; Vogel, 2014; Tarmy, 2018; Greenberger, 2015.

28 Lee, 2000.

29 Uniqlo, 2017; Steven, 2017; Campbell, 2019.

30 Scaturro, 2018: 22–27.

31 Clark, 2018.

32 The Metropolitan Museum of Art, "Savage Beauty", n.d.; Victoria and Albert Museum, n.d.

33 Petrov, 2019: 6.

34 Ibid.: 2019: 198.

35 Peirson-Smith and Peirson-Smith, 2019.

36 Vänskä and Clark, 2018; Geczy and Karaminas, 2019; Petrov, 2019: 32; McLean, 1995.

37 Geczy and Karaminas, 2019.

38 Vänskä and Clark, 2018: 7.

39 Bai, 2018.

40 Bengtsen, 2018.

41 Bernhard, 2019: 131–147.

42 Miller, 2011: 11–28.

43 Strähle and Kriegel, 2018.

44 McClendon, 2015: 15–42; Miller, 2011: 71–90, 131–154.

45 Graakjær, 2012.

46 Graakjær, 2014.

47 Graham, 2013.

48 Vernallis, 2004; Lascity, 2017; Miller, 2011: 11–28.

49 Wernick, 1991.

50 Taylor, 2004: 115–117, 132–140; See also Hollander, 1978.

Seven Names to Know in Museum Curation

1 Steele, V. (2008), "Museum Quality: The Rise of the Fashion Exhibition," *Fashion Theory*, 12(1): 7–30; *The Eye Has to Travel*.

2 Schiro, A. (1999), "Richard Martin, Curator of the Costume Institute", *The New York Times*, 9 November. Available at: www.nytimes.com/1999/11/09/arts/richard-martin-52-curator-of-the-costume-institute.html.

3 *The Metropolitan Museum of Art* (2015), "Harold Koda to Step Down After Leading Met Museum's Costume Institute for 15 Years", *The Metropolitan Museum of Art*, 15 September. Available at: www.metmuseum.org/press/news/2015/harold-koda-retirement.

4 The Museum at FIT (n.d.), "Valerie Steele—Director", Fashion Institute of Technology. Available at: www.fitnyc.edu/museum/about/director.php.

5 Wulfhart, N.M. (2019), "What Andrew Bolton Can't Travel Without", *The New York Times,* 20 April. Available at: https://www.nytimes.com/2019/04/20/travel/andrew-bolton-met-gala.html; *The Business of Fashion* (n.d.), "Andrew Bolton", *The Business of Fashion.* Available at: www.businessoffashion.com/community/people/andrew-bolton; Cassone, S. (2018), "The Met's 'Heavenly Bodies' is the Most Popular Show in the Museum's History, Drawing 1.7 Million Visitors", *ArtNet News,* 12 October. Available at: https://news.artnet.com/exhibitions/heavenly-bodies-most-visited-met-show-1370503.

6 Kerr, P. (2018), "Nathalie Bondil—Executive Director and Chief Curator at The Montreal Museum of Fine Arts', *The Montrealer,* 4 January. Available at: https://themontrealeronline.com/2018/01/nathalie-bondil-executive-director-and-chief-curator-at-the-montreal-museum-of-fine-arts/; Jacobs, J. (2020), 'Firing of Museum Director Stirs Debate and an Official Inquiry,' *The New York Times,* 22 July. Available at: https://www.nytimes.com/2020/07/22/arts/design/montreal-museum-nathalie-bondil.html

7 Farrell, A. (2019), "Dior at the V&A: Meet Oriole Cullen, The Curator Readying the Biggest Fashion Exhibition of the Year", *Elle,* 31 January. Available at: www.elle.com/uk/fashion/a25888344/dior-at-the-vanda-meet-oriole-cullen-the-curator-readying-the-biggest-fashion-exhibition-of-the-year/; Sowray, B. (2014), "How I Got Here: Oriole Cullen, Curator", *The Telegraph,* 23 January. Available at: fashion.telegraph.co.uk/news-features/TMG10589759/How-I-got-here-Oriole-Cullen-curator.html.

References

20/20 (2018), TV program ABC, 12 October.

Aaker, J. L. (1997), "Dimensions of Brand Personality", *Journal of Marketing Research,* 34(3): 347–356. doi: 10.2307/3151897

Abnett, K. (2015), "Will Mass Customization Work for Fashion?", *Business of Fashion,* 3 September. Available at: www.businessoffashion.com/articles/intelligence/mass-customisation-fashion-nike-converse-burberry

Abnett, K. (2016), "Styling Politicians in the Age of Image Wars", *Business of Fashion,* 28 July. Available at: www.businessoffashion.com/articles/intelligence/styling-politicians-donald-trump-theresa-may-hillary-clinton

ACLU (n.d.), "Tinker v. Des Moines – Landmark Supreme Court Ruling on Behalf of Student Expression". Available at: www.aclu.org/other/tinker-v-des-moines-landmark-supreme-court-ruling-behalf-student-expression

ACLU (n.d.), "All Dressed Up and Nowhere to Go: Students and Their Parents Fight School Uniform Policies". Available at: www.aclu.org/other/all-dressed-and-nowhere-go-students-and-their-parents-fight-school-uniform-policies

Adlerman, A. (2015), "*O, The Oprah Magazine* celebrates 15 years of publication", *Hearst Corporation,* 22 April. Available at: www.hearst.com/newsroom/o-the-oprah-magazine-celebrates-15-years-of-publication

Agins, T. (1999), *The End of Fashion: How Marketing Changed the Clothing Business Forever,* New York: William Marrow.

Albrecht, L. (2017), "How a Free Canvas Tote Became a Bigger Status Symbol than a $10,000 Hermès Bag", *MarketWatch,* 9 September. Available at: www.marketwatch.com/story/how-a-free-canvas-tote-became-a-bigger-status-symbol-than-a-10000-hermes-bag-2017-09-01

Allbirds (n.d.), "Our Materials." Available at: www.allbirds.com/pages/our-materials-tree

Amazon, (n.d.), "Echo Look". Available at: www.amazon.com/Amazon-Echo-Look-Camera-Style-Assistant/dp/B0186JAEWK

Anderson, B. (2006), *Imagined Communities: Reflections on the Origin and Spread of Nationalism,* Second edition, New York: Verso.

Anderson, C. (2004), "The Long Tail", *Wired,* 1 October. Available at: www.wired.com/2004/10/tail/

Arch, N. (2010), "Uniforms", in L. Skov (ed.), *Berg Encyclopedia of World Dress and Fashion: West Europe,* New York: Bloomsbury. doi: 10.2752/BEWDF/EDch8061a

Arnold, A. (2018), "*Teen Vogue* Editor-in-Chief Elaine Welteroth is Leaving Condé Nast," *The Cut,* January 11. Available at: www.thecut.com/2018/01/teen-vogue-eic-elaine-welteroth-is-leaving-cond-nast.html

Arrington, D. W. (2017), "Elsa Klensch: The Inventor of Fashion Television", *Film, Fashion & Consumption,* 6(2): 157–163. doi: 10.1386/ffc.6.2.157_1

Arthur, L. B. (1999), *Religion, Dress and the Body,* New York: Berg.

Arvidsson, A. (2005), "Brands: A Critical Perspective", *Journal of Consumer Culture,* 5(2): 235–258. doi: 10.1177/1469540505053093

Asmelash, L. (2019), "Kurt Cobain's Green Cardigan Was Sold for a Record-Breaking $334,000", *CNN,* 26 October. Available at: www.cnn.com/2019/10/26/us/kurt-cobain-cardigan-trnd/index.html.

Aspers, P. and F. Godart (2013), "Sociology of Fashion: Order and Change", *Annual Review of Sociology* 39: 171–192. doi: 10.1146/annurev-soc-071811-145526

The Associated Press (2008), "Vogue Cover with LeBron Stirs Up Controversy", *Today,* 25 March. Available at: www.today.com/news/vogue-cover-lebron-stirs-controversy-wbna23797883.

Avis, M., S. Forbes and S. Ferguson (2014), "The Brand Personality of Rocks: A Critical Evaluation of a Brand Personality Scale", *Marketing Theory,* 14(4): 451–475. doi: 10.1177/1470593113512323.

Bacon, J. (2018), "Amid Outage, Homeland Security Chief Kirstjen Nielsen 'Will Not Apologize' for Separating Families", *USA Today,* 18 June. Available at: www.usatoday.com/story/news/nation/2018/06/18/homeland-security-chief-denies-policy-separates-families-border/709378002/.

Bai, Y. (2018), "Artification and Authenticity: Museum Exhibitions of Luxury Fashion Brands in China", in A. Vänskä and H. Clark (eds), *Fashion Curating: Critical Practice in the Museum and Beyond,* New York: Bloomsbury.

Bain, M. (2018), "More U.S. School Kids Than Ever Are Wearing Uniforms The Fall", *Quartzy,* 11 September. Available at: qz.com/quartzy/1382336/school-uniforms-are-rapidly-on-the-rise-at-us-public-schools/.

Ballaster, R., M. Beetham, E. Frazer and S. Hebron (1991), *Women's World: Ideology, Femininity, and the Women's Magazine,* New York: New York University Press.

Balmer, J. M. T. and M. Burghausen (2019), "Marketing, the Past and Corporate Heritage", *Marketing Theory,* 19(2): 217–227. doi: 10.1177/1470593118790636.

Banet-Weiser, S. (2012), *AuthenticTM: The Politics of Ambivalence in a Brand Culture,* New York: New York University Press.

Barajas, J. (2015), "How Alexander McQueen's Grotesque Creations Wrecked the Runway", *PBS NewsHour,* 4 September. Available at: www.pbs.org/newshour/arts/mcqueen

Barker, J. (2018), "Under Armour, Nike, Adidas Race to 'Personalize' Products with New Technology", *The Baltimore Sun,* 3 January. Available at: www.baltimoresun.com/business/bs-bz-under-armour-customize-20171206-story.html.

Barnard, M. (2002). *Fashion as Communication,* New York: Routledge.

Barnard, M. (2010), "Fashion Statements: Communication and Culture", in R. Scapp and B. Seitz (eds), *Fashion Statements: On Style, Appearance and Reality,* New York: Palgrave Macmillan.

Barthes, R. (1977), *Image-Music-Text,* S. Heath (trans), New York: Hill and Wang.

Barthes, R. (1990), *The Fashion System,* M. Ward and R. Howard (trans), Los Angeles: University of California Press.

Barthes, R. (2012), *Mythologies,* A. Lavers (trans.), New York: Hill and Wang.

Bastos, W. and S. J. Levy (2012), "A History of the Concept of Branding: Practice and Theory", *Journal of Historical Research in Marketing,* 4(3): 347–368. doi: 10.1108/17557501211252934.

Baxter-Wright, D. (2017), "8 Reasons Nate from *The Devil Wears Prada* is the Absolute Worst", *Cosmopolitan,* 3 October. Available at: www.cosmopolitan.com/uk/entertainment/a12770393/nate-devil-wears-prada-worst/.

BBC (2018), "Melania Trump Says 'Don't Care' Jacket Was a Message", 14 October. Available at: www.bbc.com/news/world-us-canada-45853364

Becker, H. (1982), *Art Worlds,* Berkeley, CA: University of California Press.

Beebe, S. A., S. J. Beebe and D. K. Ivy (2016), *Communication: Principles for a Lifetime,* New York: Pearson.

Belk, R. W. (1998), "Possessions and the Extended Self", *Journal of Consumer Research,* 15(2): 139–168.

Belk, R. W. (2013), "Extended Self in a Digital World", *Journal of Consumer Research,* 40(3): 477–500. doi: 10.1086/671052.

Bellenger, D. N., E. Steinberg and W. W. Stanton (1976), "The Congruence of Store Image and Self Image: As It Relates to Store Loyalty", *Journal of Retailing,* 52(1): 17–32.

Bengtsen, P. (2018), "Fashion Curates Art: Takashi Murakami for Louis Vuitton", in A. Vänskä and H. Clark (eds), *Fashion Curating: Critical Practice in the Museum and Beyond,* New York: Bloomsbury

Benjamin, W. (2012), "The Work of Art in the Age of Mechanical Reproduction", in M. G. Durham and D. M. Kellner (eds), *Media and Cultural Studies Keyworks,* Malden, MA: Wiley-Blackwell.

Bennett, A. (1999), "Subcultues or Neo-Tribes? Rethinking the Relationship Between Youth, Style and Musical Taste", *Sociology,* 33(3): 599–617. doi: 101177/S0038028599000371

Bennett, A. (2011), "The Post-Subcultural Turn: Some Reflections 10 Years On", *Journal of Youth Studies,* 14(5): 493–506. doi: 10.1080/13676261.2011.559216

Berger, J. (2013), "Ways of Seeing", in L. Ouellette (ed.), *The Media Studies Reader,* 197–204, New York: Routledge.

Berger, P. L. and T. Luckmann (1966), *The Social Construction of Reality: A Treatise in the Sociology of Knowledge,* New York: Anchor.

Bernhard, E. M. (2019), *Contemporary Punk Rock Communities: Scenes of Inclusion and Dedication,* New York: Lexington Books.

Bhasin, K. (2016), "Rebel Teens are Killing Aeropostale and Some Other Clothing Giants", *The Chicago Tribune,* 3 October. Available at: www.chicagotribune.com/business/ct-teen-shoppers-retail-clothing-aeropostale-20161003-story.html

Billboard (n.d.), "Chart History; LFO". Available at: www.billboard.com/music/LFO/chart-history/hot-100/song/64130

Billboard (n.d.), "Chart History: Nirvana". Available at: www.billboard.com/music/nirvana/chart-history/TLP.

Biography.com (2014), "Diana Vreeland", *Biography.com,* 30 July. Available at: www.biography.com/people/diana-vreeland-9520769.

Black, L. (2018), "13 New Plus Size and Size Inclusive Brands that Launched in 2018", *Fashionista,* 26 December. Available at: fashionista.com/2018/12/new-plus-size-inclusive-clothing-brands-2018

Blanks, T. (2014), "Moschino", *Vogue,* 19 February. Available at: www.vogue.com/fashion-shows/fall-2014-ready-to-wear/moschino.

Blaszczyk, R. L. (2018), "The Rise of Color Forecasting in the United States and Great Britain", in R. L. Blaszczyk and B. Wubs (eds), *The Fashion Forecasters: A Hidden History of Color and Trend Prediction*, New York: Bloomsbury.

Blaszczyk, R. L. and B. Wubs (2018), *The Fashion Forecasters: A Hidden History of Color and Trend Prediction*, New York: Bloomsbury.

Blumer, H. (1969), "Fashion: From Class Differentiation to Collective Selection," *The Sociological Quarterly*, 10(3): 275–291.

Blumer, H. (1969), *Symbolic Interactionism: Perspective and Method,* Los Angeles: University of California Press.

Boellstorff, T. (2008), *Coming of Age in Second Life,* Princeton, NJ: Princeton University Press.

Bologna, C. (2018), "How Gender Reveals Became Such A Thing", *HuffPost,* 16 August. Available at: www.huffpost.com/entry/
how-gender-reveals-became-such-a-thing_n_5b4fa97be4b0b15aba8b3e46.

Bolter, J. and R. Grusin (1999), *Remediation: Understanding New Media*, Cambridge, MA: The MIT Press.

Bourdieu, P. (1984), *Distinction: A Social Critique of the Judgement of Taste,* Cambridge, MA: Harvard University Press.

Bourne, L. (2018), "When You're the First Lady, a Jacket Isn't Ever 'Just a Jacket'", *Glamour,* 25 June. Available at: www.glamour.com/story/melania-trump-jacket-first-lady-wardrobe-meaning

Box Office Mojo (n.d.), "Top Lifetime Adjusted Grosses". Available at: www.boxofficemojo.com/chart/top_lifetime_gross_adjusted/?adjust_gross_to=2019&ref_=bo_cso_ac.

boyd, d. and N. B. Ellison (2007), "Social Network Sites: Definition, History and Scholarship", *Journal of Computer Mediated Communication,* 13(1): 210–230. doi: 10.111/j.1083-6101.20067.00393.x.

Breward, C. and D. Gilbert (2006), *Fashion's World Cities,* New York: Berg.

Brewer, M. B. (1991), "The Social Self: On Being the Same and Different at the Same Time", *Personality and Social Psychology Bulletin,* 17(5): 475–482. doi: 10.1177/0146167291175001.

Brown, S., R. V. Kozinets and J. F. Sherry (2003), "Teaching Old Brands New Tricks: Retro Branding and the Revival of Brand Meaning", *Journal of Marketing,* 67(3): 19–33. www.jstor.com/stable/30040534.

Bruccullieri, J. (2019), "This Trend Forecaster's Job is to Decide What Colors We'll Be Wearing", *HuffPost,* 5 April. Available at: www.huffpost.com/entry/trend-forecasting-wgsn-jane-monnington-boddy_l_5ca63667e4b0409b0ec5762d.

Bruzzi, S. (1997), *Undressing Cinema: Clothing and Identity in the Movies,* New York: Routledge.

Buckland, S. S. (2008), "Promoting American Designers, 1940–44: Building Our Own House", in L. Welters and P. A. Cunningham (eds), *Twentieth-Century American Fashion,* 99–122, New York: Berg.

Buckley, C. and H. Clark (2018), *Fashion and Everyday Life: London and New York*, New York: Bloomsbury.

Bush, L. (2018), "Laura Bush: Separating Children from Their Parents at the Border 'Breaks My Heart'", *The Washington Post,* 17 June. Available at: www.washingtonpost.com/

opinions/laura-bush-separating-children-from-their-parents-at-the-border-breaks-my-heart/2018/06/17/f2df517a-7287-11e8-9780-b1dd6a09b549_story.html

Business of Fashion (n.d.), "Elaine Welteroth". Available at: www.businessoffashion.com/community/people/elaine-welteroth.

Campbell, C. (2009), "When the Meaning is not a Message: A Critique of the Consumption as Communication Thesis", in M. Barnard (ed.), *Fashion Theory: A Reader*, 159–169, New York: Routledge.

Campbell, J. (2019), "Celebrating Three Years of Uniqlo Tate Lates", *The Voice*, 19 October. Available at: www.voice-online.co.uk/entertainment/arts-culture/2019/10/19/celebrating-three-years-of-uniqlo-tate-lates/.

Carah, N. (2017), "Algorithmic Brands: A Decade of Brand Experiments with Mobile and Social Media", *New Media & Society*, 19(3): 384–400. doi: 10.1177/1461444815605463.

Carah, N. and D. Angus (2018), "Algorithmic Brand Culture: Participatory Labour, Machine Learning and Branding on Social Media", *Media, Culture & Society*, 40(2): 178–194. doi: 10.1177/0163443718754648.

Carah, N., S. Brodmerkel and L. Hernandez (2014), "Brands and Sociality: Alcohol Branding, Drinking Culture and Facebook", *Convergence*, 20(3), 259–275. doi: 10.1177/1354856514531531.

Carey, J. W. (2009), *Communication as Culture*, New York: Routledge.

Carpenter, D. (2007), "Montgomery Ward Brand Name is Back as an Internet and Catalog Retailer", *Deseret News*, 1 January. Available at: www.deseretnews.com/article/650219424/Montgomery-Ward-brand-name-is-back-as-an-Internet-and-catalog-retailer.html.

Carreon, J. (2019), "What Does 'Business Casual' Even Mean Anymore?", *Elle*, 9 April. Available at: www.elle.com/fashion/shopping/a27035515/business-casual-for-women/.

Carter, R. (2018), 18 June. Available at: twitter.com/CarterCenter/status/1008805106287071232/photo/1

CBS News (2019), "Meet the Ocean Cleanup Company That's Removed 4.7 Million Pounds of Trash", *CBS This Morning*, 15 June. Available at: www.cbsnews.com/news/4ocean-meet-cleanup-company-that-removed-millions-of-pounds-of-trash-2019-06-15/.

Cerini, M. (2019), "Remember When Björk Wore a Swan Dress at the Oscars?", *CNN*, 16 September. Available at: www.cnn.com/style/article/bjork-swan-dress-remember-when/index.html.

Chabbott, S. (2017), "Ashley Graham Becomes First 'Plus-Size' Model to Grace Vogue Cover", 9 February. Available at: wwd.com/business-news/media/vogue-features-first-plus-size-model-ashley-graham-on-march-2017-cover-10781777/.

Chaet, H. (2012), "The Tween Machine", *Adweek*, 25 June. Available at: www.adweek.com/brand-marketing/tween-machine-141357/

Cheney, D. (1996), *Lifestyles*, New York: Routledge.

Chernikoff, L. (2014), "'Legs in the Air? Great Let's Go': Jacky O'Shaughnessy on Modeling for American Apparel at 62", *Elle*, 19 February. Available at: www.elle.com/fashion/a14055/american-apparel-62-year-old-lingerie-model/

Chia, J. (2019), "Ashley Graham is Tired of Being Told How to Feel About Her Body", *Allure*, 18 June. Available at: www.allure.com/story/ashley-graham-cover-interview-2019

@ChurchCarlton. (2018), 18 February. Available at: twitter.com/ChurchCarlton/
    status/965416184416997376/photo/1

Church Gibson, P. (2000), "'No One Expects Me Anywhere': Invisible Women, Ageing and
    the Fashion Industry", in S. Bruzzi and P. Church Gibson (eds), *Fashion Cultures:
    Theories, Explorations and Analysis,* 79–89, New York: Routledge.

Church Gibson, P. (2012), *Fashion and Celebrity Culture,* New York: Berg.

Cillizza, C. (2018), "Melania Trumps' 'I Really Don't Care. Do U?' Jacket Was No Mistake",
    CNN, 22 June. Available at: www.cnn.com/2018/06/21/politics/melania-trump-jacket-
    border-visit/index.html

Clark, H. (2014), "Conceptual", in A. Geczy and V. Karaminas (eds), *Fashion and Art,* New
    York: Bloomsbury.

Clark, J. (2018), "Props and other Attributes: Fashion and Exhibition-making", in A. Vänskä
    and H. Clark (eds), *Fashion Curating: Critical Practice in the Museum and Beyond,* New
    York: Bloomsbury.

Clark, L. (2019), "Liz Hurley Wore 'That Dress' After Snub by Fashion Designers, Says
    Hugh Grant", *Yahoo! News,* 22 December. Available at: news.yahoo.com/liz-hurley-
    dress-designers-105229972.html

Clinton, H. (2018), 18 June. Available at: twitter.com/HillaryClinton/status/
    1008806592400314368

CNT Editors and C. Kwak (2018), "The Most Stylish Flight Attendant Uniforms", *Conde
    Nast Traveler,* 15 October. Available at: www.cntraveler.com/galleries/2015-11-06/
    the-chicest-new-airline-uniforms-from-prabal-gurung-to-christian-lacroix

Cole, D. J. and N. Deihl (2015), *The History of Modern Fashion From 1850,* London:
    Laurence King Publishing.

Cole, S. (2000), *"Don We Now Our Gay Apparel": Gay Men's Dress in the Twentieth Century,*
    New York: Berg.

Collins, A. F. (2004), "*Vanity Fair*: The early years, 1914–1936", *Vanity Fair,* September.
    Available at: www.vanityfair.com/magazine/2006/10/earlyyears

Collins, A. (2018), "Ashley Graham Lands Revlon Contract", *WWD,* 24 January. Available
    at: wwd.com/beauty-industry-news/color-cosmetics/ashley-graham-revlon-
    contract-11122981/

Colliver, V. (2016), "Fitting Rooms' New Style: Magic Mirrors, Digital Outfits", *San
    Francisco Chronicle,* 20 October. Available at: www.sfchronicle.com/business/article/
    Fitting-rooms-new-style-magic-mirrors-9984618.php?psid=8En6e

Consumerist (2013), "Is it Legal for Employers to Make Employees Pay for Uniforms?",
    Consumer Reports, 12 April. Available at: www.consumerreports.org/consumerist/
    is-it-legal-for-employers-to-make-employees-pay-for-uniforms/

Cook, D. (2004), *The Commodification of Childhood: The Children's Clothing Industry and
    the Rise of the Child Consumer,* Durham, NC: Duke University Press.

Cooley, C. H. (1902), *Human Nature and the Social Order,* New York: Charles Scribner's
    Sons.

Corrigan, P. (2008), *The Dressed Society: Clothing, the Body and Some Meanings of the
    World,* Los Angeles: Sage.

Couldry, N. and A. Hepp (2013), "Conceptualizing Mediatization: Contexts, Traditions,
    Arguments", *Communication Theory,* 23(3): 191–202. doi: 10.1111/comt.12019

Couldry, N. and A. Hepp (2016), *The Mediated Construction of Reality*, New York: Polity.

Couldry, N. and J. Turow (2014), "Advertising, Big Data and the Clearance of the Public Realm: Marketers' New Approaches to the Content Subsidy", *International Journal of Communication,* 8: 1710–1726.

Craik, J. (2005), *Uniforms Exposed: From Conformity to Transgression,* New York: Berg.

Crane, D. (2000), *Fashion and its Social Agendas: Class, Gender, and Identity in Clothing,* Chicago: University of Chicago Press.

Crane, D. (2014), "Boundaries", in A. Geczy and V. Karaminas (eds), *Fashion and Art*, New York: Bloomsbury.

Cuneo, A. Z. (2003), "Apple Transcends as Lifestyle Brand", *AdAge,* 15 December. Available at: adage.com/article/special-report-marketer-of-the-year/apple-transcends-lifestyle-brand/97129

Cupach, W. R. and S. Metts (2006), "Face Management in Interpersonal Communication", in K. M. Galvin and P. J. Cooper (eds), *Making Connections: Readings in Relational Communication*, Fourth edition, Los Angeles: Roxbury Publishing.

Currid-Halkett, E. (2017), *The Sum of Small Things: A Theory of the Aspirational Class,* Princeton, NJ: Princeton University Press.

The Cut (2008), "Meet Tavi, the 12-year-old Fashion Blogger" *The Cut,* 22 July, Available at: www.thecut.com/2008/07/meettavithe12yearoldfashio.html.

The Cut. (2008), "Tween Blogger Tavi Makes it Big with Fashion Editors", *The Cut,* 25 July. Available at: www.thecut.com/2008/07/tween_blogger_makes_it_big_wit.html

CVS (2018), "CVS Pharmacy Makes Commitment to Create New Standards for Post-Production Alternations of Beauty Imagery", 15 January. Available at: cvshealth.com/newsroom/press-releases/cvs-pharmacy-makes-commitment-create-new-standards-post-production.

CVS (2019), "CVS Phramacy Unveils New Beauty Aisles Reflecting Significant Progress in Commitment to Transparency and New Standards for Beauty Imagery", 24 January. Available at: cvshealth.com/newsroom/press-releases/cvs-pharmacy-unveils-new-beauty-aisles-reflecting-significant-progress.

Czerniawski, A. M. (2015), *Fashioning Fat: Inside Plus-Size Modeling,* New York: New York University Press.

Danesi, M. (2013), "Semiotizing a Product into a Brand", *Social Semiotics,* 23(4): 464–476. doi: 10.1080/10350330.2013.799003.

Davies, A. (2018), "People are Getting Surgery to Look Like Their Snapchat Selfies", *BBC,* 19 April. Available at: www.bbc.co.uk/bbcthree/article/9ca4f7c6-d2c3-4e25-862c-03aed9ec1082.

Davis, F. (1992), *Fashion, Culture and Identity,* Chicago: University of Chicago Press.

De Casanova, E. M. (2015), *Buttoned Up: Clothing, Conformity and White-Collar Masculinity,* Ithaca, NY: IRL Press.

De Chernatony, L. (2009), "Toward the Holy Grail of Defining 'Brand'", *Marketing Theory,* 9(1): 101–105. doi: 10.1177/1470593108100063

De Saussure, F. (1983), *Course in General Linguistics,* Roy Harris (trans), Chicago: Open Court.

Del Gandio, J. (2008), *Rhetoric for Radicals: A Handbook for 21st Century Activists,* Gabriola Island, BC: New Society Publishers.

Del Valle, G. (2019), "Virgin Atlantic Flight Attendants No Longer Have to Wear Makeup and Skirts", *Vox,* 5 March. Available at: www.vox.com/the-goods/2019/3/5/18251839/virgin-atlantic-uniform-makeup-skirts.

DeAcetis, J. (2018), "How Marine Layer Achieves Brick and Mortar Success", *Forbes,* 7 May. Available at: www.forbes.com/sites/josephdeacetis/2018/05/07/how-marine-layer-achieves-brick-and-mortar-success/#445f3d7b626d.

Deacon, D. and J. Stanyer (2014), "Mediatization: Key Concept of Conceptual Bandwagon?", *Media, Culture & Society,* 36(7): 1032–1044. doi: 10.1177/016344371452218.

Dempsey, C. (2007), "The Art of the Scarf", *Fort Worth Star-Telegram,* 24 April. Available at: www.star-telegram.com/latest-news/article3822356.html.

Denizet-Lewis, B. (2006), "The Man Behind Abercrombie & Fitch", *Salon,* 24 January. Available at: www.salon.com/2006/01/24/jeffries/.

The Devil Wears Prada (2006), Film Dir. D. Frankel, USA: Fox 2000 Pictures.

Dewey, J. (2005), *Art as Experience,* New York: TarcherPerigee.

Dirks, T. (n.d.), "Silent Films", *AMC Filmsite.* Available at: www.filmsite.org/silentfilms.html.

Dishman, L. (2015), "Why Teens Stopped Shopping at Abercrombie & Fitch and Wet Seal", *The Guardian,* 25 February. Available at: www.theguardian.com/business/2015/feb/25/clothing-retailers-teens-abercrombie-fitch-wet-seal-aeropostale-hollister

Dockers (n.d.), "Dockers Stories." Available at: www.dockers.com/US/en_US/features/guys-guide.

Dolich, I. J. (1969), "Congruence Relationships Between Self Images and Product Brands", *Journal of Marketing Research,* 6(1): 80–84.

Donnella, L. (2019), "Is Beauty in the Eyes of the Colonizer?" *NPR,* 6 February. Available at: www.npr.org/sections/codeswitch/2019/02/06/685506578/is-beauty-in-the-eyes-of-the-colonizer.

Douglas, M. and B. Isherwood (1979), *The World of Goods,* New York: Basic Books.

Doyle, S. (2016), "The True Story of How *Teen Vogue* Got Mad, Got Woke, and Began Terrifying Men Like Donald Trump", *Quartz,* 19 December. Available at: qz.com/866305/the-true-story-of-how-teen-vogue-got-mad-got-woke-and-began-terrifying-men-like-donald-trump/.

Doyle, S. A., C. M. Moore, A. M. Doherty and M. Hamilton (2008), "Brand Context and Control: The Role of the Flagship Store in B&B Italia", *International Journal of Retail & Distribution Management,* 36(7): 551–563. doi: 10.1108/09590550810880589.

Duffy, B. E. (2013), *Remake, Remodel: Women's Magazines in the Digital Age,* Chicago: University of Illinois Press.

Duffy, B. E. (2015), "Amateur, Autonomous, and Colloborative: Myths of Aspiring Female Cultural Producers in Web 2.0", *Critical Studies in Media Communication,* 32(1): 48–65. doi: 10.1080/15295036.2014.997832.

Duffy, B. E. (2017), *(not) Getting Paid to Do What You Love,* New Haven, CT: Yale University Press.

Dunn, R. G. (2008), *Identifying Consumption: Subjects and Objects in Consumer Society,* Philadelphia: Temple University Press.

Dyer, G. (1982), *Advertising as Communication,* New York: Routledge.

Ebba, O. (2010), "All 5 First Ladies Speak Out Against Family-Separation Immigration Policy", *ABC News*, 18 June. Available at: abcnews.go.com/beta-story-container/Politics/ladies-speak-family-separation-immigration-policy/story?id=55986862

Eckert, C. (1990), "The Carole Lombard in Macy's Window", in J. Gaines and C. Herzog (eds), *Fabrications: Costume and the Female Body*, New York: Routledge.

The Economist (2019), "Burqa Bans Have Proliferated in Western Europe", 9 August. Available at: www.economist.com/graphic-detail/2019/08/09/burqa-bans-have-proliferated-in-western-europe.

Edwards, A., C. Edwards, S. T. Wahl and S. A. Myers (2016), *The Communication Age: Connecting and Engaging*, Los Angeles: Sage.

Edwards, J. L. (2009), "Visual Rhetoric", in W. F. Eadie (ed.), *21st Century Communication: A Reference Handbook*, 220–227, Los Angeles: Sage.

Edwards, T. (2011), *Fashion in Focus: Concepts, Practices and Politics*, New York: Routledge.

Ehrenkranz, M. (2017), "That Totally Fake Shark Photo Isn't From Hurricane Harvey (or Any Other Hurricane)", *Gizmodo*, 28 August. Available at: gizmodo.com/that-totally-fake-shark-photo-isnt-from-hurricane-harve-1798495171.

Eicher, J. B. (2010), "Clothing, Costume, and Dress," in V. Steele (ed.), *The Berg Companion to Fashion*, New York: Berg.

Eicher, J. B. and M. E. Roach-Higgins (1993), "Definition and Classification of Dress: Implications for Analysis of Gender Roles," in R. Barnes and J. B. Eicher (eds), *Dress and Gender: Making and Meaning*, New York: Berg.

Elle (n.d.), "The Heritage". Available at: www.elleboutiqueus.com/Page/About-ELLE.

Ellison, J. (2017), "Brandy Melville and the Rise of the Instabrand", *The Financial Times*, 17 March. Available at: www.ft.com/content/9979e39e-08a1-11e7-97d1-5e720a26771b

Encyclopædia Britannica (n.d.), "HDTV". Available at: www.britannica.com/technology/HDTV.

Encyclopædia Britannica (n.d.), "Newsreel". Available at: www.britannica.com/topic/newsreel.

English, B. (2013), *A Cultural History of Fashion in the 20th and 21st Centuries* Second edition, New York: Bloomsbury.

English, J. F. (2008), *The Economy of Prestige: Prizes, Awards and the Circulation of Cultural Value*, Cambridge, MA: Harvard University Press.

Entman, R. M. (1993), "Framing: Toward Clarification of a Fractured Paradigm", *Journal of Communication*, 43(4): 51–58.

Entwistle, J. (2015), *The Fashioned Body: Fashion Dress and Modern Social Theory*, Second edition, Malden, MA: Polity.

Entwistle, J. and D. Slater (2012), "Models as Brands: Critical Thinking about Bodies and Images", in J. Entwistle and E. Wissinger (eds), *Fashioning Models: Image, Text and Industry*, 15–33, New York: Bloomsbury.

Entwistle, J. and D. Slater (2014), "Reassembling the Cultural: Fashion Models, Brands and the Meaning of 'Culture' After ANT", *Journal of Cultural Economy*, 7(2): 161–177. doi: 10.1080/17530350.2013.783501.

Everett, C. (2010), "Elle Magazine Accused of Digitally Lightening Gabourey Sidibe's Skin on October Cover", *New York Daily News*, 17 September. Available at: www.

nydailynews.com/entertainment/gossip/elle-magazine-accused-digitally-lightening-gabourey-sidibe-skin-october-cover-article-1.443873.

Ewing, M. T., C. P. Jevons and E. L. Khalil (2009), "Brand Death: A Developmental Model of Senescence", *Journal of Business Research,* 62(3): 332–338. doi: 10.1016/j. jbusres.2009.04.004.

The Eye Has to Travel (2012), Film Dir. L. I. Vreeland, B. Perlmutt and F. Tcheng, USA: Gloss Studio.

Falconer, B. (2018), "What is the Perfect Color Worth?", *The New York Times,* 28 February. Available at: www.nytimes.com/2018/02/28/magazine/what-is-the-perfect-color-worth.html.

Fandango (n.d.), "The 12 Longest Running Film Franchises". Available at: www.fandango. com/movie-photos/the-12-longest-running-film-franchises-1219

Farhi, P. (2011), "Michelle Obama's Target Trip: Critics Take Aim", 2 October. Available at: www.washingtonpost.com/lifestyle/style/michelle-obamas-target-trip-critics-take-aim/2011/10/02/gIQATrMLGL_story.html

Farooq, S. (2011), "Steve Jobs Finally Explains His Uniform", *NBC Bay Area,* 12 October. Available at: www.nbcbayarea.com/blogs/press-here/Steve-Jobs-Finally-Explains-His-Uniform-131588418.html.

Featherstone, M. (2007), *Consumer Culture and Postmodernism*, Second edition, Los Angeles: Sage.

Feiner, L. (2019), "Amazon is the Most Valuable Public Company in the World After Passing Microsoft", *CNBC,* 7 January. Available at: www.cnbc.com/2019/01/07/amazon-passes-microsoft-market-value-becomes-largest.html.

Feitelberg, R. (2019), "Tracy Reese Teams With United Airlines to Suit Up Female Employees", *WWD,* 17 January. Available at: wwd.com/fashion-news/fashion-scoops/tracy-reese-teams-with-united-airlines-to-suit-up-female-employees-1202971359/.

Feuer, J. (1995), *Seeing Through the Eighties: Television and Reaganism,* Durham, NC: Duke University Press.

Fisher, L. A. (2018), "Rihanna's Savage x Fenty Show Was an Incredibly Stunning, Inclusive Celebration of Womanhood", *Harper's Bazaar,* 12 September. Available at: www. harpersbazaar.com/fashion/fashion-week/a23108732/rihanna-savage-fenty-new-york-fashion-week/.

Folger Shakespeare Library (n.d.), *As You Like It* from Folger Digital Texts. Available at: www.folgerdigitaltexts.org/html/AYL.html.

Foss, S. K. (2004), "Framing the Study of Visual Rhetoric: Toward a Transformation of Rhetorical Theory", in C. A. Hill and M. Helmers (eds), *Defining Visual Rhetorics*, Mahwah, NJ: Lawrence Erlbaum Associates.

Foss, S. K. (2004), "Theory of Visual Rhetoric", in K. Smith., S. Moriarty, G. Barbatsis and K. Kenney (eds), *Handbook for Visual Communication: Theory, Methods and Media,* 141–152, New York: Routledge.

Foss, S. K. and C. L. Griffin (1985), "Beyond Persuasion: A Proposal for an Invitational Rhetoric", *Communication Monographs,* 62(1): 2–18. doi: 10.1080/03637759509376345.

Foucault, M. (1969), "What is an Author?". Available at: www.open.edu/openlearn/ocw/pluginfile.php/624849/mod_resource/content/1/a840_1_michel_foucault.pdf.

Fournier, S. (1998), "Consumers and Their Brands: Developing Relationship Theory in Consumer Research", *Journal of Consumer Research,* 24(4): 343–353. doi: 101086/209515

Fournier, S. and C. Alvarez (2012), "Brand as Relationship Partners: Warmth, Competence, and In-Between", *Journal of Consumer Psychology,* 22(2): 177–185. doi: 10.1016/j.jcps.2011.10.003

Fournier, S. and J. Avery (2011), "The Uninvited Brand", *Business Horizons,* 54(3), 193–207. doi: 10.1016/j.bushor.2011.01.001

Franz, J. (2005), "T.G.I. Fridays Changing its Stripes, 'Flair'", *Chicago Tribune,* 18 February. Available at: www.chicagotribune.com/news/ct-xpm-2005-02-18-0502180320-story.html

Freberg, K., K. Graham, K. McGaughey and L. A. Freberg (2011), "Who are the Social Media Influencers? A Study of Public Perceptions of Personality," *Public Relations Review,* 37(1): 90–92. doi: 10.1016/j.pubrev.2010.11.001.

Friedman, V. (2016), "Jaden Smith for Louis Vuitton: The New Man in a Skirt", *The New York Times,* 6 January. Available at: www.nytimes.com/2016/01/07/fashion/jaden-smith-for-louis-vuitton-the-new-man-in-a-skirt.html.

Friedman, V. (2018), "Met Costume Institute Embraces 'Camp' for 2019 Blockbuster Show", *The New York Times,* 9 October. Available at: www.nytimes.com/2018/10/09/arts/design/met-costume-institute-camp-2019-spring-show.html?module=inline.

Friedman, V. (2018), "Melania Trump, Agent of Coat Chaos", *The New York Times,* 21 June. Available at: www.nytimes.com/2018/06/21/style/zara-jacket-melania-trump.html

Fulcher, M. and A. R. Hayes (2018), "Building a Pink Dinosaur: The Effects of Gendered Construction Toys on Girls' and Boys' Play", *Sex Roles,* 79(5–6): 273–284: doi: 10.1007/s.11199-017-0806-3.

Funny Face (1957), Film Dir. S. Donan, USA: Paramount Pictures.

Gaines, J. (1990), "Costume and Narrative: How Dress Tells the Woman's Story", in J. Gaines and C. Herzog (eds), *Fabrications: Costume and the Female Body,* New York: Routledge.

Gaines, J. and C. Herzog (1990), *Fabrications: Costume and the Female Body,* New York: Routledge.

Gardner, B. B. and S. J. Levy (1955), "The Product and the Brand", *Harvard Business Review,* 33(2): 33–39.

Garza, F. (2019), "Send All the Influencers to Jail", *Jezebel,* 31 May. Available at: jezebel.com/send-all-the-influencers-to-jail-1835154127_jezebel_twitter.

Geczy, A. and V. Karaminas (2016), "Walter Benjamin: Fashion, Modernity and the City Street", in A. Rocamora and A. Smelik (eds), *Thinking Through Fashion: A Guide to Key Theorists,* New York: I.B. Tauris.

Geczy, A. and V. Karaminas (2018), *The End of Fashion: Clothing and Dress in the Age of Globalization,* New York: Bloomsbury.

Geczy, A. and V. Karaminas (2019), *Fashion Installation: Body, Space and Performance,* New York: Bloomsbury.

"Generation Like" (2014), Television Episode *Frontline,* 18 February. Prod. F. Koughan and D. Rushkoff. Available at: www.pbs.org/wgbh/frontline/film/generation-like/.

Genzlinger, N. (2012), "The Closet Question: Who Would Wear this Stuff?", *The New York Times,* 12 March. Available at: www.nytimes.com/2012/03/13/arts/television/fashion-star-designer-competition-series-on-nbc.html.

Gevinson, T. (2011), "I Feel Like the Photo to Accompany this Post Should be a Lot More Intense and Introspective-Seeming But Hey! Mirrors are Pretty Introspective", *Style Rookie,* 27 March. Available at: www.thestylerookie.com/2011/03/i-feel-like-photo-to-accompany-this.html.

Gieseler, C. (2017), "Gender-Reveal Parties: Performing Community Identity in Pink and Blue", *Journal of Gender Studies.* doi: 10.1080/09589236.2017.1287066.

Gillmor, D. (2004), *We the Media: Grassroots Journalism By the People, For the People,* Sebastopol, CA: O'Reilly Media.

Givhan, R. (2018), "Nothing Else Melania Trump Wears Will Ever Matter Again", *The Washington Post,* 13 July. Available at: www.washingtonpost.com/news/arts-and-entertainment/wp/2018/07/13/nothing-else-melania-trump-wears-will-ever-matter-again/

Goffman, E. (1959), *The Presentation of Self in Everyday Life,* New York: Anchor.

Goldstein, L. (1999), "The Alpha Teenager", *Forbes,* 20 December. Available at: archive.fortune.com/magazines/fortune/fortune_archive/1999/12/20/270530/index.htm.

Golfar, F. (2019), "Elizabeth Hurley on the Versace Pin Dress that Changed Everything", *Harper's Bazaar,* 25 March. Available at: www.harpersbazaar.com/fashion/designers/a26869247/elizabeth-hurley-versace-dress/.

Gonzales, E. (2017), "Christian Louboutin Responses to Cardi B's 'Bodak Yellow'", *Harper's Bazaar,* 3 October. Available at: www.harpersbazaar.com/fashion/designers/a12774913/christian-louboutin-cardi-b-bodak-yellow/

Goode, L. (2017), "Amazon's Echo Look Does More for Amazon Than it Does for Your Style", *The Verge,* 6 July. Available at: www.theverge.com/2017/7/6/15924120/amazon-echo-look-review-camera-clothes-style.

Graakjær, N. J. (2012), "Dance in the Store: On the Use and Production of Music in Abercrombie & Fitch", *Critical Discourse Studies,* 9(4): 939–406. doi: 10.1080/17405904.2012.713208.

Graakjær, N. J. (2014), "The Bonding of a Band and a Brand: On Music Placement in Television Commercials from a Text Analytical Perspective", *Popular Music and Society,* 37(5): 517–537. doi: 10.1080/03007766.2013.861242.

Graham, M. (2013), "The First 30 Videos that Played on MTV", *VH1,* 21 August. Available at: web.archive.org/web/20191211104833/www.vh1.com/news/51387/mtv-first-30-videos/.

Granata, F. (2017), *Experimental Fashion: Performance Art, Carnival and the Grotesque Body,* New York: I.B. Tauris.

Graybill, B. and L. B. Arthur (1999), "The Social Control of Women's Bodies in Two Mennonite Communities", in L. B. Arthur (ed.), *Religion, Dress and the Body,* 9–29, New York: Berg.

Greenberger, A. (2015), "A Look at the Met's Top 10 Most Visited Exhibitions of All Time", *ARTNews,* 12 September. Available at: www.artnews.com/art-news/news/a-look-at-the-mets-top-ten-most-visited-exhibitions-of-all-time-4918/.

Greenhouse, S. (2010), "Pressured, Nike to Help Workers in Honduras", *The New York Times,* 26 July. Available at: www.nytimes.com/2010/07/27/business/global/27nike.html.

Griffin, E. (2009), *A First Look At Communication Theory,* New York: McGraw-Hill.

Grindstaff, L. (2013), "Trash, Class and Cultural Hierarchy", in L. Ouellette (ed.), *The Media Studies Reader,* New York: Routledge.

Grobart, S. (2016), "Brotailers are Redefining How Guys Buy Clothes", *Bloomberg Businessweek,* 17 March. Available at: www.bloomberg.com/news/articles/2016-03-17/brotailers-are-redefining-how-guys-buy-clothes.

Groves, M. (1987), "New Buyer Sought for Abercrombie & Fitch: Oshman Pull Out of Deal to Sell Unit", *Los Angeles Times,* 25 December. Available at: www.latimes.com/archives/la-xpm-1987-12-25-fi-21031-story.html.

Gumbel, A. (2009), "The Truth about Columbine", *The Guardian,* 16 April. Available at: www.theguardian.com/world/2009/apr/17/columbine-massacre-gun-crime-us.

Hall, S, (2013), "The Work of Representations", in L. Ouellette (ed.), *The Media Studies Reader,* 171–196, New York: Routledge.

Hamilton, J. A. (1997), "The Macro-Micro Interface in the Construction of Individual Fashion Forms and Meanings", *Clothing and Textiles Research Journal,* 15(3): 164–171.

Hamilton, J. A. and J. Hawley (1999), "Sacred Dress, Public Worlds: Amish and Mormon Experiences and Commitment", in L. B. Arthur (ed), *Religion, Dress and the Body,* 31–51, New York: Berg.

Hancock, J. H. (2009), "Chelsea on 5th Avenue: Hypermasculinity and Gay Clone Culture in the Retail Brand Practices of Abercrombie & Fitch", *Fashion Practice,* 1(1): 63–86. doi: 10.2752/17593809X418702

Hancock, J. H. (2016), *Brand/Story: Cases and Explorations in Fashion Branding,* New York: Bloomsbury.

Handy, B. (2002), "Glamour with Altitude", *Vanity Fair,* October. Available at: www.vanityfair.com/news/2002/10/stewardesses-golden-era.

Hanson, R. E. (2017). *Mass Communication: Living in a Media World,* Sixth edition, Los Angeles: Sage.

Harbison, C. (2019), "Snapchat's Baby Face Filter is Just What We Needed This Friday", *Newsweek,* 24 May. Available at: www.newsweek.com/how-use-snapchat-baby-face-filter-what-app-stephen-smith-hilarious-funny-1435633.

Hare, K. (2014), "Executive Editors of *The New York Times*: Where are they now?" *Poynter,* 10 February. Available at: www.poynter.org/news/executive-editors-new-york-times-where-are-they-now.

Harper's Bazaar Staff (2014), "Diana Vreeland asks, Why don't you . . ." *Harper's Bazaar,* 20 June. Available at: www.harpersbazaar.com/culture/features/a2620/diana-vreeland-why-dont-you/.

Headlee, C. (2012), "First Black Editor-in-Chief for Conde Nast", *NPR,* 1 October. Available at: www.npr.org/2012/10/01/162088694/first-black-editor-in-chief-for-conde-nast.

Hearn, A. (2008), "'Meat, Mask, Burden': Probing the Contours of the Branded 'Self'", *Journal of Consumer Culture,* 8(2): 197–217. doi: 10.1177/1469540508090086.

Hebdige, D. (1979), *Subculture: The Meaning of Style,* New York: Routledge.

Hegarty, A. (2018), "Timeline: Immigrant Children Separated From Families at the Border", *USAToday,* 27 June. Available at: www.usatoday.com/story/news/2018/06/27/immigrant-children-family-separation-border-timeline/734014002/

Heil, E. (2018), "How Melania Trump's Jacket Choice Overtook Her Visit to the Texas Border Shelters", *The Washington Post,* 21 June. Available at: www.washingtonpost.com/news/reliable-source/wp/2018/06/21/writing-on-melania-trumps-jacket-causes-controversy-before-border-visit

Held, A. (2017), "France Aims to Get Real: Retouched Photos of Models Now Require a Label", *NPR,* 30 September. Available at: www.npr.org/sections/thetwo-way/2017/09/30/554750939/france-aims-to-get-real-retouched-photos-of-models-now-require-label.

Henderson, C. (2018), "'I Wear the Pants': Lady Gage Reveal Reason Behind Oversize Suit in Powerful Speech", *USA Today,* 17 October. Available at: www.usatoday.com/story/life/people/2018/10/17/lady-gaga-reveals-reason-behind-oversized-suit-during-powerful-speech-wear-pants/1666992002/.

Hennessy, B. (2018), *Influencer: Building Your Personal Brand in the Age of Social Media,* New York: Citadel Press.

Hepp, A., S. Hjarvard and K. Lundby (2015), "Mediatization: Theorizing the Interplay Between Media, Culture and Society", *Media, Culture & Society,* 37(2): 314–324. doi: 10.1177/0163443715573835.

Hofstede, G. (2011), "Dimensionalizing Cultures: The Hofstede Model in Context", *Online Readings in Psychology and Culture,* 2(1). doi: 10.9707/2307-0919.1014.

Hollander, A. (1978), *Seeing Through Clothes,* New York: Penguin Books.

Hollander, A. (1994), *Sex and Suits: The Evolution of Modern Dress,* New York: Kodansha International.

Hollenbeck, C. R., C. Peters and G. M. Zinkhan (2008), "Retail Spectacles and Brand Meaning: Insights from a Brand Museum Case Study", *Journal of Retailing,* 84(3): 334–353. doi: 10.1016/j.jretai.2008.05.003.

Holt, D. B. (2002), "Why Do Brands Cause Trouble? A Dialectical Theory of Consumer Culture and Branding", *Journal of Consumer Research,* 29(1): 70–90. doi: 10.1086/339922.

Holt, D. B. (2004), *How Do Brands Become Icons: The Principles of Cultural Branding,* Cambridge, MA: Harvard Buiness School Press.

Holt, D. B. (2006), "Toward a Sociology of Branding", *Journal of Consumer Culture,* 6(3): 299–302. doi: 10.1177/1469540506068680.

hooks, b. (2013), "The Oppositional Gaze: Black Female Spectators", in L. Ouellette (ed.), *The Media Studies Reader,* 171–196, New York: Routledge.

Horyn, C. (2011), "Galliano Case Tests Dior Brand's Future", *The New York Times,* 1 March. Available at: www.nytimes.com/2011/03/02/fashion/02galliano-dior.html.

How I Built This (2017), Podcast, *NPR,* 7 August. Available at: www.npr.org/2017/09/21/541686055/rent-the-runway-jenn-hyman.

Hudson, B. T. and J. M. T. Balmer (2013), "Corporate Hertiage Brands: Mead's Theory of the Past", *Corporate Communications: An International Journal,* 18(3): 347–361. doi: 10.1108/CCIJ-Apr-2010-0027.

Hudson, D. L. and M. Ghani (2017), "Clothing, Dress Codes & Uniforms", *Freedom Forum Institute,* 18 September. Available at: www.freedomforuminstitute.org/first-amendment-center/topics/freedom-of-speech-2/k-12-public-school-student-expression/clothing-dress-codes-uniforms/.

Hughes, A. (2016), "Ashley Graham Launches Swimsuits for All Collection", *WWD,* 21 May. Available at: wwd.com/fashion-news/fashion-scoops/ashley-graham-swimsuits-for-all-collection-10436519/.

Hume, L. (2010), "Dress and Religious Practices", in J. B. Eicher and P. G. Tortora (eds), *Berg Encyclopedia of World Dress and Fashion: Global Perspectives,* New York: Bloomsbury. doi: 10.2752/BEWDF/EDch10010.

Hume, L. (2013), *The Religious Life of Dress,* New York: Bloomsbury.

Ibrahim, B. (2019), "Pantone's Color of the Year is a Vibrant Start to 2019", *CNN,* 3 January. Available at: www.cnn.com/2019/01/03/cnn-underscored/pantone-color-year-2019-living-coral/index.html.

Ilyashov, A. (2015), "Here's to the End of Fashion's Social-Media 'Voices'", *Refinery 29,* 11 August. Available at: www.refinery29.com/en-us/2015/08/92216/dkny-pr-girl-account-disappears

Italie, L. (2019), "Billy Porter Speaks on Oscars Gown and Social Media Hate", *Associated Press,* 26 February. Available at: www.apnews.com/c87bf643d7824a18ad5f5db99c6d029a.

Jacobs, A. (2019), "Tycoon of the Pre-Owned", *The New York Times,* 23 January. Available at: www.nytimes.com/2019/01/23/style/the-real-real.html.

Jeffers McDonald, T. (2010), *Hollywood Catwalk: Exploring Costume and Transformation in American Film,* New York: I.B. Tauris.

Jenkins, H. (2006), *Convergence Culture: Where Old and New Media Collide,* New York: New York University Press.

Jenss, H. (2015), *Fashioning Memory: Vintage Style and Youth Culture,* New York: Bloomsbury.

Johnson, K. K. P. (2010), "Politics and Fashion", in V. Steele (ed.), *The Berg Companion to Fashion,* London: Bloomsbury Academic.

Johnston, C. (2018), "Amazon Opens a Supermarket with No Checkouts", *BBC,* 22 January. Available at: www.bbc.com/news/business-42769096.

Johnston, P. (2019), "Untuckit, One on Line Only, is Now at 51 Brick and Mortar Stores and Counting", *Stores,* 15 January. Available at: stores.org/2019/01/15/shirttails-out-storefronts-in/.

Kadaba, L. S. (2019), "Casual Friday? At More and More Top Workplaces It's Casual Every Day", *The Philadelphia Inquirer,* 19 April. Available at: www.philly.com/business/top-workplaces/top-workplaces-dress-codes-casual-friday-every-day-millennials-gen-z-20190419.html.

Kaiser, S. B. (1997), *The Social Psychology of Clothing: Symbolic Appearances in Context,* New York: Fairchild.

Kaiser, S. B. (2012), *Fashion and Cultural Studies,* New York: Berg.

Kaiser, S. B., R. H. Nagasawa and S. S. Hutton (1991), "Fashion, Postmodernity and Personal Appearance: A Symbolic Interactionist Formulation", *Symbolic Interaction,* 14(2): 165–185.

Kalbaska, N., T. Sádaba and L. Cantoni (2018), "Fashion Communication: Between Tradition and Digital Transformation," *Studies in Communication Sciences,* 18(2): 269–285. doi: 10.24434/j.scoms.2018.02.005.

Kanai, A. (2016), "Why Ashley Graham Doesn't Like the Term 'Plus Size'", *Cosmopolitan,* 9 April. Available at: www.cosmopolitan.com/style-beauty/a54313/ashley-graham-april-2016/.

Kaplan, S. (2015), "The Rise and Fall of Abercrombie's 'Look Policy'", *The Washington Post,* 2 June. Available at: www.washingtonpost.com/news/morning-mix/wp/2015/06/02/the-rise-and-fall-of-abercrombies-look-policy/

Karimzadeh, M. and J. Naughton (2010), "Calvin Klein's Big Move: Ck One Turns Lifestyle Brand", *WWD,* 27 September. Available at: wwd.com/fashion-news/denim/calvin-kleins-big-move-ck-one-turns-lifestyle-brand-3306215/.

Kaufman, A. (2017), "How *Teen Vogue*'s Elaine Welteroth is Shaking up Expectations for a New Generation of Young Women", *Los Angeles Times,* 6 December. Available at: www.latimes.com/entertainment/la-et-mn-teen-vogue-elaine-welteroth-20171206-story.html.

Kaufman, L. and C. H. Deutsch (2000), "Montgomery Ward to Close Its Doors", *The New York Times,* 29 December. Available at: www.nytimes.com/2000/12/29/business/montgomery-ward-to-close-its-doors.html

Kawamura, Y. (2005), *Fashion-ology: An Introduction to Fashion Studies,* New York: Berg.

Keblusek, L. and H. Giles (2017), "Dress Style Code and Fashion", *Oxford Research Encyclopedia of Communication.* doi: 10.1093/acrefore/9780190228613.013.448.

Keefer, A. (2018), "How the Ultimate Shark Photo Went Viral", *National Geographic,* 8 November. Available at: www.nationalgeographic.com/animals/2018/07/great-white-shark-meme-news-photography-animals-peschak/.

Keller, K. L. (2012), "Understanding the Richness of Brand Relationships: Research Dialogue on Brands as Intentional Agents", *Journal of Consumer Psychology,* 22(2): 186–190. doi: 10.1016/j.jcps.2011.11.011.

Kervyn, N., S. T. Fiske and C. Malone (2012), "Brands as Intentional Agents Framework: How Perceived Intentions and Ability Can Map Brand Perception", *Journal of Consumer Psychology,* 22(2): 166–176. doi: 10.1016/j.jcps.2011.09.006.

Kesvani, H. (n.d.), "The Man Who Coined the Term 'Metrosexual' on the Word Being MIA from the 'Queer Eye' Reboot", *MEL.* Available at: melmagazine.com/en-us/story/the-man-who-coined-the-term-metrosexual-on-the-word-being-mia-from-the-queer-eye-reboot.

Killing Us Softly 4: Advertising's Image of Women (2010), Film Dir. S. Jhally, USA: Media Education Foundation.

Klara, R. (2015), "How Bloomingdale's Plain Paper Shopping Bags Became So Incredibly Iconic", *Adweek,* 2 November. Available at: www.adweek.com/brand-marketing/how-bloomingdale-s-plain-paper-shopping-bags-became-so-incredibly-iconic-167867/

Klein, N. (2009), *No Logo,* New York: Picador.

Knobloch, L. K. and D. H. Solomon (2002), "Information Seeking Beyond Initial Interaction: Negotiating Relational Uncertainty Within Relationships," *Human Communication Research,* 28(2): 243–257.

Kotler, P. (2003), *Marketing Insights from A to Z: 80 Concepts Every Manager Needs to Know,* Hoboken, NJ: John Wiley & Sons.

Kozinets, R. V., J. F. Sherrt, B. DeBerry-Spence, A. Duhachek, K. Nuttavuthisit and D. Storm (2002), "Themed Flagship Brand Stores in the New Millennium: Theory, Practice, Prospects", *Journal of Retailing,* 78(1): 17–29. doi: 10.1016/S0022-4359(01)00063-X.

Kreps, D. (2019), "Kurt Cobain's Sweater From Final Photoshoot Sells for $75,000 at Auction", *Rolling Stone,* 19 May. Available at: www.rollingstone.com/music/music-news/kurt-cobain-sweater-auction-837291/.

Kreps, D. (2019), "Kurt Cobain's 'Unplugged' Sweater Heads to Auction Again, Never Been Washed", *Rolling Stone,* 9 October. Available at: www.rollingstone.com/music/music-news/kurt-cobain-unplugged-sweater-auction-896937/.

KTRK (2017), "Remembering Our Favorite Stores that Closed", 6 March. Available at: abc13.com/shopping/remembering-our-favorite-stores-that-closed/1787167/

Kuczynski, A. (2005), "A Dark, Secluded Place", *The New York Times,* 7 July. Available at: www.nytimes.com/2005/07/07/fashion/thursdaystyles/a-dark-secluded-place.html.

Kwan, A. (2008), "Young Fashion Bloggers are Worrisome Trend to Parents", *USAToday,* 12 August. Available at: usatoday30.usatoday.com/tech/webguide/internetlife/2008-08-12-girl-fashion-blogs_N.htm.

Lantz, J. (2016), *The Trendmakers: Behind the Scenes of the Global Fashion Industry,* New York: Bloomsbury.

Lascity, M. E. (2017), "Brand References and Music Video Intertextuality: Lessons from *Summer Girls* and *She Looks So Perfect*", *Film, Fashion & Consumption,* 6(2): 105–122. doi: 10.1386/ffc.6.2.105_1.

Lascity, M. E. (2018), "'Cool' Workings: Glamour Labor and Identity Issues in Fashion Branding", *Fashion Theory.* doi: 10.1080/1362704X.2018.1488415.

Lascity, M. E. (2019), "Lifestyle Journalism as Brand Practice: The Cases of Uniqlo and Abercrombie & Fitch", in L. Vodanovic (ed.), *Lifestyle Journalism: Social Media, Consumption and Experience,* New York: Routledge.

Laver, J. (1937), *Taste and Fashion: From the French Revolution to the Present Day,* London: George G. Harrap and Co.

Lee, A. (2000), "Art for Armani's Sake", *Salon,* 18 October. Available at: www.salon.com/2000/10/18/armani/.

Legal Information Institute (n.d.), "Tinker v. Des Moines Independent Community School Dist." Available at: www.law.cornell.edu/supremecourt/text/393/503.

Lester, T. L. (2011), "A Real Life Pan Am Stewardess On What it was Like to Wear That Famous Uniform", *Glamour,* 10 October. Available at: www.glamour.com/story/a-real-life-panam-stewardess-o.

Levine, M. (1998), *Gay Macho: The Life and Death of the Homosexual Clone,* New York: New York University Press.

Levy, S. J. (1959), "Symbols for Sale", *Harvard Business Review,* 37(4): 117–124.

Lewis, R. (2013), "The Modest Fashion Blogosphere: Establishing Reputation, Maintaining Independence", in D. Bartlett, S. Cole and A. Rocamora (eds), *Fashion Media: Past and Present,* 165–174, New York: Bloomsbury.

Lewis, T. (2008), *Smart Living: Lifestyle Media and Popular Expertise,* New York: Peter Lang.

Lewis, V. D. (2003), "Dilemmas in African Diaspora Fashion", *Fashion Theory,* 7(2): 163–190. doi: 10.2752/136270403778052113.

Lipovetsky, G. (1994), *The Empire of Fashion: Dressing Modern Democracy,* C. Porter (trans), Princeton, NJ: Princeton University Press.

Littlejohn, S. W. (1996), *Theories of Human Communication,* New York: Wadsworth.

Lorenz, T. (2019), "The Real Difference Between Creators and Influencers", *The Atlantic,* 31 May. Available at: www.theatlantic.com/technology/archive/2019/05/how-creators-became-influencers/590725/.

Lowery, S. A. and M. L. DeFleur (1995), *Milestones in Mass Communication Research: Media Effects,* Third edition, White Plains, NY: Longman.

Lowry, C., L. Parker, K. Chirico, A. Bagg, S. Watson and M. J. Foronda (2014), "This is What 'One Size Fits All' Actually Looks like on All Body Types", *Buzzfeed,* 3 December. Available at: www.buzzfeed.com/candacelowry/heres-what-one-size-fits-all-looks-like-on-all

Lurie, A. (1981), *The Language of Clothes,* NY: Random House.

Lury, C. (2004), *Brands: The Logos of the Global Economy,* New York: Routledge.

Lury, C. (2009), "Brand as Assemblage: Assembling Culture", *Journal of Cultural Economy,* 2(1–2): 67–82. doi: 10.1080/17520250903064022.

Lury, C. and L. Moor (2010), "Brand Valuation and Topological Culture", in M. Aronczyk and D. Powers (eds), *Blowing up the Brand: Critical Perspectives and Promotional Culture,* 29–52, New York: Peter Lang.

Luther, M. (2010), "Fashion Journalism," in V. Steele (ed.), *The Berg Companion to Fashion,* New York: Bloomsbury.

Lutz, A. (2013), "Abercrombie & Fitch Refuses to Make Clothes for Large Women", *Business Insider,* 3 May. Available at: www.businessinsider.com/abercrombie-wants-thin-customers-2013-5

Luvaas, B. (2016), *Streetstyle: An Ethnography of Fashion Blogging,* New York: Bloomsbury.

Macarthur, K. (2005), "McDonald's Plans to Reinvent Employee Uniforms", *AdAge,* 4 July. Available at: adage.com/article/news/mcdonald-s-plans-reinvent-employee-uniforms/46205.

McCammon, S. (2018), "First Ladies Unite Against Separating Children at Border", *NPR,* 19 June. Available at: www.npr.org/2018/06/19/621349853/first-ladies-unite-against-separating-children-at-border.

McClendon, A. (2015), *Fashion and Jazz: Dress, Identity and Subcultural Improvisation,* New York: Bloomsbury.

McCombs, M. E. and D. L. Shaw (1993), "The Evolution of Agenda-setting Research: Twenty-five Years in the Marketplace of Ideas", *Journal of Communication*, 43(2): 58–67.

McCracken, G. (1986), "Culture and Consumption: A Theoretical Account of the Structure and Movement of the Cultural Meaning of Consumer Goods," *Journal of Consumer Research*, 13(1): 71–84.

McCracken, G. (1988), *Culture and Consumption: New Approaches to the Symbolic Character of Consumer Goods and Activities,* Bloomington, IN: University of Indiana Press.

McCracken, G. (2005), *Culture and Consumption II: Markets, Meaning and Brand Management,* Bloomington, IN: Indiana University Press.

McFadden, R. D. (2014), "Joan Rivers, a Comic Stiletto Quick to Skewer, Is Dead at 81", *The New York Times,* 4 September. Available at: www.nytimes.com/2014/09/05/arts/television/joan-rivers-dies.html.

McGregor, J. (2012), "The Art of Mark Zuckerberg's Hoodie", *The Washington Post,* 10 May. Available at: www.washingtonpost.com/blogs/post-leadership/post/the-art-of-mark-zuckerbergs-hoodie/2012/05/09/gIQAhBCnDU_blog.html.

McGregor, J. (2014), "Abercrombie & Fitch CEO Mike Jeffries Steps Down", *The Washington Post,* 9 December. Available at: www.washingtonpost.com/news/on-leadership/wp/2014/12/09/abercrombie-fitch-ceo-mike-jeffries-steps-down/

McGregor, J. and T. Telford (2019), "'All the Men are Psyched' about Goldman Sachs' Relaxed Dress Code. For Everyone Else, It's Complicated", *The Washington Post,* 15 March. Available at: www.washingtonpost.com/business/economy/all-the-men-are-psyched-about-goldman-sachs-relaxed-dress-code-for-everyone-else-its-complicated/2019/03/15/9d24da8a-41de-11e9-a0d3-1210e58a94cf_story.html.

McIntyre, M. P. (2016), "Looking the Part: Negotiating Work Clothes, Gender and Expertise in Retail", *Fashion Practice,* 8(1): 117–134. doi: 10.1080/17569370.2016.1147698.

Mackinney-Valentin, M. (2017), *Fashioning Identity: Status Ambivalence in Contemporary Fashion,* New York: Bloomsbury.

McLean, F. (1995), "A Marketing Revolution in Museums?", *Journal of Marketing Management,* 11(6): 601–661. doi: 10.1080/0267257X.1995.9964370

McMillan, J. (2019), "In Gender-Swap Photo Filers, Some Trans People See Therapy", *Associated Press,* 17 May. Available at: www.apnews.com/71cd88bf196e45a2aa2c55ed05beb96a

MacNaughton, W. (2018), "How Pantone Picked "Living Coral' as the 2019 'Color of the Year'", *The New York Times,* 5 December. Available at: www.nytimes.com/2018/12/05/business/pantone-2019-color-of-the-year-living-coral.html.

McNeil, P. (2016), "Georg Simmel: The 'Philosophical Monet'", in A. Rocamora and A. Smelik (eds), *Thinking Through Fashion: A Guide to Key Theorists,* New York: I.B. Tauris.

McNeil, P. and S. Miller (2014), *Fashion Writing and Criticism: History, Theory, Practice,* New York: Bloomsbury.

McQuail, D. and S. Windahl (1993), *Communication Models for the Study of Mass Communication,* New York: Longman.

McRobbie, A. (1998), *British Fashion Design: Rag Trade or Image Industry?,* New York: Routledge.

McVeigh, B. J. (2010), "Individualizing Japanese Student Uniforms", in J. E. Vollmer (ed.), *Berg Encyclopedia of World Dress and Fashion: East Asia,* New York: Bloomsbury. doi: 10.2752/BEWDF/EDch6411

Maffesoli, M. (2016), "From Society to Tribal Communities," *The Sociological Review,* 64(4): 739–747. doi: 10.1111/1467-954X.12434.

Magsaysay, M. (2018), "The Unglamorous Reality of Being a Stylist to the Stars", *Business of Fashion,* 9 October. Available at: www.businessoffashion.com/articles/intelligence/the-unglamorous-reality-of-being-a-stylist-to-the-stars

Maheshwari, S. (2019), "They See It. They Like It. They Want It. They Rent It", *The New York Times,* 8 June. Available at: www.nytimes.com/2019/06/08/style/rent-subscription-clothing-furniture.html.

Martin, M. (2019), "How Christian Siriano Broke the Internet with His Inclusive Design at the Oscars", *NPR,* 3 March. Available at: www.npr.org/2019/03/03/699861599/how-christian-siriano-broke-the-internet-with-his-inclusive-design-at-the-oscars.

Massoni, K. (2010), *Fashioning Teenagers: A Cultural History of* Seventeen *Magazine,* Walnut Creek, CA: Left Coast Press.

Mauss, M. (1973), "Techniques of the Body", *Economy and Society,* 2(1): 70–88. doi: 1080/0385147300000003.

Mean Girls (2004), Film Dir. M. Waters, USA: Paramount Pictures.

Meinhold, R. (2013), *Fashion Myths: A Cultural Critique,* New York: Transcript-Verlag.

Mejía, P. (2019), "Hot Topic is Still Hot", *The New York Times,* 6 April. Available at: www.nytimes.com/2019/04/06/style/hot-topic-stores.html

Melchior, M. R. (2014), "Understanding Fashion and Dress Museology", in M. R. Melchior and B. Svensson (eds), *Fashion and Museums,* New York: Bloomsbury.

Memmott, M. (2013), "75 years ago, 'War of the Worlds' Started a Panic. Or Did It?" *NPR,* 30 October. Available at: www.npr.org/sections/thetwo-way/2013/10/30/241797346/75-years-ago-war-of-the-worlds-started-a-panic-or-did-it.

Mercer, B. (2018), "Is the High School Letterman's Jacket a Sign of the Patriarchy?" *SFGate,* 20 October. Available at: www.sfgate.com/opinion/article/high-school-letterman-jacket-patriarchy-abc-housew-13320883.php.

Mercer, J. (2010), "A Mark of Distinction: Branding and Trade Mark Law in the U.K. from the 1860s", *Business History,* 52(1): 17–42. doi: 10.1080/00076790903281033.

"The Merchants of Cool" (2001), Television Episode *Frontline,* 27 February. Prod. B. Goodman and R. Dretzin. USA: WGBH. Available at: www.pbs.org/wgbh/pages/frontline/shows/cool/.

The Metropolitan Museum of Art (n.d.), "Hat". Available at: www.metmuseum.org/art/collection/search/83437.

The Metropolitan Museum of Art (n.d.), "Alexander McQueen: Savage Beauty". Available at: web.archive.org/web/20120711012413/blog.metmuseum.org/alexandermcqueen/about/.

Miles, C. and T. Nilsson (2018), "Marketing (as) Rhetoric", *Journal of Marketing Management,* 34(15–16): 1259–1271. doi: 10.1080/0267257X.2018.1544805.

Miller, D. (2010), *Stuff,* Malden, MA: Polity.

Miller, D. and S. Woodward (2012), *Blue Jeans: The Art of the Ordinary,* Los Angeles: University of California Press.

Miller, J. (2011), *Fashion and Music,* New York: Bloomsbury.

Miller, J. (2016), "Sigmund Freud: More than a Fetish: Fashion and Psychanalysis", in A. Rocamora and A. Smelik (eds), *Thinking Through Fashion: A Guide to Key Theorists,* New York: I.B. Tauris.

Miller, S. (2013), "Taste, Fashion and the French Fashion Magazine", in D. Bartlett, S. Cole and A. Rocamora (eds), *Fashion Media: Past and Present,* 13–21, New York: Bloomsbury.

Miller, S. and P. McNeil (2018), *Fashion Journalism: History, Theory and Practice,* New York: Bloomsbury.

Moeslein, A. (2018), "Why Blake Lively's Been Wearing So Many Suits Lately: An Investigation", *Glamour,* 14 September. Available at: www.glamour.com/story/why-blake-lively-has-been-wearing-suits-a-simple-favor.

Moor, L. (2007), *The Rise of Brands,* New York: Berg.

Moore, K. and S. Reid (2008), "The Birth of Brand: 4000 Years of Branding", *Business History,* 50(4): 419–432. doi: 10.1080/00076790802106299.

Mull, A. (2019), "The Mystery of Business Casual", *The Atlantic,* 22 April. Available at: www.theatlantic.com/health/archive/2019/04/allbirds-rothys-silicon-valley-shoe-fashion/587428/.

Mulvey, L. (1999), "Visual Pleasure and Narrative Cinema", in L. Braudy and M. Cohen (eds), *Film Theory and Criticism: Introductory Readings,* New York: Oxford University Press.

Munich, A. (2011), *Fashion in Film,* Bloomington, IN: Indiana University Press.

Nakassis, C. V. (2012), "Brand, Citationality, Performativity", *American Anthropologist,* 114(4): 624–638. doi: 10.1111/j.1548-1433.2012.01511.X.

Nededog, J. (2013), "'Scandal's' Kerry Washington on Olivia Reclaiming the White Hat: 'It's a Conflict and It's Exciting'", *The Wrap,* 30 August. Available at: www.thewrap.com/scandals-kerry-washington-olivia-reclaiming-white-hat-it-s-conflict-and-it-s-exciting-video/.

Neff, G., E. Wissinger and S. Zukin (2005), "Entrepreneurial Labor Among Cultural Producers: 'Cool' Jobs in 'Hot' Industries", *Social Semiotics,* 15(3): 307–334. doi: 1080/10350330500310111.

Negrin, L. (2014), "Aesthetics", in A. Geczy and V. Karaminas (eds), *Fashion and Art*, New York: Bloomsbury.

Neighbors (2014), Film Dir. Nicholas Stroller, USA: Universal Pictures.

Neil, D. (2009), "When Cars were America's Idols", *Los Angeles Times*, 1 June. Available at: articles.latimes.com/2009/jun/01/business/fi-gm-history1.

New York Public Library (n.d.), "The Gutenberg Bible". Available at: www.nypl.org/events/exhibition/2009/05/31/gutenberg-bible.

The New York Times (1988), "Abercrombie Chain Bought", 18 January. Available at: www.nytimes.com/1988/01/16/business/company-news-abercrombie-chain-bought.html.

The New York Times (2018), "Ashley Graham Unfiltered", 5 September. Available at: www.nytimes.com/interactive/2018/09/04/style/ashley-graham-body-positive-movement-ar-ul.html.

Nichols, T. (2017), *The Death of Expertise: The Campaign Against Established Knowledge and Why it Matters,* Oxford, UK: Oxford University Press.

Nike (2018), "Nike Manufacturing Map." Available at: manufacturingmap.nikeinc.com

Nudd, T. (2015), "McDonald's Launches the Big Mac Lifestyle Collection for Fans of Beefy, Cheesy, Everything", *Adweek,* 24 March. Available at: www.adweek.com/creativity/mcdonalds-launches-big-mac-lifestyle-collection-fans-beefy-cheesy-everything-163655/.

O'Connor, C. (2014), "Abercrombie & Fitch CEO Jeffries Out as Struggling Teen Chain Tries to Save Itself", *Forbes,* 9 December. Available at: www.forbes.com/sites/clareoconnor/2014/12/09/abercrombie-fitch-ceo-jeffries-out-as-struggling-teen-chain-tries-to-save-itself/#6a66043d54ff

O'Malley, K. (2018), "Blake Lively Has Finally Explained Why She's Been Wearing All Those Suits This Season", *Elle,* 9 November. Available at: www.elle.com/uk/fashion/celebrity-style/a23078799/blake-lively-explained-suits-fashion./

O'Neal, G. S. (1999), "The African American Church, its Sacred Cosmos, and Dress", in L. B. Arthur (ed.), *Religion, Dress and the Body,* 117–134, New York: Berg.

O'Neal, G. S. (2010), "African American", in P. G. Tortora (ed.), *Berg Encyclopedia of World Dress and Fashion: The United States and Canada,* 536–545, New York: Bloomsbury.

Obama, M. (2018), 18 June. Available at: twitter.com/MichelleObama/status/1008768272895012867

Okawa, T. (2008), "Licensing Practices at Maison Christian Dior", in R. L. Blaszczyk (ed.), *Producing Fashion: Commerce, Culture and Consumers,* 82–107, Philadelphia: University of Pennsylvania Press.

Ong, T. (2018), "Amazon Patents a Mirror that Dresses You In Virtual Clothes", *The Verge,* 3 January. Available at: www.theverge.com/circuitbreaker/2018/1/3/16844300/amazon-patent-mirror-virtual-clothes-fashion.

Ong, T. (2018), "Amazon's Echo Look Style Assistant Gets a Little Bit Smarter", *The Verge,* 7 February. Available at: www.theverge.com/2018/2/7/16984218/amazons-echo-look-collections-feature-curated-content-vogue-gq.

Oppenheimer, M. (2017), "The Downsides of School Uniforms", *The New Yorker,* 6 September. Available at: www.newyorker.com/culture/culture-desk/the-unquestioned-goodness-of-school-uniforms.

Opree, S. J. and R. Kühne (2016), "Generation Me in the Spotlight: Linking Reality TV to Materialism, Entitlement, and Narcissism", *Mass Communication and Society,* 19(6): 10.1080/15205436.2016.1199706.

Ortved, J. (2018), "See the Art that Tavi Gevinson Collects", *The New York Times,* 3 January. Available at: www.nytimes.com/2018/01/03/arts/design/tavi-gevinson-rookie-brooklyn.html.

Palladino, G. (1999), *Teenagers: An American History,* New York: Basic Books.

Palmer, A. and H. Clark (2005), *Old Clothes, New Looks: Second Hand Fashion,* New York: Berg.

Pantone (n.d.), "About Pantone". Available at: www.pantone.com/about/about-pantone.

Paoletti, J. (2012), *Pink and Blue: Telling the Boys from the Girls in America,* Bloomington, IN: Indiana University Press.

Paoletti, J. B. (2015), *Sex and Unisex: Fashion, Feminism and the Sexual Revolution,* Bloomington, IN: Indiana University Press.

Pardes, A. (2018), "With an Eco-Friendly Sneaker, Rothy's Trends on New Ground", *Wired,* 13 September. Available at: www.wired.com/story/rothys-sneaker/.

Parker, B. T. (2009), "A Comparison of Brand Personality and Brand User-Imagery Congruence", *Journal of Consumer Marketing,* 26(3): 175–184. doi: 10.1108/07363760910954118.

Patterson, M. (1999), "Re-appraising the Concept of Brand Image", *The Journal of Retail Brand Management,* 6(6): 409–426. doi: 10.1057/bm.1999.32.

Patterson, T. (2019), "Goldman Sachs, Patagonia and the Mysteries of 'Business Casual'", *The New Yorker,* 8 May. Available at: www.newyorker.com/culture/on-and-off-the-avenue/goldman-sachs-patagonia-and-the-mysteries-of-business-casual.

Pearson, J. and R. Davilla (2001), "The Gender Construct: Understanding Why Men and Women Communicate Differently", in L. P. Arliss and D. J. Borisoff (eds), *Women and Men Communicating: Challenges and Changes*, Second edition, Long Grove, IL: Waveland Press.

Peirson-Smith, A. F. and B. O. Peirson-Smith (2019), "Back to the Future: The Critical Role of Fashion Archives in Preserving, Curating and Narrating Fashion Stories", presented at Popular Culture Association Annual Conference, Washington, DC.

Peretz, H. (1995), "Negotiating Clothing Identities on the Sales Floor", *Symbolic Interaction,* 18(1): 19–37.

Peter, J. (2018), "'Nipplegate' Revisited: What Really Happened Between Janet Jackson and Justin Timberlake?", *USA Today,* 31 January. Available at: www.usatoday.com/story/sports/nfl/2018/01/31/nipplegate-revisited-what-really-happened-between-janet-jackson-and-justin-timberlake/1083557001/.

Petrov, J. (2019), *Fashion, History, Museums: Inventing the Display of Dress,* New York: Bloomsbury.

Pettegree, A. (2014), *The Invention of News: How the World Came to Know About Itself,* New Haven, CT: Yale University Press.

Pettinger, L. (2004), "Brand Culture and Branded Workers: Service Work and Aesthetic Labour in Fashion Retail", *Consumption, Markets and Culture,* 7(2): 165–184. doi: 10.1080/1025386042000246214.

Pham, M. T. (2015), *Asians Wear Clothes on the Internet: Race, Gender and the Work of Personal Style Blogging,* Durham, NC: Duke University Press.

Pine, B. J. and J. H. Gilmore (2011), *The Experience Economy,* Second edition, Boston, MA: Harvard Business Review Press.

Plante, S. G. (2017), "The Impossible Question of Public School Uniforms", *Racked,* 3 May. Available at: www.racked.com/2017/5/3/15518542/public-school-uniforms-education-policy

Polan, B. and R. Tredre (2009), *The Great Fashion Designers,* New York: Berg.

Polhemus, T. (1994), *Street Style: From Sidewalk to Catwalk,* London. Thames & Hudson.

Polhemus, T. (1996), *Style Surfing: What to Wear in the 3rd Millennium,* London: Thames & Hudson.

Polhemus, T. (2011), *Fashion & Anti-fashion,* Open Source.

Pooley, J. (2010), "The Consuming Self: From Flappers to Facebook", in M. Aronczyk and D. Powers (eds), *Blowing Up the Brand: Critical Perspectives on Promotional Culture,* New York: Peter Lang.

Pooley, J. and M. J. Socolow (2013), "The Myth of the *War of the Worlds* Panic," *Slate,* 28 October. Available at: www.slate.com/articles/arts/history/2013/10/orson_welles_war_of_the_worlds_panic_myth_the_infamous_radio_broadcast_did.html.

Poster, M. (2001), *What's the Matter with the Internet?,* Minneapolis, MN: University of Minnesota Press.

Potter, W. J. (2014), "A Critical Analysis of Cultivation Theory", *Journal of Communication,* 64(6): 1015–1036. doi: 10.1111/jcom.12128.

Pouillard, V. and K. J. Trivette (2018), "Tobé Coller Davis: A Career in Fashion Forecasting in America", in R. L. Blaszczyk and B. Wubs (eds), *The Fashion Forecasters: A Hidden History of Color and Trend Prediction,* New York: Bloomsbury.

"The Power of Style" (2017), TV Episode First Ladies Revealed, *Smithsonian Channel.* www.smithsonianchannel.com/videos/the-first-presidential-wife-to-be-called-the-first-lady/56839

Powers, D. and A. Pattwell (2015), "Immortal Brands? A Temporal Critique of Promotional Culture", *Popular Communication,* 13(3): 202–215. doi: 10.1080/15405702.2015.1048343.

Pujalet-Plaà, E. (2010), "New Look", in V. Steele (ed.), *The Berg Companion to Fashion,* New York: Bloomsbury.

Quick, R. (1999), "Fashion Coup at 'Dawson's Creek': American Eagle Becomes Clothier", *The Wall Street Journal,* 22 June. Available at: www.wsj.com/articles/SB930001940814263371.

Raphael, R. (2019), "Big Beauty Brands Eagerly Join the CVS Photoshop Ban", *Fast Company,* 24 January. Available at: www.fastcompany.com/90295860/big-beauty-brands-like-covergirl-and-revlon-eagerly-join-the-cvs-photoshop-ban.

Rees, A. (2013), "Abercrombie Caves on Sizing Policies, Will Stock Larger Sizes", *Cosmopolitan,* 8 November. Available at: www.cosmopolitan.com/politics/news/a16373/af-caves/

Rees-Roberts, N. (2018), *Fashion Film: Art and Advertising in the Digital Age,* New York: Bloomsbury.

Reese, S. D. (2001), "Framing Public Life: A Bridging Model for Media Research", in S. D. Reese, O. H. Gandy and A. E. Grant (eds), *Framing Public Life: Perspectives on Media and Our Understanding of the Social World,* Mahwah, NJ: Erlbaum.

Reich, S. M., R. W. Black and R. Foliaki (2018), "Constructing Difference: Lego® Set Narratives Promote Stereotypic Gender Roles and Play", *Sex Roles*, 79(5–6): 285–298. doi: 10.1007/s11199-017-0868-2.

Reyer, C. (2017), "When Hollywood Glamour Was Sold at the Local Department Store", *Smithsonian Magazine,* 23 February. Available at: www.smithsonianmag.com/arts-culture/when-hollywood-glamour-was-sold-local-department-store-180962262/.

Ritchie, D. (1986), "Shannon and Weaver: Unravelling the Paradox of Information," *Communication Research*, 13(2): 278–298.

Ritzer, G. and N. Jurgenson (2010), "Production, Consumption, Prosumption: The Nature of Capitalism in the Age of the Digital 'Prosumer'", *Jorunal of Consumer Culture,* 10(1): 13–36. doi: 10.1177/1469540509354673.

Ritzer, G., P. Dean and N. Jurgenson (2012), "The Coming Age of the Prosumer", *American Behavioral Scientist,* 56(4): 379–398. doi: 10.1177/0002764211429368.

Roach, M. E. and J. B. Eicher (2007), "The Language of Personal Adornment," in M. Barnard (ed.), *Fashion Theory: A Reader*, New York: Routledge.

Roberson, D. (2018), Podcast "Olivia Pope Hangs Up Her White Hat for Good", *The Takeaway,* WNYC, 20 April. Available at: www.wnycstudios.org/podcasts/takeaway/segments/olivia-pope-hangs-her-white-hat-good.

Rocamora, A. (2012), "Hypertextuality and Remediation in the Fashion Media: The Case of Fashion Blogs", *Journalism Practice,* 6(1): 92–106. doi: 10.1080/17512786.2011.622914.

Rocamora, A. (2017), "Mediatization and Digital Media in the Field of Fashion", *Fashion Theory,* 21(5): 505–522. doi: 10.1080/1362704X.2016.1173349.

Rocamora, A. (2018), "Mediazation and Digital Retail", in A. Geczy and V. Karaminas (eds), *The End of Fashion: Clothing and Dress in the Age of Globalization,* New York: Bloomsbury.

Rose, M. (2000), "In 'Real Simple,' a Rare Misstep for Time Inc", *The Wall Street Journal,* 7 June, B1.

Rose, M. (2003), "In Hopeful Sign, Time is Testing New Magazines", *The Wall Street Journal,* 29 January, B1.

Ross, H. (2018), "I Have A Lot of Pent-Up Feelings About Nate in 'The Devil Wears Prada'", *Man Repeller,* 5 November. Available at: www.manrepeller.com/2018/11/nate-the-devil-wears-prada-adrian-grenier.html.

Rothy's (n.d.), "Sustainability." Available at: rothys.com/sustainability.

Roy, J. (2014), "Urban Outfitters' AWFUL BLOOD-spattered Kent State Sweatshirt is Now For Sale on eBay", *New York,* 15 September. Available at: nymag.com/daily/intelligencer/2014/09/urban-outfitters-kent-state-sweatshirt-on-ebay.html.

Rubin, J. (2014), "Smells Like Teen Spirit: Inside the Secretive World of Brandy Melville", *Racked,* 24 September. Available at: www.racked.com/2014/9/24/7575693/brandy-melville

Rubin, S. (1996), "Stone's Eye-Popping Oscar Duds? A $22 Shirt From the Gap", *SFGate,* 28 March. Available at: www.sfgate.com/entertainment/article/Stone-s-Eye-popping-Oscar-Duds-A-22-Shirt-2988053.php.

Sabin, S. (2019), "A Tough Task for FTC: Regulating Instagram When Anyone Can Be an Influencer", *Morning Consult,* 28 May. Available at: morningconsult.com/2019/05/28/a-tough-task-for-ftc-regulating-instagram-when-anyone-can-be-an-influencer/.

The Salvation Army (n.d.), "Our History". Available at: www.salvationarmyusa.org/usn/history-of-the-salvation-army/.

Saviolo, S. and A. Marazza (2013), *Lifestyle Brands: A Guides to Aspirational Marketing,* New York: Palgrave Macmillan.

Sawyer, J. (2017), "Louis Vuitton Launches New 'Make It Yours' Customizations Campaign", *HighSnobiety,* 6 June. Available at: www.highsnobiety.com/2017/06/06/louis-vuitton-make-it-yours-campaign/.

Scaturro, S. (2018), "Confronting Fashions Death Drive: Conversation, Ghost Labor, and the Material Turn within Fashion Curation", in A. Vänskä and H. Clark (eds), *Fashion Curating: Critical Practice in the Museum and Beyond,* New York: Bloomsbury.

Scharrer, E. and G. Blackburn (2018), "Cultivating Conceptions of Masculinity: Television and Perceptions of Masculine Gender Role Norms", *Mass Communication and Society,* 21(2): 149–177. doi: 10.1080/15205436.2017.1406118.

Schivinski, B. and D. Dabrowski (2016), "The Effect of Social Media Communication on Consumer Perceptions of Brands", *Journal of Marketing Communications,* 22(2): 189–214. doi: 10.1080/13527266.2013.871323.

Schor, J. (2004) *Born to Buy,* New York: Scribner.

Seaver, N. (2017), "Algorithms as Culture: Some Tactics for the Ethnography of Algorithmic Systems", *Big Data & Society,* 4(2): 1–12. doi: 10.1177/2053951717738104.

Sellers, P. (2004), "eBay's Secret", *Fortune,* 18 October. Available at: archive.fortune.com/magazines/fortune/fortune_archive/2004/10/18/8188091/index.htm.

Sender, K. (2012), *The Makeover: Reality Television and Reflexive Audiences,* New York: New York University Press.

Shackelford, K. (2014), "Mary Beth and John Tinker and *Tinker v. Des Moines*: Opening the Schoolhouse Gates to First Amendment Freedom", *Journal of the History of the Supreme Court,* 39(3): 372–385.

Shah, K. (2016), "How Beautyblender Changed Makeup Sponges Forever", *Racked,* 17 May. Available at: www.racked.com/2016/5/17/11513412/beautyblender-makeup-sponges-countouring-rea-ann-silva.

Sheftalovich, Z. (2016), "Australia's Lesson in Burkinui Politics", *Politico,* 23 August. Available at: www.politico.eu/article/australias-lesson-in-burkini-politics-muslim-immigrants-cronulla-beach-riots-france-solution/.

Sheppard, M. (2014), "Virgin Glamour: Launching our New Vivienne Westwood Designed Uniforms", *Ruby: A Blog by Virgin Atlantic,* 4 July. Available at: blog.virginatlantic.com/virgin-glamour-launching-our-new-vivienne-westwood-designed-uniforms/.

Simmel, G. (1904 1957), "Fashion", *The American Journal of Sociology,* 62(2): 541–558.

Simonson, I. and E. Rosen (2014), *Absolute Value: What Really Influences Customers in the Age of (Nearly) Perfect Information,* New York: HarperBusiness.

Singer, M. (2017), "How Models Like Ashley Graham and Gigi Hadid are Democratizing Fashion", *Vogue,* 8 February. Available at: www.vogue.com/article/model-diversity-ashley-graham-gigi-hadid-kendall-jenner-march-cover.

Singer, O. (2019), "A Singular Vision: Ashley and Mary-Kate Olsen on Bringing The Row to London", *Vogue,* 6 April. Available at: www.vogue.co.uk/article/the-olsen-twins-speak-fashion-and-their-singular-vision-in-creating-the-row.

Sirgy, M. J. (1982), "Self-Concept in Consumer Behavior: A Critical Review", *Journal of Consumer Research,* 9(3): 287–300.

Slater, D. (2002), "Capturing Marketing from the Economists", in P. du Gay and M. Pryke (eds), *Cultural Economy: Cultural Analysis and Commercial Life,* 59–77, Los Angeles: Sage.

Smith, G. D. and L. E. Stedman (1981), "Present Value of Corporate History", *Harvard Business Review,* 59(6): 164–173.

Smith, K. M., J. M. McClain and M. E. Lascity (2019), "Oscar PR Girl: How Interconnected Social Media Platforms Humanized the Oscar de la Renta Brand Identity", *Fashion, Style & Popular Culture,* 5(2): 261–278. doi: 10.1368/fspc.5.2.261_1

Solomon, D. and J. Theiss (2013), *Interpersonal Communication: Putting Theory into Practice,* New York: Routledge.

Spellings, S. (2018), "Uniqlo's Newest Collaboration is More than Just Modest", *The Cut,* 16 August. Available at: www.thecut.com/2018/08/hana-tajima-and-uniqlo-release-new-collection-for-fall-2018.html.

Spinner, L., L. Cameron and R. Calogero (2018), "Peer Toy Play as a Gateway to Children's Gender Flexibility: The Effect of (Counter)Stereotypic Portrayals of Peers in Children's Magazines", *Sex Roles,* 79(5–6): 314–328. doi: 10.1007/s11199-017-08883-3.

Spiridakis, E. (2008), "Post Adolescents", *T* Magazine, 13 August. Available at: www.nytimes.com/2008/08/17/style/tmagazine/17tween.html.

Steele, V. (2008), "Museum Quality: The Rise of the Fashion Exhibition", *Fashion Theory,* 12(1): 7–30. doi: 10.2752/175174108X268127.

Stern, B. (2006), "What Does *Brand* Mean? Historical-Analysis Method and Construct Definition", *Journal of the Academy of Marketing Science,* 34(2): 216–223. doi: 10.1177/0092070305284991.

Steven, R. (2017), "Tate Modern and Uniqlo on One Year of Tate Lates and the Key to a Good Partnership", *Creative Review,* 27 October. Available at: www.creativereview.co.uk/tate-modern-uniqlo-tate-lates/?mm_5dc0ddc7a2633=5dc0ddc7a2635.

Stone, G. P. (1995), "Appearance and the Self", in M. E. Roach-Higgins, J. B. Eicher and K. K. P. Johnson (eds), *Dress and Identity,* 19–39, New York: Fairchild.

Strähle, J. and A. Kriegel (2018), "Fashion and Music: A Literature Review", in J. Strähle (ed.), *Fashion and Music,* Singapore: Springer.

Strate, L. (2004), "A Media Ecology Review", *Communication Research Trends,* 23(2). Available at: cscc.scu.edu/trends/v23/v23_2.pdf

Strings, S. (2019), *Fearing the Black Body: The Racial Origins of Fat Phobia,* New York: New York University Press.

Stutesman, D. (2011), "Costume Design, or, What Is Fashion in Film?", in A. Munich (ed.), *Fashion in Film,* Bloomington, IN: Indiana University Press.

Sullivan, A. (2016), "Karl Marx: Fashion and Capitlaism", in A. Rocamora and A. Smelik (eds), *Thinking Through Fashion: A Guide to Key Theorists,* New York: I.B. Tauris.

Sullivan, E. (1997), "Historical Overview of the Academic Costume Code", *American Council on Education.* Available at: www.acenet.edu/news-room/Pages/Historical-Overview-Academic-Costume-Code.aspx

Sundén, J. (2003), *Material Virtualities: Approaching Online Textual Embodiment,* New York: Peter Lang.

Syme, R. (2018), "The Algorithmic Emptiness of Allbirds Shoes", *The New Yorker,* 12 November. Available at: www.newyorker.com/culture/on-and-off-the-avenue/the-optimized-anti-style-of-allbirds-shoes

Tarmy, J. (2018), "The Most-Visited Exhibition in Met Museum History", *Bloomberg,* 11 October. Available at: www.bloomberg.com/news/articles/2018-10-11/heavenly-bodies-was-the-met-s-most-visited-exhibition-ever.

Tashjian, R. (2019), "How Jennifer Lopez's Versace Dress Created Google Images", *GQ,* 20 September. Available at: www.gq.com/story/jennifer-lopez-versace-google-images.

Taylor, A. (2016), "The Surprising Australian Origin Story of the 'Burkini,'" *The Washington Post,* 17 August. Available at: www.washingtonpost.com/news/worldviews/wp/2016/08/17/the-surprising-australian-origin-story-of-the-burkini/.

Taylor, L. (2004), *The Study of Dress History,* New York: Manchester University Press.

Television Academy (n.d.), "Project Runway", Available at: www.emmys.com/shows/project-runway.

This Film is Not Yet Rated (2006), Film Dir. K. Dick, USA: IFC.

Thomas, D. (2002), "The Power Behind the Cologne", *The New York Times Magazine,* 24 February. Available at: www.nytimes.com/2002/02/24/magazine/the-power-behind-the-cologne.html

Thompson, D. (2019), "Are Influencers the Future of Online Commerce?", *The Atlantic,* 6 June. Available at: www.theatlantic.com/ideas/archive/2019/06/influencers-frauds-or-the-future-of-online-commerce/591133/.

Thornton, S. (1996), *Club Cultures: Music, Media and Subcultural Capital,* Hanover, NH: Wesleyan University Press.

Tietjen, A. (2017), "Cindy Crawford Reflects on MTV's 'House of Style'", *WWD,* 22 August. Available at: wwd.com/eye/people/cindy-crawford-reflects-on-mtv-house-of-style-10963951/.

TIME (1977), "Abercrombie's Shuts Its Doors", *TIME,* 28 November. Available at: content.time.com/time/magazine/article/0,9171,919168,00.html.

Tinker v. Des Moines www.law.cornell.edu/supremecourt/text/393/503.

Tolentino, J. (2019), "The Age of Instagram Face", *The New Yorker,* 12 December. Available at: www.newyorker.com/culture/decade-in-review/the-age-of-instagram-face.

Trenholm, S. (2014), *Thinking through Communication: An Introduction to the Study of Human Communication,* New York: Pearson.

Trong, S. (2011), "Tavi Gevinson Explains Her New Website, Rookie", *The Cut,* 5 September. Available at: www.thecut.com/2011/09/tavi_gevinson_explains_her_new.html.

Troy, N. (2003), *Couture Culture: A Study in Modern Art and Fashion,* Cambridge, MA: The MIT Press.

Trump, D. J. (2018), 21 June. Available at: twitter.com/realDonaldTrump/status/1009916650622251009

Tschorn, A. (2018), "How Well-Suited Director Paul Feig Takes His Styles Cures from Classical Hollywood", *Los Angeles Times,* 6 September. Available at: www.latimes.com/fashion/la-ig-paul-feig-20180906-story.html.

Tseëlon, E. (2016), "Jean Baudrillard: Post-modern Fashion as the End of Signification", in A. Rocamora and A. Smelik (eds), *Thinking Through Fashion: A Guide to Key Theorists,* 215–232, New York: I.B. Tauris.

Tulloch, C. (2011), "Style-Fashion-Dress: From Black to Post-Black", *Fashion Theory,* 14(3): 273–303. doi: 10.1752/175174110X1271241152019.

Turow, J. (2011), *The Daily You: How the New Advertising Industry is Defining Your Identity and Your Worth,* New Haven, CT: Yale University Press.

Twohey, M. (2010), "Petite Teen Becomes Big Voice in Fashion World", *The Seattle Times,* 12 January. Available at: www.seattletimes.com/life/lifestyle/petite-teen-becomes-big-voice-in-fashion-world/.

Uhlirova, M. (2013), "100 Years of the Fashion Film: Frameworks and Histories", *Fashion Theory,* 17(2): 137–157. doi: 10.2752/175174113X13541091797562.

Uniqlo (2017), "Uniqlo Renews Sponsorship of Popular 'Uniqlo Free Friday Nights' at MOMA", *Uniqlo News,* 29 January. Available at: www.uniqlo.com/us/en/uniqlo-free-friday-nights-at-moma.html.

Uniqlo (n.d.), "Airism". Available at: www.uniqlo.com/us/en/page/airism.html.

United States Courts (n.d.), "Facts and Case Summery – Tinker v. Des Moines". Available at: www.uscourts.gov/educational-resources/educational-activities/facts-and-case-summary-tinker-v-des-moines.

Van Dyke, M. B. (2014), "Urban Outfitters Features 'Vintage' Red-stained Kent State Sweatshirt", *BuzzFeed,* 15 September. Available at: www.buzzfeed.com/mbvd/urban-outfitters-features-vintage-red-stained-kent-state-swe.

Van Meter, J. (2019), "Plus One! Ashley Graham on Modeling and Becoming a New Mom", *Vogue,* 6 December. Available at: www.vogue.com/article/ashley-graham-cover-january-2020.

Vanderschoot, K. J. (2018), "Mizzen+Main's First Brick and Mortar is Good News for the Men of Dallas", *D Magazine,* November. Available at: www.dmagazine.com/publications/d-magazine/2018/november/mizzenmains-first-brick-and-mortar-is-good-news-for-the-men-of-dallas/.

Vänskä, A. and H. Clark (2018), *Fashion Curating: Critical Practice in the Museum and Beyond,* New York: Bloomsbury.

Veblen, T. (1899 2009), *The Theory of the Leisure Class,* The Floating Press.

Vernallis, C. (2004), *Experiencing Music Video: Aesthetics and Cultural Context*, New York: Columbia University Press.

Vernuccio, M. (2014), "Communicating Corporate Brands Through Social Media: An Exploratory Study", *International Journal of Business Communication,* 51(3): 211–233. doi: 10.1177/2329488414525400.

Victoria and Albert Museum (n.d.), "Alexander McQueen: Savage Beauty", Available at: www.vam.ac.uk/content/exhibitions/exhibition-alexander-mcqueen-savage-beauty/about-the-exhibition/.

Vogel, C. (2014), "Met's Costume Institute to be Renamed for Anna Wintour", *The New York Times,* 14 January. Available at: artsbeat.blogs.nytimes.com/2014/01/14/mets-costume-institute-to-be-renamed-for-anna-wintour/.

Wahba, P. and D. Skariachan (2013), "Analysis: New Tastes, Nimble Fashion Rivals Squeeze Top U.S. Teen Chains", *Reuters,* 21 August. Available at: www.reuters.com/article/us-usa-retail-teens-analysis/analysis-new-tastes-nimble-fashion-rivals-squeeze-top-u-s-teen-chains-idUSBRE97L04620130822

Walker, M. (2010), "Miniskirt", in V. Steele (ed.), *The Berg Companion to Fashion*, Oxford, UK: Bloomsbury Academic.

Walmart (n.d.), "Our History." Available at: corporate.walmart.com/our-story/our-history.

Warner, H. (2009), "Style Over Substance? Fashion, Spectable and Narrative in Contemporary U.S. Television", *Popular Narrative Media,* 2(2). doi: 10.3828/pnm.2009.5.

Warner, H. (2014), *Fashion on Television: Identity and Celebrity Culture,* New York: Bloomsbury.

Warner, P. C. (2008), "The Americanization of Fashion: Sportswear, the Movies and the 1930s", in L. Welters and P. Cunningham (eds), *Twentieth-Century American Fashion,* New York: Bloomsbury. doi: 10.2752/9781847882837.

Weaver, D. H., M. E. McCombs and C. Spellman (1975), "Watergate and the Media: A Case Study of Agenda-Setting", *American Politics Quarterly,* 3(4): 458–472.

Weaver, H. (2018), "Did Melania Trump Just Undercut Her Border Visit With a Very Poorly Chosen Jacket?", 21 June. Available at: www.vanityfair.com/style/2018/06/melania-trump-i-dont-really-care-jacket-border-visit

Webster, E. (2010), "School Uniforms in New Zealand", in M. Maynard (ed.), *Berg Encyclopedia of World Dress and Fashion: Australia, New Zealand and the Pacific Islands,* New York: Bloomsbury. doi: 10.2752/BEWDF/EDch7053

Webster, N. S. (2015), "1999: Our Last Innocent, Giddy Summer", *The Daily Beast,* 25 May. Available at: www.thedailybeast.com/1999-our-last-innocent-giddy-summer

Wernick, A. (1991), *Promotional Culture: Advertising, Ideology and Symbolic Exchange,* Thousand Oaks, CA: Sage.

WGSN, (n.d.), "Industries". Available at: www.wgsn.com/en/industry/.

Wigley, S. M., K. Nobbs and E. Larsen (2013), "Marking the Marque: Tangible Branding in Fashion Product and Retail Design", *Fashion Practice,* 5(2): 245–264. doi: 10.2752/175693813X13705243201577.

Wilkinson, I. (2011), "Diana Vreeland: New Documentary Traces 'Vogue' Fashion Empress's Legacy", *The Daily Beast,* 2 September. Available at: www.thedailybeast.com/diana-vreeland-new-documentary-traces-vogue-fashion-empresss-legacy.

Williams, C. (2016), "Timeline: Delta's Journey to New Uniforms", *News Hub,* 25 October. Available at: news.delta.com/timeline-deltas-journey-new-uniforms.

Willingham, A. (2018), "Social Media Filters Mess with Our Perceptions So Much, There's Now a Name for It", *CNN,* 10 August. Available at: www.cnn.com/2018/08/10/health/snapchat-dysmorphia-cosmetic-surgery-social-media-trend-trnd/index.html.

Wilson, E. (2003), *Adorned in Dreams: Fashion and Modernity,* New York: I.B. Tauris.

Wilson, E. (2004), "Magic Fashion", *Fashion Theory,* 8(4): 375–385. doi: 10.2752/136270404778051609.

Wissinger, E. A. (2015), *The Year's Model: Fashion, Media and the Making of Glamour,* New York: New York University Press.

Wolgast, S. L. (2009), "The Intercollegiate Code of Academic Costume: An Introduction", *Transactions of the Burgon Society,* 9: 9–37. doi: 10.4148/2475-7799.1070.

Wright, C. R. (1960), "Functional Analysis and Mass Communication", *The Public Opinion Quarterly,* 24(4): 605–620.

Yagou, A. (2010), "Girls' Uniforms in Greek Schools", in D. Bartlett and P. Smith (eds), *Berg Encyclopedia of World Dress and Fashion: East Europe, Russia and the Caucasus,* New York: Bloomsbury. doi: 10.2752/BEWDF/EDch9089

Zimmerman, L. K. (2017), "Preschoolers' Perceptions of Gendered Toy Commercials in the U.S.", *Journal of Children and Media,* 11(2): 119–131. doi: 10.1080/17482798.2017.1297247.

Zukin, S. (2005), *Point of Purchase: How Shopping Changed American Culture,* New York: Routledge.

Index